DATE DUE

Demco, Inc. 38-293

EUGENE O'NEILL

A CRITICAL STUDY

EUGENE O'NEILL

A Critical Study

Sophus Keith Winther

DEPARTMENT OF ENGLISH, UNIVERSITY OF WASHINGTON
SEATTLE

NEW YORK
RUSSELL & RUSSELL
1961

TO

MABEL ELINE

Preface to the Second Edition

No MODERN man of letters has aroused a wider range of critical interest than has Eugene O'Neill. This is as true in the field of scholarly criticism as it is in the publications addressed to the popular reader. The list of scholars who have undertaken the serious study of his plays increases with each passing year. Two books devoted to a detailed study have appeared recently; others, are near completion. Biographical study is growing in volume. At least three books dealing with his life are at present being written. This year the whole issue of *Modern Drama,* a magazine devoted exclusively to the criticism of this genre was given over to articles on O'Neill's plays.

Now that all of O'Neill's work is published, the errors of an interpretation based on a single play need not occur. When *Days Without End* first appeared there were many predictions made that O'Neill had returned to the bosom of the Mother Church. This amused him, but he was also a trifle disappointed that the critics couldn't understand that he was not writing a confession of faith but a modern version of a morality play. He did not return to his childhood faith. His intellectual frame of reference out of which he created his dramas was the poetry and the philosophy of the

Preface to the Second Edition

Nineteenth Century. The books that expressed best for him the meaning of life are listed in the stage directions for *A Long Day's Journey Into Night*. They are referred to often and in many plays, but more often in the strictly autobiographical dramas.

Throughout the years I have followed the work of the many writers who have made critical studies of O'Neill. In the final chapter on the four plays published since the first edition of this book I owe much to other critics and to at least two biographers, C. Bowen and Agnes Bolton. I am indebted to the books on O'Neill by Edward A. Engel, Doris V. Falk, Horst Frenz and the scholarly studies in professional journals by Doris Alexander. I must mention especially the friendly interest of Professor Cyrus Day, and the serious critical studies of Joseph Wood Krutch.

All that has been done so far is a mere introduction. In every graduate school in the country young students are working on O'Neill. There are hundreds of Master's Theses filed in graduate libraries, and there is a growing number of Doctor's Theses under development here and abroad. The life and dramas of O'Neill invite the analysis of serious literary criticism.

University of Washington, 1961.   S.K.W.

Table of Contents

EUGENE O'NEILL

A CRITICAL STUDY

I

The Destructive Power of the Romantic Ideal

"Romantic imagination! It has ruined more lives than all the diseases! Other diseases, I should say! It's a form of insanity." *Strange Interlude*

I

CRITICAL thought in this modern world has been a relentless enemy of the romantic ideal, and no modern writer has attacked it more consistently or more bitterly than Eugene O'Neill. The exaggerated romanticism which enveloped the American theater a generation ago nurtured the mind of his youth and provoked the rebellion of his maturity. Against that tradition his dramas are a direct challenge. He hates the false dreams and false ideals and false endings that have dominated the American stage and are still the inspiration of the Movies.

To O'Neill these ideals are not harmless entertainment, but a virulent disease that has eaten into the core of life, rotting and destroying the only hope for salvation that is possible for man. O'Neill believes that man's hope lies in his being willing to face life as it is, accepting

3

its limitations and, on the foundations of these very
shortcomings, erecting a new world free from the tyranny of romantic dogmatism.

The creative imagination will not always obey the
logic of cold reason, and nothing is more characteristic
of O'Neill than the conflict between his criticism of the
romantic ideal and the manner in which he .succumbs,
at times, to its seductive appeal. I doubt if there is a character in the whole range of his work who could be described as truly realistic in the sense that Bazarov, Pelle,
or Sister Carrie might be called realists. Perhaps the
greatness of O'Neill's characters lies in this very fact:
that they are too complex, too involved with the cross
currents of life to be purely one thing or the other. Their
conflicts give them a quality which inspires confidence
in their humanity and enlists the reader's sympathy and
understanding in a way that more consistent and unified personalities never could.

A study of the men and women that move through
the world of O'Neill's dramas reveals some noteworthy
characteristics that many of them have in common. One
is impressed by the courage and fortitude with which
they face the unfavorable circumstances of the world in
which they live. They are determined to give life meaning and value in defiance of a world that is impersonal
and unconcerned about the ambitions of human beings.
It is not this characteristic that I wish to emphasize at
this point but something that is purely physical and, at
the same time, suggests a hidden romantic passion in
the nature of O'Neill. Buried deep in his inner being is

a love for some quality that the materialistic interpretation of life does not seem to bring out in its proper perspective.

In order to discover just what this is, it will be necessary to note, in some detail, his descriptions of the leading characters in many different plays to observe what physical characteristics they have in common. In the pursuit of this study a curious fact comes to light. No matter who the character may be or what his occupation or position in the social order is, the favorite character of an O'Neill play has dreamy eyes. His characters live in two worlds: one the outward world of physical reality, the other, a world of unfulfilled and passionate desire. This latter world is the one which the dreamer wishes for with all the pent-up powers of his being. To this world he will sacrifice all that life has given him, for there is nothing in life that for a moment is comparable to the genuine reality of his dream. Captain Bartlett commits murder because his longed-for dream of pirate treasure seems to have come true, and in another play, another sea captain sacrifices the sanity of his wife in order that his desire for a full load of whale oil may become a reality.

2

Before analyzing further the manner in which the romantic dream is both the victory and the despair of the O'Neill hero, it will be important to note from direct example to what extent the characteristic of the dreamy eyes appears consistently throughout the plays. In *Lazarus Laughed,* Miriam's mask is described in these words: "The eyes of the mask are almost closed. Their gaze turns within, oblivious to the life outside, as they dream down on the child forever in memory at her breast." And in *The Great God Brown* Margaret is described in these words: "She is almost seventeen, pretty and vivacious, blonde, with big romantic eyes, her figure lithe and strong, her facial expression intelligent but youthfully dreamy, especially now in the moonlight." While Dion's face is not described by the word "dreamy," a synonym serves to convey the same idea. "His face is masked. The mask is a fixed forcing of his own face—dark, spiritual, poetic, passionately supersensitive, helplessly unprotected in its childlike, religious faith in life."

In *Diff'rent,* Emma Crosby appears as "a slender girl of twenty. . . . Her face, in spite of its plain features, gives an impression of prettiness, due to her large, soft blue eyes which have an incongruous quality of absentminded romantic dreaminess about them!" And in *Welded,* Michael Cape is likewise a member of the race of dreamers, tortured dreamers, for it is a part of the dreamer's character that he lives in a world of conflict and divided ends. Cape is "tall and dark. His unusual face is a harrowed battlefield of supersensitiveness, the features at war with one another—the forehead of a thinker, the eyes of a dreamer, the nose and mouth of a sensualist. . . . There is something tortured about him—a passionate tension, a self-protecting, arrogant defiance of life and his own weakness, a deep need for love as a faith in which to relax."

Robert, in *Beyond the Horizon,* "is a tall slender young man of twenty-three. There is a touch of the poet about him expressed in his high forehead and wide, dark eyes." A more complex character, but no less of a thwarted romanticist than Robert, is Stephen Murray in *The Straw.* He is a "tall, slender, rather unusual-looking fellow with a pale face, sunken under high cheek bones, lined about the eyes and mouth, jaded and worn for one still so young. His intelligent, large hazel eyes have a tired, dispirited expression in repose, but can quicken instantly with a concealment mechanism of mocking, careless humor whenever his inner privacy is threatened. . . . He is staring into the fire, dreaming, an open book lying unheeded on the arm of his chair."

Juan Ponce de Leon, in *The Fountain,* is described in the following manner: "His countenance is haughty, full of a romantic adventurousness and courage; yet he gives the impression of disciplined ability, of a confident self-mastery—a romantic dreamer governed by the ambitious thinker in him." And twenty years later "His hair and beard are gray. His expression and attitude are full of great weariness. His eyes stare straight before him blankly in a disillusioned dream."

And so it is from beginning to end in this world of Eugene O'Neill. His chief characters are poetic dreamers, ill-fitted to cope with a world that is inimical to poetry. These men and women drift down the stream of life, fighting desperately to maintain their position and, in spite of the current, to reach the happy shore of their dreams. They present one of the strange anomalies of life, in that their dream embodies all that is beautiful and good, and just because of that they are destroyed. As is true of the great heroes of all tragedies, and especially Shakespeare's, they are destroyed by their virtues. Marsden in *Strange Interlude* is another member of the hapless company of idealists who are incapable of accepting the reality of the world and are destroyed by their own dreams of beauty. He is described: "His face is too long for its width, his nose is high and narrow, his forehead broad, his mild blue eyes those of a dreamy self-analyst, his thin lips ironical and a bit sad. There is an indefinable feminine quality about him, but it is nothing apparent in either appearance or act." He is a man fascinated by his own idealism and at the same time conscious of the limitations of his ideal. Speaking of Nina he says, "But sometimes the scent of her hair and skin . . . like a dreamy drug . . . dreamy! . . . there's the rub! . . . all dreams with me! my sex life among the phantoms!"

Even the unimaginative Mrs. Fife in *Dynamo* is not wholly of this world of reality, for beneath her calm exterior there lies the shadow of something unrealized. "Her eyes are round and dark blue. Their expression is blank and dreamy."

The great Marco who could see nothing in the eyes of the beautiful princess, though it was his duty to study them every day, was in his youth of a poetic nature. His father said of him: "But still heedless. A dreamer!" Even old Ephraim Cabot in *Desire Under the Elms* is described in these words: "His eyes have taken on a strange, incongruous dreamy quality."

This poetic, dreamy-eyed hero of the O'Neill play possesses a strange quality of unreality that a careless reader might call a false idealization, but a closer examination brings to light the fact that in their very romance there is something of the eternal idealist that is as much a true quality of human nature as are the more clearly perceived realistic attributes. Don Quixote is a foolish idealist tilting at windmills, but he is also the embodiment of man's undying hopes, dreams, aspirations. And there is something of the Don Quixote in Eugene O'Neill, something that transcends the confident security of the casual critic who sees only bloodshed, terror and defeat in the plays of this modern dramatist. The tendency in much of the criticism of O'Neill's work has been to overlook the delicate beauty of his chief characters and it has concentrated instead upon his use of profanity. The manner in which the critic overlooks the poetic quality of O'Neill's characters and stresses instead the less important suggests the story of the director who strove for originality in his production of *Hamlet* by giving the lead to Guildenstern. The following quotation illustrates the point:

> "O'Neill has undoubtedly a considerable gift for language; he loves the flavor of words, and uses with fine effect speech that smacks of the soil or has the tang of the

sea in it. His tendency to interlard his pages with profanity has given offense in some quarters, and even his
admirers have not always found it easy to justify its use.
Clayton Hamilton's explanation has more than a modicum of truth in it: 'It is, I think, his sense of literary style
that accounts for his fondness for obscene phrases and
profane ejaculations, more than any wish to shock the
ladies in the audience or to assert his unconventionality.
Most of the swearing is done from an obscure desire to
revel in the sound of words.' Yet, while it seems clear
that O'Neill is using coarse, profane language as an artist
to re-create the actual speech of his rough characters, one
feels that such language could be properly indicated with
a less generous supply of profanity." (C. H. Whitman,
Appendix to *Seven Contemporary Plays,* Houghton Mif-
flin Company, 1931. p. 556.)

Note the reference to "rough characters," as though
that were an accepted truth. It is a common misunderstanding which is based on an uncritical analysis. That
they speak their native tongue cannot be denied, nor
can it be a fault; but to reason from that to roughness
must seem strange when one reviews the deep, generous, intensely sympathetic nature that one finds in
almost every play that O'Neill has written.

This failure to recognize the beauty and sympathy
in O'Neill has often led to strange generalizations.
There is already a critical tradition established with
reference to his language as illustrated above. Another
tradition, equally unjustified in its emphasis, refers to
the grimness of his tragedies, and like the attitude to-

wards his language misconstrues his characters. Again Whitman may be used for a typical illustration:

> "The plays of O'Neill are for the most part unpleasant plays, wrought out of the agony and pain of life. His most successful characters are people of rather primitive instincts, misfits, suffering from disease, economic inhibitions, frustrations, from soul-destroying powers which they cannot understand. These poor souls are usually beaten in the battle of life by a force either within or outside themselves that makes for their confusion and ruin. In fact, few plays of our day have such a plethora of murders, violent deaths, suicides and insanity." (*Ibid.* p. 555.)

This I take to be a true description of a certain important phase of O'Neill's work, but that it should be cited as an example of his limitations in itself seems strange. If the nature of O'Neill's characters is evidence of their unfitness for artistic purposes, then they go to an honored death in company with some of the most tortured souls that have ever inspired the love and sympathy of mankind: Macbeth, Hamlet, Antony and a thousand others in drama, poetry and novel. It is the very fact that they are tortured by "soul-destroying powers which they cannot understand" that makes them the embodiment of man's tragic struggle against an unfriendly universe, that gives them universality, that arouses tragic pity, and makes us understand more clearly than we ever understood before just what it means to be human.

3

O'Neill's plays are a direct protest against the romantic ideal with its exaggerated hopes and its false values and its tendency to deny that man is first and fundamentally the product of his animal heritage. But since O'Neill is an artist and not a mere essayist developing a thesis, his sympathies are with the very dreamer out of whom his tragedy grows. O'Neill, the rebel against the romantic ideal, is himself an idealist at heart. What he says of Juan Ponce de Leon might be said of him: "Soldier of iron—and dreamer." The two are ever at war with each other and in that strife lies the reason for O'Neill's greatness. He is complex, intricate, a divided personality, a man at war with himself, and just because of that, an artist who can portray man's tragic struggle with the forces of life.

Throughout the whole of O'Neill's work, men and women characters are brought to a tragic end because they ask more from life than life can offer them. They are incapable of reconciling themselves to the limitations of the world in which they live. The narrow confines of their environment irk them, and they dream beyond the horizon into an imaginative world where all is beautiful and good. Living in this divided world, the one of reality, the other of imagination, they are continually tortured by the passionate longing of their dreams and the grim reality of their immediate surroundings.

It always seems as though O'Neill began by conceiv-

ing a theme in which he would completely condemn
the romantic ideal. He gives the impression that he
would try to show how his characters are brought to
a sad end because they were incapable of reconciling
themselves to the reality of the world in which they
actually lived. But, in the end, his drama leaves the
impression that the disaster which grew out of the
dream was somehow a justification in itself, or if not
wholly a justification, nevertheless an inevitable out-
come of a particular type of human being.

Juan Ponce de Leon is a typical example. In the beginning of the play Juan is the soldier of iron sufficient
unto himself. He has no need for love and is perfectly
reconciled to leaving Spain and Maria de Cordova. She
understood his weakness when she told him: "You are
noble, the soul of courage, a man of men. You will go
far, soldier of iron—and dreamer. God pity you if these
two selves should ever clash!" He was young, brave,
full of enthusiasm and self-confidence. He had not
yet reached the age nor suffered the experience which
makes it necessary to hope beyond the possibility of
achievement in order to make life endurable at all.
He is even convinced of his own realism and con-
temptuous of the dreamer, saying of Columbus: "He
was riding his flea-bitten mule as if he were a Caesar
in triumph. His eyes were full of golden cities." And
Juan laughs at such a man, one who will not accept the
reality of sense experience. He claims for himself a
philosophy of sterner stuff, a conviction that "We do
what we must—and sand covers our bodies and our

deeds." He scorns beauty as he renounced love, assuming a conscious pose that almost verges on bravado, little realizing that the day is coming when love, beauty, youth, the age-old phantoms which he condemns shall become his reality and his cross. His poetic friend Luis knows this, and his tender heart yearns for Juan when he says: "Juan, why do you always sneer at beauty—while your heart calls you liar."

Twenty years later as Governor of Porto Rico, the character of the poetic dreamer is gradually getting possession of the realist, but not without conflict and protest. Nano, an Indian, tells him of Cathay, pointing to the west. But now it is not only Cathay that intrigues his imagination, for in the same direction as the fabled cities Nano also tells of the spring of eternal youth. Juan is skeptical, saying: "The old trick of poets—evasion of facts!" Nevertheless he is impressed, saying: "Where there is so much smoke, there must be a spark of fire." In one breath he condemns the dreamer, scorning all that is not "fact," in the next he yearns for "the King's patent to discover new lands! I would sail tomorrow for Cathay—or for the moon!" And as he reminisces about the past, his anger rises against Columbus who has been free to follow the life of the discoverer while Juan has been condemned to remain behind. He calls Columbus a dreamer and of himself says: "I would succeed! I am no visionary chasing rainbows. I tell you I loathe this place! I loathe my petty authority! By God, I could sink all Porto Rico under the sea for one glimpse of Cathay!" And then, as if the visionary had gained complete power, assuming the reality of a Cathay somewhere, he says: "I begin to dread—another failure. I am too old to find Cathay."

As his hope of finding Cathay grows dim, a newer and still more romantic dream takes its place. Nano's words about the spring of eternal youth bear fruit in the mind of Juan, when the daughter of his old sweetheart arrives at Porto Rico. Beatrice is the image of her mother, and at last Juan realizes that love is everything for him. Cathay with its wealth and honor is as nothing compared with his desire for youth. And all the time he is incapable of seeing any other dream but his own. He scorns Luis' dream of Heaven saying:

> JUAN. Have you talked with men who saw Him in the manger, or on the cross?
> LUIS. Juan, this is blasphemy!
> JUAN. Then let it be! I have prayed to Him in vain.
> LUIS. Juan!
> JUAN. Let me be damned forever if Nature will only grant me youth upon this earth again!
> LUIS. Juan! You defy your God!
> JUAN. There is no God but Love—no heaven but youth!

He goes on a futile quest for the spring, secretly fearing failure. At the spring where he has been led by the treacherous Nano, he drinks. Before daring to look at his reflection, he must urge himself on by saying, "Coward! How often have you looked death in the face? Are you afraid of life?" And later when the grim truth is forced upon him his answer to himself is, "Fool! Why did I look? I might have died in my dream."

In the end he must witness the cycle complete. His young nephew, as the lover of Beatrice, speaks to him of honor and the glory of serving Spain and, as Juan in his youth might have said, the nephew now speaks:

> NEPHEW. I do not care for riches; and as for Golden Cities, I only wish to plant Spain's banner on their citadels!
> JUAN. Brave dreams! Echoes blown down the wind of years.

Juan's romantic dream made his life a tragedy, but at the same time his dream gave to his life the greatest and most genuine value it possessed. On the one hand, O'Neill has written a play which deals with the emptiness of the romantic ideal, but at the same time he has made a hero out of his dreamer. He has made life into a fool's dream and a philosopher's tragedy. As a thinker Juan is a child; as a poetic dreamer he is noble, brave and inspiring. It is as though O'Neill had failed to do the thing he set out to accomplish and in his failure achieved his real success. Just as Juan failed to find the secret of eternal youth, but found instead that "One must accept, absorb, give back, become oneself a symbol! Juan Ponce de Leon is past! He is resolved into the thousand moods of beauty that make up happiness —color of the sunset, of tomorrow's dawn, breath of the great Trade wind—sunlight on the grass, an in-

sect's song, the rustle of leaves, an ant's ambitions."
So in the end O'Neill the poet of reality is in a very
true sense also the dreamer-poet. Like one of his great
masters, Conrad, he is both realist and romanticist. He
is aware of this conflict and has consciously striven to
reveal it in his plays, for he holds that man's passional
will to believe is as much a factor in the interpretation
of life as is that of critical reason.

4

No single idea has made so deep and abiding an impression on the mind of O'Neill as that of the destructive power of the romantic ideal, or the power of
illusion to lead man to deny the reality which lies about
him at every hand, and in the strength of his denial
to create a world of fantastic dreams as a substitute for
that reality. If O'Neill has an affirmative philosophy,
it is to accept reality and to deny the illusion. But, as
I have indicated before, he cannot escape from the love
of the illusion. The people who interest him are the
very ones who "follow the gleam" to a tragic end. In
that aspect of his philosophy lies his genuine strength
as a dramatist, for the essence of life is its psychological
inconsistency and not its exemplification of logic.

Barrett Clark in stating the general theme of illusion
in O'Neill writes: "Once again, as in *Beyond the Horizon,* the playwright shows his characters basing their
lives upon illusion. Sometimes this takes the form of a
dream of beauty, sometimes it is love, sometimes physi-

cal passion. In the later plays we shall find Ponce de
Leon in quest of the illusion of love and fame, Marco
Polo after the illusion of power, Lazarus after a solution
of the problem of life everlasting, and Reuben Light
in *Dynamo* after a religion that he can believe in; but
always it is the quest that counts—the pursuit that never
ends, the search for happiness, the hope for an ultimate
meaning and justification of life." (Clark, p. 101.) And
Beyond the Horizon provides an excellent opportunity
for studying O'Neill's use of illusion. His chief character, Robert Mayo, "is a tall, slender young man of
twenty-three. There is a touch of the poet about him
expressed in his high forehead and wide, dark eyes."
He is a dreamer who is not reconciled to the life of
the farm, who is forever striving for a life that is more
than a life, but not realizing that such a life is no life
at all. Andrew, his brother, says to him, "You do take
the prize for day-dreaming." And Robert's explanation
is that "There's something calling me—(*He points to
the horizon*) Oh, I can't just explain it to you, Andy."

   Robert's dreams are nebulous, living only as vague
longings in the mind of one who is unable to accept
the reality of the world that lies about him. Reality
teaches him nothing about the world in general. The
immediate experience is to him as it is to the mystic,
a matter of little consequence when contrasted to the
creations of his imagination. To his brother he says:

   "Supposing I was to tell you that it's just Beauty that's
   calling me, the beauty of the far off and unknown, the

mystery and spell of the East which lures me in the books I've read, the need of the freedom of great wide spaces, the joy of wandering on and on—in quest of the secret which is hidden over there, beyond the horizon?"

He abandons his chance to test his dream of what lies "Beyond" in order to follow another dream equally evanescent and futile, that of a love that will answer all the needs of life. The bitter tragedy of his love follows as a natural consequence of his false idealism and his everlasting inability to accept life as a reality. He grows to hate his home and all that it demands of him. His dreaming makes him ineffectual. The hills that surround his farm are "Like the walls of a narrow prison yard shutting me in from all the freedom and wonder of life!" He never realizes that life itself is a prison, and that there is no escape beyond the horizon, except the escape that comes with death, an escape that brings peace, but without the realization of what it has brought—obliteration of both pain and the hope of happiness.

As one dream fades, another comes to take its place. Sick unto death he sees an escape by hoping for a new life in the city with Ruth. He tells her that "Life owes us some happiness after what we've been through. It must! Otherwise our suffering would be meaningless —and that is unthinkable." Futile as his hope is for a new life in the city, it is not so far divorced from reality as is his illusion about the nature of the universe and his own suffering. It is always the final gesture of the romantic idealist to assume that his suffering bears some compensating virtue and that the universe is built upon an ethical plan. Of all the bitter disillusionment that the Roberts of this world must go through, this is the hardest for them: to come to the realization that there is no connection between what man desires from life and what he gets; that the universe as such is impersonal and takes no account of man's hopes and fears, joys and despairs.

But this illusion of a new life in the city meets with the same defeat as did all the other forms of escape from reality with which Robert had deluded himself. At last he realizes that his life is over and that death is to be his reward; death is to be the unthinkable meaning to life, after all. Once more, and for the last time, he avoids the issue, and this time it can do him no harm, for it is the end. Consumption has brought him to the end of his struggle. With his last strength he has dragged himself out of the house and into the open where he can see his beloved hills and sky. His last words are: "Don't you see . . . I'm freed from the farm —free to wander on and on—eternally! . . . Isn't it beautiful beyond the hills? I can hear the old voices calling me to come—and this time I'm going! It isn't the end . . . ! I've won my trip—the right of release— beyond the horizon!"

In his introduction to *Contemporary American Drama,* Quinn says of this conclusion:

The great motive of the play "is Robert Mayo's aspiration, his vision of the great adventure 'beyond the horizon'—which he had dreamed as a boy at the window at sunset, and which he had given up at the call of Ruth's passion for him." (Quinn, Intro. p. XIX.) Thus Quinn's sympathetic interpretation makes Robert's death a victory at last. This seems hardly consistent with the spirit of the play which emphasizes from the first the futility of the romantic illusion. Instead of being a victory, this is the most tragic touch of all; the bitter irony that summarizes the whole play. The false idealism that ruined his life and condemned him to the narrow futility of the New England farm was with him even in death.

In another place Quinn comes back to the same theme, writing: "O'Neill knows that the most precious gifts to humanity are the illusions that keep us alive, and he fulfills the most severe test of tragedy, which has come down to us from the Greeks, that it purifies us through our sympathy with suffering." (*Ibid*. Vol. II. p. 172.) It is true that O'Neill knows how prone man is to live in an atmosphere of illusion, and it may be true that O'Neill has his own fondness, secretly buried, for these same illusions, but in this play, as in the main body of his work, he reveals the tragic futility of these illusions. If *Beyond the Horizon* means anything as an interpretation of life, it is just the opposite of what Mr. Quinn suggests. O'Neill has no more vindicated Robert than Shakespeare vindicated Hamlet, who wanted to punish his mother and avenge his father's death by killing the King, but in the end really killed the King to avenge the death of his mother. *Beyond the Horizon* is an exemplification of the de-

structive power of the romantic ideal, and its final
ironic touch is Robert's triumphant cry, "It isn't the
end." At last he has an illusion that no one can dispute,
a safe illusion, an illusion that has no meaning for the
living.

5

Welded is a direct attack upon the romantic ideal
and its destructive power. In this case it is the romantic
ideal that destroys married love and turns what might
have been happiness into madness and fury. The two
leading characters, Michael and Eleanor, found in their
love the inspiration to great creative work, but they
also found in their passion that which turned their
victory into dust and ashes. They could not accept love
as a limited good in itself, but must, because of their
exaggerated idealism, exalt it into a symbol that was
beyond the possibility of achievement.

John, the old manager and devoted but unrequited
lover of Eleanor, expresses the bitter truth that his two
friends cannot accept. He says that it is necessary to
"face the truth in yourself." This they cannot do,
for his statement requests them to take a realistic attitude towards their love, even demands that they try
to understand themselves as normal human beings. And
these two will never understand themselves. Life has
made them into dreamers who substitute for reality the
glittering ideals of their imagination, and then when
these ideals clash with actual experience they are hurt,

wounded and utterly despondent without being able to understand why it is so.

O'Neill in his description of Michael Cape gives the reader a clear understanding of his meaning. The same conflict that is so apparent in all of his principal characters is emphasized in the following description of Michael: "the forehead of a thinker, the eyes of a dreamer, the nose and mouth of a sensualist. One feels a powerful imagination tinged with somber sadness— a driving force which can be sympathetic and cruel at the same time. There is something tortured about him —a passionate tension, a self-protecting, arrogant defiance of life and his own weakness, a deep need for love as a faith in which to relax." Michael is a poorly integrated personality, full of unresolved conflicts, incapable of achieving a harmony between his emotional reactions and his intellectual convictions. From the very moment of his appearance until the end of the play he is restless, indecisive, ineffectual. He is at war with himself and, in the bitterness of his contempt for himself, he brews the vile poison which destroys the beauty of his love for Eleanor.

Their conflict with each other begins when, instead of dealing with their present interests, they turn like defeated idealists to reminiscing about the past—their own past. But in exploring the past they are led by their memories to a reality that is fixed and cannot be subjected to the illusion of future hopes. For the idealist to look backward is fatal. The past does not accommodate itself to the ideal. Michael is not aware of this

difference, and as a consequence he is shocked and
disturbed when he finds that in exploring bygone days
with his wife he runs into conflicts with his dreams.
He says to her: "I wanted to dream with you in our
past—to find there—a new faith—" The "new faith"
proves a mockery. Its pursuit involves the inexorable
logic which is the destruction of faith. Eleanor calls
him a "relentless idealist" and such he is, one who
blindly, emotionally pursues the unattainable. He is a
man who has too much intelligence to live by faith,
and too little intelligence to live by reason. He must
indulge in the dangerous business of making idols
which his reason constantly convinces him are really
clay. In speaking of the marriage, he says: "We'd tend
our flame on an altar, not in a kitchen range!" But
even as he says it, he recognizes its futility and gives to
his words a "half-mocking" accent. The words spring
from the heart, but they are checked and colored by
the reason. *"He forces a grin—then abruptly changes
again, with a sudden fierce pleading,* 'It has been what
we dreamed, hasn't it Nelly?'" Eleanor's reply seems
to indicate that she understands their trouble better
than he does when she says: "Sometimes I think we've
demanded too much." To him the fault lies in the
very nature of life, and like the true idealist he must
personify it, saying: "It seems at times as if some jealous
demon of the commonplace were mocking us." Eleanor
tells him that he is "too severe. Your ideal is too in-
human." He knows this rationally, but it does not prevent his feeling "How intolerably insulting life can be."

His actions throughout the play bear out this interpretation of his character. When he quarrels with
Eleanor, he decides to destroy this romantic ideal which
is tearing and twisting his life into a tragedy, and the
only conceivable way for him is to defile his ideal by
contact with a prostitute. In this case his ideal or romantic conception of the prostitute is as far from the
truth of reality as are his other ideals of life. When he
meets the prostitute he is revolted by the same conflicts
that make his life with his wife intolerable. The prostitute is simple and straight-forward. She analyzes him
in the terms of experiences which she understands and
says: "I'm wise to what's wrong with you. You been
lappin' up some bum hooch." Which is just another
and more realistic way of saying that his romantic ideal
has distorted his conception of reality. Before her he is
as ineffectual as with Eleanor. He leaves without getting what he came for, and returns once more to his
wife.

Eleanor's life story is almost the same as that of her
husband. Defeated and disappointed in life until she
met Michael, she made out of him an ideal in which
she hoped to hide her past failures. She says: "I began
living in you. I wanted to die and become you!"
Through the development of this ideal she soon
reached the point where it was as impossible for her
as it was for Michael to deal with the problems of reality, and then began that series of experiences by which
each successfully crucifies the other on the cross of
false ideals.

6

From the early one-act plays to *Mourning Becomes Electra,* O'Neill deals with romantic illusions that destroy the possibility of happiness. It is as though he would say: "Man is incapable of accepting the reality of the world as it is, and in that fact lies the germ of his inevitable tragedy." From Yank who cursed the life of the sea and dreamed of how nice it would be to "have a farm with a house of your own with cows and pigs and chickens, 'way in the middle of the land where yuh'd never smell the sea or see a ship" to General Mannon, O'Neill's men and women follow the gleam of unreal ideals to their destruction. This is not literally true of Yank, but it is true of his brother seaman Chris Christopherson. He lived in a fool's paradise believing that because his daughter was on one of those marvelous farms that Yank speaks of she would be safe and happy. He says to Marthy: "Ay bet you she's fine, good, strong gel, pooty like hell! Living on farm made her like dat. And Ay bet you some day she marry good, steady land fellar here in East, have home all her own, have kits—and den Ay'm ole grandfader, py golly! And Ay go visit dem every time Ay gat in port near!" How his illusion compared with reality everyone knows. All of Chris' years of fine illusions could not make up for the terrible agony of the revelation that followed from Anna's love for Burke.

In the little play *Ile,* Mrs. Keeney is brought to disaster by her faith in a false dream. The loneliness of the life on her husband's whaler drives her to insanity. If we ask, "How does it happen that a woman ever persuaded herself and her husband that she would enjoy a trip to the whaling seas?" the answer is given in her own words: "I used to dream of sailing on the great, wide, glorious ocean. I wanted to be by your side in the danger and vigorous life of it all. I wanted to see you the hero they make you out to be in Homeport. And instead—all I find is ice and cold—and brutality. . . . Oh, I know it isn't your fault, David. You see, I didn't believe you. I guess I was dreaming about the old Vikings in the story-books and I thought you were one of them."

A little later in one brief speech she fully explains herself to the reader, without doing so to herself, "I used to think Homeport was a stupid, monotonous place. Then I used to go down on the beach, especially when it was windy and the breakers were rolling in, and I'd dream of the fine free life you must be leading. I used to love the sea then. But now—I don't ever want to see the sea again."

Even as she analyzes her own false ideals she unconsciously clings to those of the story-books, believing in Vikings that lead free, romantic and beautiful lives. Reality has made her believe that her husband is a brute, when in truth he is just a good, able and tenacious captain of a whaling ship. In spite of her invidious reference to him in contrast with the Vikings, I believe that it is quite clear from the story that any Viking expedition would not have hesitated in accepting the services of Captain Keeney.

Robert, Juan, Chris and Mrs. Keeney are members of the same family of romantic dreamers. Their tragedy grows out of their false romanticizing. It does not follow that, if they had been uncompromising realists, life would then have been one long and beautiful bed of roses, but it appears plain that in all cases their lives would have been happier, and in all cases free from the terrible consequences of their romantic actions.

But the end of this subject has not yet been reached. Captain Bartlett in *Gold* was guilty of murder and ruined his family, finally losing his mind in the pursuit of a romantic illusion. Like the others he was a dreamer who worked in one world and lived in another. His real business was trading in oil, but as he puts it—meditating aloud over a cache of gilded junk which he believes is gold: "I've been dreamin' o' this for years. I never give a damn 'bout the oil—that's just trade—but I always hoped on some voyage I'd pick up ambergris—a whole lot of it—and that's worth gold!" For years he had nourished this dream of pirates' gold until it had become an obsession with him. When two of his crew told him that his find was only brass and junk, he was ready to commit murder. They were the voices of reality speaking the truth, the one thing that the romantic dreamer hates above all things. Later when he is practically insane the doctor who has been studying the case analyzes him clearly, saying to the Captain's son: "No, your father won't let himself look the facts in the face. If he did, probably the shock would kill him. That darn dream of his has become his life."

Captain Bartlett knew in his heart that his dream was false but through so many years he had nursed his illusion of finding gold or ambergris that he grasped frantically at the opportunity of self-vindication. Having once consented to the murder of two of his crew in defense of his illusion, he was all the more determined to make his dream come true. In the end he admitted that he was "afeered to show" the anklet that he had brought home with him from the treasure chest, because he knew it was not gold.

In his case, then, as in the others, his life was a tragedy, because he could not bring himself to accept the ordinary limitations of this world. He had to create a dream world, a world of illusion, and in this dream he destroyed himself and brought unhappiness and death to others.

It is a far cry from the brutal, uneducated and uncultured Captain Bartlett to the learned and refined anthropologist, Curtis Jayson, in *The First Man.* They are quite as different as two people could be in manners, training, habits, social and cultural background, but they have one fatal flaw in common. Both of them are romanticists, dreamers, followers of an illusion that serves as a shield to protect them from reality. In *The First Man,* O'Neill accounts for Curtis' behavior by giving us some insight into his past. After the first fifteen lines of exposition comes the following dialogue:

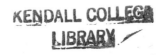

MARTHA. Do tell me what he was like at Cornell.

BIGELOW. A romanticist—and he still is!

MARTHA. What! That sedate man! Never!

CURTIS. Don't mind him, Martha. He always was crazy.

BIGELOW. Why did you elect to take up mining engineering at Cornell instead of a classical degree at the Yale of your fathers and brothers? Because you had been reading Bret Harte in prep. school and mistaken him for a modern realist. You devoted four years to grooming yourself for another outcast of Poker Flat.

*   *   *   *

CURTIS. What next?

BIGELOW. Next? You get a job as engineer in that Goldfield mine—but you are soon disillusioned by a laborious life where six-shooters are as rare as nuggets. You try prospecting. You find nothing but different varieties of pebbles. But it is necessary to your nature to project romance into these stones, so you go in strong for geology. As a geologist, you become a slave to the Romance of the Rocks. It is but a step from that to anthropology—the last romance of all. There you find yourself—because there is no further to go.

And then as the play goes on a little further, Martha brings out one more evidence of the extent to which her husband has abandoned himself to a romantic ideal, and at the same time, she unconsciously reveals that she belongs to the same school of dreamers as her husband. She tells how they had two children, who at the ages of two and three respectively died of pneumonia. Then she says: "We swore we'd never have children again—to steal away their memory. It wasn't what you thought—romanticism—that set Curt wandering—and me with him. It was a longing to lose ourselves—to forget." And what could be better evidence of life's illusion than her own attempt at denial?

Martha has decided to compromise with the memories of the past and is expecting another baby. When Jayson learns of this he cries: "You have blown my world to bits." Tragedy follows rapidly, helped on by the false standards and conventional illusions of Curtis' family.

This play seems quite defective from the point of view of real tragedy, due to the fact that it is overworking the theme of false illusions. In the end, Curtis leaves on his great anthropological expedition, a true dreamer to the end.

The Straw emphasizes the same note. Bill Carmody says of his little daughter, "You're a Cullen like your mother's people. They always was dreamin' their lives out." And so are all the principal characters in the play. Dreaming of health, love, truth, beauty and other impossible ideals for them to achieve. Murray, the hero of the play, is described in these words: "He is staring into the fire, dreaming, an open book lying unheeded on the arm of his chair." For a brief space it seems as though Eileen and Murray will escape together from the disaster that tuberculosis threatens, and they might have escaped if Murray had been enough of a realist to understand himself and accept his normal human limi-

tations. He is not. Eileen suffers a relapse. Too late
Murray discovers that he is really in love with her. In
spite of the doctor's statement that Eileen will die,
Murray says: "I'll make Eileen get well, I tell you!
Happiness will cure! Love is stronger than— (*He suddenly breaks down before the pitying negation she cannot keep from her eyes. . . .*) Oh, why did you give me
a hopeless hope?" And Miss Gilpin answers, "Isn't all
life just that—when you think of it?" The play ends
with Murray nursing the illusion that Eileen may live,
and Eileen with the illusion that Murray is suffering
from a relapse into the condition that characterized
him when she first knew him, and that now she must
take care of him to help him back to health. The whole
thing a "hopeless hope."

7

The play which gives the most complete expression
to the destructive power of the romantic ideal is *Strange
Interlude*. Nina's tragic life was not of her own making. She was brought up in a home that reflected the
atmosphere of a romantic detachment from reality.
Her father, a university professor, was a master in the
art of unreality. His room which provides the opening
scene of the play is described in these words: "The
atmosphere of the room is that of a cosy, cultured retreat, sedulously built as a sanctuary where, secure with
the culture of the past at his back, a fugitive from
reality can view the present safely from a distance, as

a superior with condescending disdain, pity and even amusement." This room is but a symbol of the theory of life that molded the character of Nina, laid the foundation of her philosophy of life—her ethics and her knowledge of other men and women. For all outward purposes the professor's ideal seemed perfect. He was kind, generous and considerate to all people, and inculcated these virtues in his daughter, along with the ideal of good conduct and the virtue of obedience. The professor saw no flaw in his theory of life. He may have realized that it made no close contact with reality, but since he desired to live a life apart from the crass, uncultured world, it seemed a real advantage to be free from the voice of the world that lay beyond the seclusion of his study.

The day was to come when his ideal proved but a weak fortification against the assertions of reality. Nina, obedient to her father's ideals, did not marry the young aviator who was assigned to war duty in France. Gordon restrained his love and passion for Nina, because the old professor brought forth the impressive machinery of his fixed romantic ideal in battle array against Gordon's impetuous desire. The professor appealed to Gordon's honor and all the romantic illusions which honor implied.

Thus the professor won a victory. His ideal had worked perfectly, and when Gordon was killed in France he was glad that his daughter was not made a widow with a child to care for, which might very easily have been the case had the professor not interfered, or better still had not the whole tradition of his life stood out against the passionate cry of youthful love.

Time passed. Suddenly, without warning, the whole romantic edifice of the professor's philosophy came toppling about his head. Nina in a passion of fury denounced his whole system. All the pent-up anguish that had accumulated, after she realized the falsity of her father's romantic ideal, burst forth with bitterness and hatred, poured out in one of the cruelest speeches in all of O'Neill's plays—a speech that gives Nina relief as it condemns to death all that her old father had held dear, all that he had gained from life. His work had not given him wealth, nor power, but in place of these goods it had given him a knowledge of human nature—or so he thought—and now in his old age, his daughter, his one great victory in life, takes all this from him in a single moment and leaves him stripped as naked as a pauper on the brink of his grave, a grave that in a few months will receive his dead body, and his dead works, and his dead ideals. Professor Leeds had been trying to convince Nina that she owed nothing to Gordon and that her idea of nursing wounded soldiers as a compensation for what she did not give Gordon was absurd. He kept up the argument until Nina was goaded into saying the things that she had really wished to spare her father:

PROFESSOR LEEDS. It seems to me when you gave him your love, he got more than he could ever have hoped—

NINA. I gave him? What did I give him? It's what I didn't give! That last night before he sailed—in his arms until my body ached—kisses until my lips were numb—knowing all that night—something in me knowing he would die, that he would never kiss me again—knowing this so surely yet with my cowardly brain lying, no, he'll come back and marry you, you'll be happy ever after and feel his children at your breasts looking up with eyes so much like his, possessing eyes so happy in possessing you! But Gordon never possessed me! I'm still Gordon's silly virgin! And Gordon is muddy ashes! And I've lost my happiness forever! All that last night I knew he wanted me. I knew it was only the honorable code-bound Gordon, who kept commanding from his brain, no, you mustn't, you must respect her, you must wait till you have a marriage license!

*　　*　　*　　*

Gordon wanted me! I wanted Gordon! I should have made him take me! I knew he would die and I would have no children, that there would be no big Gordon or little Gordon left to me, that happiness was calling me, never to call again if I refused! And yet I did refuse! I didn't make him take me! I lost him forever! And now I am lonely and not pregnant with anything at all, but—but loathing! Why did I refuse? What was that cowardly something in me that cried, no, you mustn't, what would your father say?

In fleeing from the tragic consequences of one illusion, Nina rushes into the fatal grip of another even more fantastic because it is more uncommon. The pas-

sion for vicarious atonement takes a peculiar form, but
not strange to those who understand the elements of
abnormal psychology. She says: "I must learn to give
myself, do you hear—give and give until I can make
that gift of myself for a man's happiness without
scruple, without fear, without joy except in his joy!"
Her father's ideal has become so vile to her that it
pained every nerve in her body, an agony that only the
most exaggerated indulgence could alleviate.

Shortly after Nina's departure the old professor dies.
The illusion which had sheltered him for so many
years, which had won for him many battles with the
harsh world, had failed him at the crucial moment—
it could not win for him the one big battle which
should have been the crowning victory of his life.

And Nina fares no better. Her first adventure proves
to be incomplete. To satisfy her longing she finally
marries a man, who, for the moment, seems to be a
solution to her restless disillusion with the past. Of
him she says: "I only married him because he needed
me—and I needed children!" This might have been a
real solution for Nina had not Sam brought her in
contact with another family that, like her father's, only
in a far graver sense, had based its life upon a falsifica-
tion of reality.

Mrs. Evans, Sam's mother, had been tricked into
marrying a man who came from a long line of insane
ancestors. His excuse for marrying Mrs. Evans without
telling her the truth was, as she puts it: "He said he
loved me so much he'd have gone mad without me,

said I was his only hope of salvation." This romantic ideal proved a failure. Mr. Evans became insane, and to perpetuate the false ideal of life, Sam was sent away from home, never to discover the skeleton in his family closet.

The false ideal of Nina's own family life was now combined with that of her husband's. Her only solution was to fall back on science, get rid of the life within her and begin anew.

From beginning to end, the play is an attack upon the falsity of the romantic ideal. Nina, her father, Mrs. Evans, Marsden, and even Dr. Darrell have their lives twisted, warped, and in a sense destroyed by an attempt to escape from reality. Dr. Darrell sees the full implication of this ideal for all of them when he says, "Romantic imagination! It has ruined more lives than all the diseases! Other diseases, I should say! It's a form of insanity."

The ending of the play is in keeping with the spirit of the piece as a whole. The romantic imagination goes on in the lives of the younger generation. Dr. Darrell asks for one thing only from life: "Oh, God, so deaf and dumb and blind! . . . teach me to be resigned to be an atom!" And for Marsden it is the same. His summary is the final culmination of his life of romantic illusions. He says to Nina: "So let's you and me forget the whole distressing episode, regard it as an interlude, of trial and preparation, say, in which our souls have been scraped clean of impure flesh and made worthy to bleach in peace." And Nina replies: "Strange

interlude! Yes, our lives are merely strange dark interludes in the electrical display of God the Father!"

8

Dynamo, which follows *Strange Interlude,* is no exception to the rule. The characters in this play are even
more violently and passionately the children of illusion
than any of the other characters that O'Neill has created. The illusion is so exaggerated that the characters
fail to be convincing as human beings. Each in his own
way is destroyed by the passion of his desire for a life
that is no life at all, a life of romantic dreams. Religion,
love, sex are all distorted and fantastic ideals to these
characters. With great passion for the ideal but with
neither knowledge or understanding of reality they
squirm and writhe in their futile struggle with a reality
that they can neither comprehend nor master.

The confused world in which these characters move
has made the play introspective to the point where it
failed as an actual stage play—a rare thing in O'Neill's
dramas—but this does not mean that as far as a study
of O'Neill is concerned it is not valuable. It may mean
just the reverse. The time may come when the student
of O'Neill will find in this one play a key to much
that is of real importance in explaining O'Neill. As a
play it marks the end of one period in the development
of his technique and the beginning of another. To
some it has been the *reductio ad absurdum* of the
"aside" technique. But such a position is in itself of

no value, for any method of artistic representation if pushed far enough resolves either in chaos or childish simplicity, depending upon its adaptability to deal with human psychology. In this particular play it is the conflict between the real and the ideal that results in confusion.

9

From *Dynamo* to *Mourning Becomes Electra* is an easy transition. The incest theme began in *Dynamo,* and in a sense wrecked the play, only to find its proper expression in the story of General Mannon's family. The tragedy that ends with Lavinia's resolve to "Live alone with the dead, and keep their secrets" began in the home of her grandfather long before she was born. Ezra Mannon as a child had been in love with Marie Brantôme, but it was his uncle, David, who was the successful lover. So deep was Abe Mannon's resentment against this brother who had stolen the affection of the young woman that he himself had loved—loved in the thwarted Mannon sense of love, which dares not face the truth—that he drove him and his sweetheart from his home, and eventually destroyed the house in order that all memory of the cursed experience might be obliterated forever from his life.

In that episode begins the false romantic ideal which finds its culmination years later in the grandson as accomplice in the murder of his uncle and the long series of crimes that follow. From the beginning the misfortunes of the Mannons grow out of an inability to face the reality of life. They live by false Puritan standards of behavior. They did not know and could not learn that man as a psychological phenomenon is doomed to disaster if compelled to live within the confines of a limited creed. One by one "Death came tacitly and took them" from the sunlight of a world they had never seen except through the colored glass of the "Meeting House" windows. They didn't know what it was all about until too late to learn a new way of life.

The world tour of Orin and Lavinia is one of the great tragic conceptions of O'Neill, for these two children are doubly doomed because they do not know that their tragedy lies within, and that were they able to flee from the planet itself they would still bear it with them. As they travel they make one faint gesture in the direction of freedom, but the scars of the past had left a tissue which inhibited forever a turn into a new world. I refer to the Islands of the South Seas that had been so dear to the memory of Captain Brant, and dear also to the imagination of O'Neill as they were to Melville, one of the very few authors that are mentioned by name in O'Neill's plays. No single passage in the play touches the heart more than Orin's sad speech in which he tells of these Islands with a bitterness born of his disillusionment. For, as he says "They turned out to be Vinnie's islands, not mine. They only made me sick—and the naked women disgusted me. I guess I'm too much of a Mannon, after all, to turn into a pagan." To Lavinia they were real, they were an escape, so she thought, from all that had cursed her family for generations. They were to her all that her young lover had promised her, but she could not accept that which she wanted. The cruel hand of tradition led her back to her doom, where she told Peter the story of the Islands in these words:

> LAVINIA (*Dreamily*) I loved those Islands. They finished setting me free. There was something there mysterious and beautiful—a good spirit—of love—coming out of the land and sea. It made me forget death. There was no hereafter. There was only this world—the warm earth in the moonlight—the trade wind in the coco palms—the surf on the reef—the fires at night and the drum throbbing in my heart—the natives dancing naked and innocent—without knowledge of sin. (*She checks herself abruptly and frightenedly.*)

It is a characteristic of the Mannons that they knew or realized in a dim sort of way what was wrong with them, but always the realization came too late to set straight their crooked path of life. General Mannon discovered a new philosophy on the night that he was murdered, a discovery that, made twenty years earlier, would have saved him and his family. And what may be said of him in this respect may be said of many of O'Neill's characters with reference to the romantic ideal. An uncritical analysis might lead a reader to believe that O'Neill had stacked the fates against them. The opposite is really true, for it is typical of the ro-

mantic dreamer that he does not, nor can he, comprehend the falsity of his position until it is put to the
crucial test, and then it is too late to turn back. It is
O'Neill's clear development of this point that gives
tragic reality to his work, and it is the failure to grasp
this truth which has led many people to condemn him.
But he is too much of an artist not to realize truly a
fact of life that is the very essence of his own nature.
He is the romantic dreamer who knows the deadly
power of the dream's appeal. In his life, as in his work,
he has striven against it, and out of the struggle he has
created the bitter tragic beauty of his art. He never
forgets that life will exact a double toll from those who
believe that dreaming of what life ought to be will
make it other than it is.

II

The Anathema of Puritanism

"I'm not asking God or anybody for forgiveness.
I forgive myself! I hope there is a
hell for the good somewhere."
Mourning Becomes Electra

O'NEILL's scope is greater and his penetration more profound than is indicated by his rebellion against the romantic dogma. The main currents of modern thought flow clearly and swiftly across the plains over which his creative spirit broods. He welcomes with a fierce enthusiasm as well the object of his hatred as the material of love. Beauty and ugliness stir his imagination— it is the stuff on which his dreams are made. There is the enthusiasm of the reformer in his spirit, and the power of the artist to give that spirit scope.

The rebellion of the modern world against the romantic ideal has found a dramatic interpretation in O'Neill. The range of his voice is not limited to this one note, but soars to include the whole trend of modern man's attempt to liberate himself from the shackles of dead traditions. In order to do this, much of modern thought has been first a protest and secondly an affirmation. A glance in memory at the literature and art of modern times emphasizes the prominence of this theme of rebellion. From Butler, Hardy, Gorky, Ibsen, Hauptmann, and Anatole France to Anderson and Dreiser in America the voice of modern literature has been a voice of splendid and vitriolic defiance of conventional standards and dogmas. O'Neill belongs in this tradition. He is firm and sure in his denial. His rebellion is pointed and bitter, but it is no more important to an interpretation of his significance than is his affirmation of life's values. The positive value grows out of his negative criticism which is varied and profound.

Another phase of this spirit of protest finds its vent in an outspoken condemnation of the Puritan ideal. The Puritan ideal like that of the romantic dreamer represents to O'Neill a barrier on the road to the good life. Puritanism, as it emphasizes the value of self-abnegation, is distasteful to him. Puritanism, in so far as it stands for a doctrine of suppression, he condemns as a distinct force for evil. He abjures a "thou shalt not" philosophy, because it is a positive evil that endangers the only good that is possible in life, and that is happiness. Puritanism inhibits, forbids, denies, and inhibition and denial lead to fear, prejudice and narrow hatred, thwarted personality, and a beggar's attitude at the door of life. Life will not be had in its fullest sense by the hands of the beggar. Its richest gifts are only for those who demand a right to love, beauty, joy and happiness. Puritanism destroys all these goods.

And Puritanism has infected the modern world,

fastening itself like a deadly parasite upon the skin of civilization. It has made man afraid of himself. It has made him believe that there is virtue in denying himself the real pleasure and beauty that might be possible in rare moments during his struggle with an unfriendly universe. He resorts to suppression, believing that what is not seen is therefore properly destroyed. But as John Dewey says, "Suppression is not annihilation. 'Psychic' energy is no more capable of being abolished than the forms we recognize as physical. If it is neither exploded nor converted, it is turned inwards, to lead a surreptitious, subterranean life." (*Human Nature and Conduct,* p. 156.) This in the end leads to pathological symptoms that manifest themselves in strange ways which to the unwary or the self-deceived appear to have no connection with the original suppression.

The character of Dion (*The Great God Brown*) is understandable in the terms of an enforced Puritanism which made him deny the best part of himself in order to conform to the demands of a Puritan society which professed values that were essentially destructive. He summarizes these in a few words: "Wake up! Time to get up! Time to exist! Time for school! Time to learn! Learn to pretend! Cover your nakedness! Learn to lie! Learn to keep step! Join the procession! Great Pan is dead! Be ashamed!" This is the essence of the Puritan philosophy. Because it goes contrary to life's urge to express itself in active creative forms, Puritanism must forever wear a mask to conceal itself from the truth of life, or life in the character of Dion must

wear a mask to conceal itself from the death-in-
Puritanism in the character of Margaret. Puritanism is
the avowed enemy of Pan. It cannot afford to be naked
and carefree. It must assume the virtues it does not
possess, or call its vices virtues. It must "be ashamed."

Death, not life, becomes the companion of these
"ashamed" ones, and like Caligula *(Lazarus Laughed)*
they cling to death as the symbol of their power. With
him they would say, if they were as realistic and articu-
late as he: "You have murdered my only friend, Lazarus! Death would have been my slave when I am
Caesar. He would have been my jester and made me
laugh at fear!" The words of Lazarus explain the
witch-burning Puritans:

> CALIGULA. Then if there is no death, O Teacher, tell
> me why I love to kill?
> LAZARUS. Because you fear to die!

The Puritan with his eyes focused on death fosters all
that is deadly and destructive. He cannot grasp the
doctrine of Lazarus who says: "Love is man's hope—
love for his life on earth, a noble love above suspicion
and distrust!"

In *Lazarus Laughed* there is an Aged Jew who
expresses the Puritan doctrine as he shakes his fist at
the followers of Lazarus:

> "They come to him and work for nothing! For noth-
> ing! And they are glad, these undutiful ones! While they
> sow, they dance! They sing to the earth when they are

plowing! They tend his flocks and laugh toward the
sun!"

Laughter, happiness, joy in beauty are things to be
feared and hated by the Puritans. The Puritans closed
the theaters and threw out the music from the churches,
and white-washed the paintings, but that was only the
external symbol of their real crime. They stifled the
spirit of life at its source, and it is against this grosser
crime that O'Neill directs his scorn. I do not mean to
imply that O'Neill takes a thesis and writes a play to
illustrate his meaning in the manner of Ibsen or Galsworthy. His primary interest lies in the tragedy of life,
not in the teaching of some social doctrine, but in the
development of his tragic theme he analyzes the social
structure. In this he follows the sure practice of all
great artists, for it is only in presenting man against
the background of his biological and environmental
heritage that drama gains a great or a universal significance. O'Neill does not moralize, but his plays have
a great moral significance.

There are times when O'Neill does allow his thesis
to become more important than the drama itself. In
Dynamo it is quite apparent that he forgot that the
play is the thing. He had a good subject, a subject that
would lend itself to an excellent essay for a journal in
sociology, but as a play it did not "come off." He
wanted to show how the destruction of one religious
ideal demands the creation of a new one to take its
place. The theme is a good one, for if man is forever

doomed to be the slave of some personified force outside himself, then the end of one tragedy is but the
beginning of another. And so it was in the case of
Reuben Light. In his life, as in the case of all life,
religion and love were strangely mixed. It was love that
aroused Reuben to the realization that the Puritan doctrine of his father was a narrow, mean and ugly religion. Reuben liberated himself with apparent ease
from the thraldom of a fixed dogma, but he could not
escape the deeper and the more deadly implications of
his father's religion. He did not realize that when he
had denied the existence of the Christian God, he had
achieved only a verbal release. The really mordant
power of the old belief had been so deeply impressed
upon him that he did not even know that it existed.
He rebelled against the old Puritan God, and boldly
declared himself free. In reality he was as much a slave
as ever, only now he was dangerous to himself and to
society, for his freedom was merely verbal. In his heart
he still carried the real doctrine of the Puritan. He was
still a slave to a doctrine that life is essentially evil, and
that sex is the source of all that is vile and degenerate
in man. As an avowed Christian there was a certain
kind of effective unity to his life; as a rebel he thought
himself free, while in his behavior he was a slave.

The happiness that should have come from his new
life was destroyed at every turn by the teachings of the
past, and by the longing for a guiding principle that
his ignorance of philosophy made it impossible for him

to develop. Freedom without knowledge is dangerous and destructive.

Reuben's struggle is blind and hopeless. His conception of love turns to a sexual debauchery, a fact that he dimly understands and finally tries to solve by inventing the new God of mechanical power. But the influence of the past had not yet finished its sport with him. A love for his mother which likewise he did not understand made him turn in his despair to the mother of the girl he should have loved, and whom he would have loved had it not been for the depravity of his puritanical father. Obedient to the teachings of his father even when he thinks that he has abandoned them, he savagely reduces his love for Ada to an ugly debauchery, and in despair turns to her mother.

He renounced a God that he hated, but he had been so completely enslaved and broken by the old belief that freedom was impossible for him. His new God of science was a device for escaping the judgment of a sin-sick soul. It was also a means of escape from another deadly result of his puritanical training, the love for his mother.

O'Neill evidently began the theme of *Mourning Becomes Electra* in *Dynamo*. This love helps to complicate the life of Reuben, but it also confuses the original theme, and is one of the principal causes of its failure as a play. He gave the action of the drama more than the traffic would bear. This makes the play interesting from the point of view of studying O'Neill's conception of Puritanism, but it also makes the play futile as real drama.

Puritanism becomes the embodiment of all that is evil and degenerate in the life of man. Under the guise of its pretended ideals, man is being led to destruction. To O'Neill, Puritanism in its emphasis upon the life hereafter has destroyed life here; it is to him not a religion of salvation but a religion of death. Brigadier-General Mannon expresses what he had learned about the religion of Puritanism, and in the light of the treatment this theme gets in other plays, it may be taken as a fair statement of O'Neill's conception of Puritanism and its destructive power:

> MANNON. It was seeing death all the time in this war got me to thinking these things. Death was so common, it didn't mean anything. That freed me to think of life. Queer, isn't it? Death made me think of life. Before that life had only made me think of death!
> CHRISTINE. Why are you talking of death?
> MANNON. That's always been the Mannons' way of thinking. They went to the white meeting-house on Sabbaths and meditated on death. Life was a dying. Being born was starting to die. Death was being born. How in hell people ever got such notions! That white meeting-house. It stuck in my mind—clean-scrubbed and whitewashed—a temple of death! But in this war I've seen too many white walls splattered with blood that counted no more than dirty water. I've seen dead men scattered about, no more important than rubbish to be got rid of. That made the white meeting-house

seem meaningless—making so much solemn fuss over death!

General Mannon had to live to old age and go through two wars before he realized that he had been the victim of a tragic ideal. Love as an end in itself had gradually found a home in his heart. But too late. Even as he talks of the new happiness that he thinks is in store for him now that he has triumphed over the tyranny of death, the reality of it hangs over him ready to receive him into its black shroud before the red-streaked dawn shall welcome the new day.

As the tragedy in the House of Mannon grew out of a puritanic philosophy, so likewise did the tragedy in the House of Leeds. (*Strange Interlude.*) Professor Leeds lived his life in a "cosy, cultured retreat, sedu-lously built as a sanctuary where, secure with the cul-ture of the past at his back, a fugitive from reality can view the present safely from a distance." But he was not secure, for the nemesis of a false ideal pursued him, and, unknown to him, betrayed his own desire for happiness by leading him to interfere with the life of his daughter, Nina. This interference in the interests of the Puritan ideal destroyed her happi-ness and laid the sure foundation for the inevitable tragedy which was to follow.

And all this has a very close relationship to Nietzsche, whose teaching has always been a guiding spirit to O'Neill. It is significant that the proud, defiant O'Neill should have walked on the heights with Zarathustra, one who also hated the Puritans and their negative philosophy. How like the words of Mannon quoted above are these from Zarathustra:

> "There are the terrible ones who carry about in themselves the beast of prey, and have no choice except lusts or self-laceration. . . .
>
> There are the spiritually consumptive ones: hardly are they born when they begin to die, and long for doctrines of lassitude and renunciation.
>
> They would fain be dead, and we should approve of their wish! Let us beware of awakening those dead ones, and of damaging those living coffins!" (*Zarathustra*, Mod. Lib. ed. p. 60.)

This gospel of death spreads its sinister atmosphere over the lives of so many of O'Neill's characters that it might almost be called the greatest evil in the imaginative world of his dramas. It makes his world into a little city of dreadful nights where monsters of death and clay-footed idols move with incredible swiftness to dash out sunlight, beauty and happiness.

This world of O'Neill is bowed down under the heavy load of wrong ideals. Like Bunyan's Pilgrim, it toils under the burden of an almost unbearable load of sins, sins that have made the "happy isles" into shadows of the valley of death. But as is always the case with O'Neill the sins which he condemns, which he dramatizes so well, are the virtues of the past grown old, haggard, lean and skull-faced, virtues that may have served a need in older civilizations, but in the modern world have become parasitic tumors, swelling the body to ugly proportions, or appearing in the form of infected scabs that turn man into a disease and life into a dismal swamp. Opposed to this deadly menace in the world of O'Neill is the vital force of a new paganism, an old philosophy made new, a philosophy which will no longer make love "a shameless ragged ghost of a word—begging at all doors for life at any price!"

III

Religion

"I ain't never took much stock in the truck them
sky-pilots preach."

Bound East for Cardiff

I

PURITANISM is a convenient term to use in describing a
character trait of Western civilization, especially with
reference to American culture. The sense in which it
is used in the preceding chapter may have little historical validity, but modern usage has given it a special
connotation that justifies the sinister implications of
the previous discussion. That O'Neill dramatizes a
certain phase of our culture, a phase which is expressed
in the terms of a narrow ascetic ideal, seems clearly
established. That he looks upon this manifestation in
our culture as destructive, even deadly, is also certain.
To some extent it must also be clear that Puritanism is
one form of the romantic ideal. It is an escape from the
reality of life through the doorway of self-denial and
flagellation.

The transition is easily made from this subject to

religion as still another form of escape from reality. O'Neill's attitude towards the organized form of modern Christianity has always impressed me as of paramount importance in explaining the man and the significance of his work. No writer seriously occupied with an interpretation of modern life can avoid a consideration of this particular aspect of it. The Church has always professed to have a solution to man's apparently inescapable dilemma, and no doubt there have been times in the history of civilization when it did provide a very real answer. Perhaps it is true that in the Middle Ages Christianity was a genuine answer to man's eternal enigma. But as Western civilization came into the true heritage of its purely Western culture, the romantic, other-worldly religion of the East lost its influence in direct proportion to the success of the very culture which it professed to nurture. If survival of our particular civilization is to be used as a standard of worth, then it might very well be said that in our struggle to achieve material triumph over the outward aspects of nature, we are doing the very things which will lead to our ultimate annihilation. The more successful we are in the invention of machinery—machinery in every sense of the word—the more we divorce man from the very things that make for his physical and mental health. Not only that, but we seem to be driven by this machinery to take an active part in self-destruction, not being willing to wait for physical deterioration and nervous insanity to do its slow but sure work.

On these problems O'Neill has expressed himself in no uncertain terms in such plays as *The Hairy Ape* and *Strange Interlude*. But Religion itself as a destructive power is my particular concern in this chapter. The other problems of the economic struggle and war will be discussed later. O'Neill has not over-emphasized the problems of modern Christianity, but his plays give ample evidence that even from the very first he was interested in the effect of Christian doctrine upon the lives of his characters. This is just what one might expect from a dramatist who makes the material of his art man's struggle with the shadowy, indefinable and inevitable forces of life. When I use religion in dealing with this phase of O'Neill's plays, I mean by it just what he does: modern institutionalized Christianity. The careful reader of his plays will find ample evidence that he has no quarrel with Jesus as a social teacher. O'Neill's view of organized Christianity could be expressed in the words from Renan's *Life of Jesus:* "Even in our days, troubled days, in which Jesus has no more authentic followers than those who seem to deny him, the dreams of an ideal organization of society, which have so much analogy with the aspirations of primitive Christian sects, are only in one sense the blossoming of the same idea." The idea referred to is the Kingdom of God, which to O'Neill means social justice and individual freedom. What O'Neill does quarrel with is the idea of a professed religion that on Sunday preaches "One thing thou lackest: go, sell whatsoever thou hast and give to the poor, and thou shalt have treasure in heaven: and come, follow me;" a Sunday religion which on Monday is translated into the doctrine of rugged individualism, a doctrine which holds that profits made through buying cheap and selling dear is the secure end of salvation. O'Neill sees only the elements of tragedy in a philosophy which is incompatible with the exigencies of a fixed social practice. This theme which is present more by implication than in fact in the early plays grows to real tragic proportions in *Mourning Becomes Electra.*

2

As the good ship *Glencairn* moved through the fog, bound east for Cardiff, one of her sailors, Yank, lay dying. He knew that he would never again see that eastern port which now was a port of memories, memories of hates and loves, memories of lights and shadows. His ship was bound east, but he was "going west," and he knew it. All of Driscoll's talk about how Yank would be on deck in a day or two "chippin' rust . . . wid the best av us" did not delude Yank from his firm conviction that all the dirty work of a sailor's life was over for him. In his own way he was making a few of life's last reckonings; he was making his last summary. Yank was evaluating the Christian dogma in simple terms. He puts it in plain language, saying: "I was just thinkin' it ain't as bad as people think—dyin'. I ain't never took much stock in the truck them sky-pilots preach. I ain't never had religion; but I know whatever

it is what comes after it can't be no worser'n this."
He has stated in these few words a true empirical
position, measuring the dogma by what life really is
in experience, and this is what O'Neill always does. By
this standard the promise of religion is immediately
divorced from the reality of the world, a separation that
can't be glossed over except by those who are more
interested in a promised escape than in the bitter
knowledge which is the fruit of truth.

I have no intention of pushing the implications of
the situation in *Bound East for Cardiff* beyond the
limits of what is justified by the materials of the play
itself. If this were the only play in which a reference
of this kind occurred, I would admit that nothing of
any importance to O'Neill's attitude on Christianity
could legitimately be inferred. But it is not the only
play which makes definite use of Christianity in the
interpretation of man's tragedy. This is the rule of his
art, not the exception.

3

In *The Rope,* a trick play of no great importance,
the incongruity between Christian text and human
practice is used as the principal characteristic of Abraham Bentley. Bentley is sixty-five, bald, tottering, and
the very apotheosis of bitterness and hate. O'Neill has
carefully made his language from biblical text. "He
will visit thine iniquity—" is the theme of the old man's
discourse. All that Christianity has done for him is to

give him an adequate vehicle for his hate, bitterness
and love of revenge. When Luke, his son, returns,
Abraham is overjoyed and shouts:

> BENTLEY. Bring forth the best robe, and put it on
> him; and put a ring on his hand, and shoes on his
> feet: And bring hither the fatted calf, and kill it; and
> let us eat and be merry: For this my son was dead,
> and is alive again; he was lost, and is found.
> LUKE. Yuh're still spoutin' the rotten old Word o' God
> same's ever, eh? Say, give us a rest on that stuff, will
> yuh?

"The rotten old Word o' God" is so in this case not
because of anything that is intrinsically corrupt in its
nature, but because it is perverted in the mouth of a
vicious and depraved old man, who has all his life used
the language of Christianity as an end in itself. It has
never occurred to him that there need be any connection between what one says and what one does. Apparently Abraham Bentley found the excellent texts
of the Bible useful only as convenient language with
which to condemn the behavior of others.

The Rope is ironic melodrama, but it reveals a point
of view towards the Christian faith that pervades the
atmosphere of all of O'Neill's work. Like most of the
leading writers of the modern world, O'Neill is not a
Christian in the conventional understanding of Christianity. Rather he is an artist who is concerned with
the problem of man's relation to his universe. He is
seeking an answer to this puzzle. One way he is sure

will not solve the riddle, and that is the way of traditional Christianity. He is sure that man's solution to life's enigma will not be answered in the terms of the old faith, but he is also certain that instead of being helpful, this old form of an other-worldly religion is a bar across the road to happiness. As popularly conceived, it is an active force for evil, a force that leads man to make dangerous denials, and finally to the inhibition of those qualities that alone might make the brief span of this life gleam with occasional moments of real beauty, a beauty that would come through an admission that we are human and through a vigorous affirmation of our humanity. This theme which is faintly suggested here grows and develops into one of major importance in later plays, notably *Dynamo,* and the character of Abraham Bentley is a prophecy of one of O'Neill's major creations, old Ephraim Cabot in *Desire Under the Elms.*

4

The avaricious mendacity of the Church is a predominant theme in *The Fountain,* a beautiful romantic historical drama of the days of Columbus. Although this play deals with Ponce de Leon and his search for the spring of eternal youth, there is a sort of minor theme, a theme of hate, revenge, bitterness and noble ideals fallen from high estate into grasping greed for power. This is Christianity, which serves as a chorus of evil to the noble deeds of Ponce de Leon. In almost every scene the beauty of Juan's character and aspiration is thwarted by the ugliness and crime of the Church as exemplified in the actions of her leaders. This note is emphasized in the opening scene when Diego Menendez is introduced. He is "a Franciscan monk, about the same age as Juan and Luis. He has a pale, long face, the thin, cruel mouth, the cold, self-obsessed eyes of the fanatic." This monk is raging with fury against a Moorish poet whose songs suggest some of the strange, appealing beauty of the pagan ideal that Menendez and his kind are so anxious to crush forever. His hatred of the poet goes beyond all bounds when he hears him relate the story of the spring of youth, a spring which destroys the marks of old age and revives the power and passion of youthful love. The monk shouts "Idolatry," and later when the friends of the poet are not on their guard, Menendez kills the poet. Luis calls him "miserable bigot" and would have stabbed him in return had he not been restrained by Juan. Held back by force he breaks into tears as the self-righteous murderer says: "What, a soldier of Christ weep for an infidel!"

This pitiless bigotry, which from a pure dramatic point almost carries off the scene that should have been centered upon the conflict between the "soldier of iron —and dreamer" in Juan Ponce de Leon, is an indication of a theme that echoes through the whole play. It may be argued that as good drama the play suffers from the recurrence of this note of bitterness towards the Church which creeps into almost every scene. On

the other hand it gives to the play a certain grim vitality, and a critical truth that is a rich intellectual
compensation for whatever flaw it may have from the
dramatic point of view. It serves to show off the character of Juan, and it helps one to understand O'Neill
better. It is quite plain that his sympathies are with
Juan, who progresses more and more away from the
professed practices of the Church until as Governor
of Porto Rico, he finds that he is directly opposed to
all that the Church practices, and revolted by cruelty
and murder for the sake of bigotry and power. Even
his good friend, Luis, has deserted him by becoming a
Dominican and preaching: "You must renounce in
order to possess." Juan replies: "The world would be
stale indeed if that were true! I fight the battles; you
monks steal the spoils! I seek to construct; you bind
my hands and destroy!"

I find no difficulty here in knowing where O'Neill's
sympathies lie, nor in understanding why he has made
so much of the greed of the Church enriched by cruelty
and power. It is not alone the poor natives of Porto
Rico in the sixteenth century that arouse the sympathies
of O'Neill as expressed in the philosophy of Juan, but
it is helpless natives everywhere crushed by the powerful twins of the modern world: Christianity and Capitalism. In the mind of O'Neill these two forces are
evil in that they tend to destroy beauty, love of liberty,
and all that affirms the goodness of this life in this
world.

His bitterest condemnation he puts in the mouth of

a native Indian who tries to explain to his chieftain
what the white man believes, basing his interpretation,
very naturally, upon the white man's practices:

> NANO. Their devils make them strong. But they are
> not true warriors. They are thieves and rapers of
> women.
> CHIEF. Have they no God?
> NANO. Their God is a thing of earth! It is this! *(He
> touches a gold ornament that the CHIEF wears.)*
> MEDICINE MAN *(Mystified)* Gold? Gold is sacred
> to the Sun. It can be no God itself.
> NANO *(Contemptuously)* They see only things, not
> the spirit behind things. Their hearts are muddy as a
> pool in which deer have trampled. Listen. Their Medi-
> cine Men tell of a God who came to them long ago
> in the form of a man. He taught them to scorn things.
> He taught them to look for the spirit behind things.
> In revenge, they killed him. They tortured him as a
> sacrifice to the Gold Devil. They crossed two big
> sticks. They drove little sticks through his hands and
> feet and pinned him on the others—thus.

This may not be good imitation of native language,
but the idea is plain enough, and the direct criticism
reveals something of what O'Neill himself thinks of
Christianity when it is judged by its practice in contrast
with its professed doctrine. Nor should the reader fail to
observe that while the criticism of organized Christianity is acrid, the feeling towards Jesus is by implication
one of great admiration. O'Neill pays his deepest respect to the one who tried to see the "spirit behind

things." It is only because O'Neill respects Jesus for his genuine social philosophy that he can hate so openly those who have perverted the honest, simple teachings of the Galilean to the base uses of exploitation.

This point of view is further borne out by the descriptive terms used in identifying the leading Christians of the play: "They are the type of adventurous cavaliers of the day—cruel, courageous to recklessness, practically uneducated—knights of the true Cross, ignorant of and despising every first principle of real Christianity—yet carrying the whole off with a picturesque air." The Father Superior is described as "a portly monk with a simple round face, gray hair and beard. His large eyes have the opaque calm of a ruminating cow's." And these characters are well fitted for the work they do, which O'Neill is careful to point out is not in harmony with a single "principle of real Christianity." From this it might be inferred that with "real Christianity" O'Neill might be in perfect harmony. No doubt this is true, but that does not change my major premise, that with modern or ancient organized and institutionalized Christian practice, he is at odds, even actively opposed to it. Even though he may admire the earnest, sincere personality of Jesus, he would still be opposed to that aspect of his philosophy which emphasizes other-worldliness and the negation of purely human values.

The scornful attitude O'Neill always assumes in characterizing his religious men and women almost makes them typical of a class that is physically repulsive and spiritually vicious. The terms used above to describe the Father Superior indicate the type. Lily in *The First Man* says, "What ridiculous things funerals are, anyway! That stupid minister—whining away through his nose! Why does the Lord show such a partiality for men with adenoids, I wonder!" Dion in *The Great God Brown* expresses his opinion of Christians when, in heaping the bitterest denunciation he can think of upon himself, he says, "Behold your man —the sniveling, cringing, life-denying Christian slave you have so nobly ignored in the father of your sons!"

In *Dynamo* a minister of the Gospel is a principal character. "He is a man in his early sixties, slightly under medium height, ponderously built. His face is square, ribbed with wrinkles, the forehead low, the nose heavy, the eyes small and gray-blue, the reddish hair grizzled and bushy, the stubborn jaw weakened by a big indecisive mouth. His voice is the bullying one of a sermonizer who is the victim of an inner uncertainty that compensates itself by being boomingly overassertive." A page further on he is described as staring "before him with the resentful air of one brooding over a wrong done him and unsuccessfully plotting revenge."

The actual behavior of Reverend Light does not fail to support the details of this description. He is narrow-minded, selfish, cruel and tactless. Like all the people that O'Neill definitely designates as Christians, he is sadistic in his reactions to other people. It is as though O'Neill believed that the inevitable Christian brooding over the terrible tortures of hell-fire could produce no other result than sadism. An uncritical reader might hold that this is a mark of prejudice and narrowness on the part of O'Neill. I rather think not. It simply means that he is bound by the truth of human psychology. Thus when he introduces a character who is a Christian of the type who takes delight in his faith in hell, he is by very definition a sadist. But since all people are sadists to a certain extent it resolves itself into a matter of degree. The professional preachers of hell fire are just more so than those who have neither the time nor the inclination to feed and encourage the inevitable heritage of life's struggle for existence. But it is also quite clear that O'Neill finds nothing to admire in these Christian types which he introduces.

A specific example of Reverend Light's thoughts will illustrate the foulness and the cruel vanity of his mind. He is speaking to himself, brooding over his hatred of the atheist who is his next-door neighbor:

If it weren't for my cloth I'd have beaten his face to a bloody pulp! . . . I'd . . . (Suddenly horrified at himself) A murderer's thoughts! . . . Lord God, forgive me! . . .

*   *   *   *

But, Lord, Thou knowest what a thorn in the flesh that atheist, Fife, has been since the devil brought him next door! . . .
How long, O Lord? . . . does not his foul ranting begin to try Thy patience? . . . is not the time ripe to smite this blasphemer who defies Thee publicly to strike

him dead? . . . Lord God of Hosts, why dost Thou not strike him? . . . If Thou didst, I would proclaim the awful warning of it over all America! . . . I would convert multitudes, as it was once my dream to do! . . .

It should be noted here, that in contrast to the brutal Reverend Light, Mr. Fife, the atheist, is a "practical joker" with "a biting tongue, but at bottom is a good-natured man except where the religious bigotry of his atheism is concerned." Fife is sure of himself, generous in his dealings with other people, and not worried over the state of his own soul nor that of any other man. Fife has his limitations, but no reader would ever prefer the world made on the pattern of Reverend Light to a world fashioned after the model of Mr. Fife. In the plays of O'Neill the characters who are definitely portrayed as Christians are invariably less admirable than those who are not so designated. If this fact were taken literally, it might indicate an ungenerous or false attitude on the part of O'Neill. Perhaps it does, but more critically, it may mean that true Christianity does not fatten on a system of brutality and exploitation.

5

Dion in *The Great God Brown* never tires of heaping his scorn upon a doctrine that is directly opposed to the pursuit of beauty as a good in itself. He hates the cringing, beggarly attitude that is forever asking permission to live, that is forever accepting the tragedies of life with bowed head and an unrebellious spirit. He is not deluded with the hope that the rebellion will change that which is fixed in the past, but he does seem to believe that in the act of rebellion there is a self-respecting virtue. Like Milton's Satan he would say:

> "Immortal hate,
> And courage never to submit or yield,
> And what is else not to be overcome."

Dion is openly rebellious. He has asked life for an answer, and the reply has been an insult. He looks to the way that the Church points, reading from the New Testament: " 'Come unto me all ye who are heavy laden and I will give you rest.' I will come—but where are you, Savior? (*He tosses the Testament aside contemptuously*) Blah! Fixation on old Mama Christianity! You infant blubbering in the dark, you!" No answer here for the free spirit to treasure. To Dion it means that if he will give up that which he prizes most he can have that for which he has no desire. He paraphrases with contempt, "Blessed are the meek for they shall inherit graves! Blessed are the poor in spirit for they are blind!" He calls the conforming and successful Brown "One of God's mud pies," and when Brown says to him, "After all, I couldn't keep chasing after you and be snubbed every time. A man has some pride!", Dion replies, "(*bitterly mocking*) Dead wrong! Never more! None whatever! It's unmoral! Blessed are the poor in spirit, Brother!"

In *Strange Interlude* when Christianity is put to a crucial test it fails to satisfy the demands of those in sore need. O'Neill's men and women demand more from life than is prescribed for man within the limits of an ascetic dogma. When Nina is put to the terrible test of sacrificing the life she bears within her, she realizes that there is no God that can help her and says: "I don't believe in God the Father!" and Mrs. Evans replies, "And I don't believe in Him, neither, not any more. I used to be a great one for worrying about what's God and what's devil, but I got richly over it living here with poor folks that was being punished for no sins of their own, and me being punished with them for no sin but loving much. Being happy, that's the nearest we can ever come to knowing what's good! Being happy, that's good! The rest is just talk!"

Bitter experience had taught Mrs. Evans that faith in Christianity was no solution to the problems that are fundamentally biological. Genes have no respect for dogmas and doctrines. And knowing that to her sorrow, she warns Nina of the sad truth.

In this situation, as in all others of a similar tragic nature in the plays of O'Neill, the solution is always in harmony with the modern world of science. It may be that the solution is not successful, quite often it is not, but at least his characters face the issue squarely. They realize that primitive incantations cannot change biological functions any more than they can produce rain or still the waves of the sea. O'Neill does not use Christianity as a solution to tragedy, because he has no faith in it as a solution to life's complex problem in this modern world. He does not believe in it, because he is a part of this modern world, a world which has abandoned faith in the interests of technology. He might be willing to admit that this is in itself a tragedy, but he would hold that even if it is, that would not change the fact that it is true. Technology has become our God, and for ages to come we are doomed to be her slave. O'Neill is as skeptical of any ultimate solution to life through science, as he is definitely critical of the religious dogmas of the past. His tragedy goes deeper than that. He rejects Christianity first of all, because it is a passive and a negative religion which emphasizes resignation. His characters are never resigned. They are active and affirmative even in the presence of defeat. They meet destruction and death with high heads, bitter words and an undaunted courage. From Yank to Lavinia they are nobly defiant, never asking forgiveness; like Christopherson who never missed an opportunity to hurl his hatred at the "ole davil, sea," so do they all defy an unfriendly and immutable universe.

6

God, as deity, is a word that is often on the lips of O'Neill's characters, but when they speak of God, it is with neither reverence nor love, but with hatred and bitterness. These men and women of the world of Eugene O'Neill have lost all faith in a beneficent ruler of the universe, or a ruler of any kind. God remains only

as a symbol of a faith that is either dead or dying, but
since the terminology of any faith always lingers like a
ghost to haunt the spirit of man long after the actual
belief itself has passed away, so in O'Neill's plays men
and women use God as a significant symbol for the un-
named forces of evil. It does not follow that O'Neill
therefore believes that there is an active and conscious
power of evil in the world that is supernatural and bent
upon inflicting pain and suffering upon the helpless
spirit of man. To him the universe is unmoral. His
universe is not concerned about the hopes and fears, desires and aspirations of man. Whatever hope there may
be for man in the dramatic picture of the world that
O'Neill has given us arises out of the very fact that the
universe is without any particular purpose as far as
man is concerned. It leaves man free to create his own
ideals, and to bend the forces of nature to his own uses,
reversing the order of the primitive past, thereby making man the master and nature his slave.

In the transition period of man's history as a thinking animal, which is the modern period of which
O'Neill writes, man is still more rebellious and defiant
than actively concerned with a constructive program.
He is busy sweeping away the débris of a civilization of
erroneous conceptions, false beliefs and fatal superstitions. Only the simple are still living with confidence
in the world of a conscious ruling power that watches
over the destinies of men. There is a slight ironical
touch in the fact that one of the few characters in the
multitude that move across the complex stage of

O'Neill's world who expresses an earnest faith is not even given a name. She is merely Woman, and she is a prostitute. When Cape and Eleanor had torn their love to shreds in a bitter and terrible quarrel, Cape runs from his home to seek consolation in the arms of a prostitute. With masochistic fury he wants to insult and injure Eleanor, himself and all that he counts most beautiful in life. He picks a woman from the street and goes with her to her room. There in boasting of his despair, he says, "Hell is my home! I suspect we're fellow-citizens."

> WOMAN *(Superstitiously)* You oughtn't to say them things.
> CAPE *(With dull surprise)* Why?
> WOMAN. Somep'n might happen. *(A pause)* Don't you believe in no God?

This is the exception and not the rule, for usually there is open and vigorous protest or ironical scorn associated with the name of God. Darrell *(Strange Interlude)* is typical when he says, "Oh, God, so deaf and dumb and blind! . . . teach me to be resigned to be an atom!" This speech of Darrell's is in harmony with Lily *(The First Man)* when she is revolted by the suffering of Jayson's wife in child-birth. Figuratively speaking she puts the blame on God, saying: "I hereby become a life-member of the birth-control league. Let's let humanity cease—if God can't manage its continuance any better than that!"

In *All God's Chillun Got Wings* there is a bitter

treatment of God from the irony of the title to the final note of the tragedy. All God's children may have wings, but as far as this play is concerned they are the wings of evil. Gentleness, honesty, virtue, generosity and real beauty of character were brittle weapons in Jim's hands as he battled against the white man's racial prejudice. Jim's summary tells all. Ella says to him: "Will God forgive me, Jim," and he replies, "Maybe He can forgive what you've done to me; and maybe He can forgive what I've done to you; but I don't see how He's going to forgive—Himself." Nor could any-one see it judging from the basis of this play. To O'Neill it is quite plain that there is no shop in this world at which man can purchase salve of forgiveness; there is no such commodity for sale. Be it for good or ill, man must face the truth.

Another variant of this same concept of God as un-feeling and unsympathetic is revealed in *Desire Under the Elms*. In this play, as in all the others, the implica-tion is in reality that the world is godless, but since the drama must use the indirect method, O'Neill often makes it appear that there is a malignant force that rules the world. Such primitivism is not a part of his realistic system. On the other hand, it would be futile to at-tempt an evaluation of Ephraim Cabot in *Desire Under the Elms* without considering the implications of that Old Man of Iron's conception of God. Ephraim was above all things consistent. He never allowed his re-ligion to interfere with his practice. Those who think that Ephraim was not truly religious and point to his sex life, his cruelty, hatred and hard unsympathetic nature as evidence of their thesis do not take into account who or what his God was. But Ephraim knew. He describes Him in plain words:

> Wall—this place was nothin' but fields o' stones. Folks laughed when I tuk it. They couldn't know what I knowed. When ye kin make corn sprout out o' stones, God's livin' in yew! They wa'n't strong enuf fur that! They reckoned God was easy. They laughed. They don't laugh no more. Some died hereabouts. Some went West an' died. They're all under ground—fur follerin' arter an easy God. God hain't easy. An' I growed hard. . . . God's hard, not easy! God's in the stones! Build my church on a rock—out o' stones an' I'll be in them! That's what He meant t' Peter! Stones. I picked 'em up an' piled 'em into walls. Ye kin read the years o' my life in them walls, every day a hefted stone, climbin' over the hills up and down, fencin' in the fields that was mine, whar I'd made thin's grow out o' nothin'—like the will o' God, like the servant o' His hand. It wa'n't easy. It was hard an' He made me hard fur it.

And the God that rules over the world of Eugene O'Neill's plays is very much like the old man, Ephraim Cabot himself, or like Ephraim's God, which is much the same thing. By inference this means no God at all in the modern world, for by the painless road of least resistance we long ago abandoned in theory the old God of the Puritans, substituting the easy, friendly, good-health-physical-culture God of the modern Y. M. C. A. And for this deity O'Neill has no need. He has

made his dramas an interpretation of the modern
world, and in the modern world the anthropomorphic
rulers are swiftly receding into the limbo of all forgotten things.

But O'Neill will not allow our old gods to pass away
silently and without rebuke. Their long, cruel reign has
left deep scars and the spirit of man rises in indignant
and bitter rebellion. O'Neill the artist interpreting the
new courage of a new world carries with him some of
the hatred of the old, for as all great and broad-sweep-
ing conceptions of life are born out of the hell of pain,
so with O'Neill. This lack of disinterestedness would
by a Matthew Arnold be condemned as evidence of a
limitation in his work as a dramatist. The artist should
hold himself aloof from the struggle; he should reflect
life, not evaluate it. He should leave the problem of
values to the professor of ethics. So many would hold,
and on this very basis much has been written in condemnation of O'Neill. I hold that such a position is absurd in the light of what great art has been in the past.
Milton and Dante, Goethe and Byron would have no
meaning apart from the milieu that nurtured them. I
do not mean to imply that O'Neill is a second Milton
nor anybody else than himself, but that he is the living
embodiment of this modern world is the theme that I
do hold, and that he has given vitality and meaning to
this world in his plays. As Nathan writes: "The life
that he so produces is often not to the taste of the
American audience, for it is not always a sweet and
pretty life—the life which that audience cherishes

across the footlights—but life it is none the less. It pulses from his stages; it quivers from his adjectives and verbs. And it makes his manuscripts warm, beating and vital things. Many American plays have heart. It has remained for O'Neill, to no little extent, to add the blood." (Preface to *The Moon of the Caribbees,* Mod. Lib. Ed.)

Since O'Neill is very definitely caught in the mad struggle of modern life, it is only reasonable to expect him to reflect its passion in reason, for since it is an age of critical evaluation, there is passion and even hatred in its highest critical moments. Criticism does not sit serene and holy and self-righteous in its court of justice. It is an age of militant aggressive criticism, not an age of cool self-composed and secure judgments as those that emanated from the critics of the eighteenth century. This is the age of Mencken in criticism. A criticism that waves high its banner at every victory won from the fortification of entrenched traditionalism. It is typical that as the defeated one flees with the torn and scattered pages of Aristotle and Boileau, he trails a smoke screen to protect his retreat.

O'Neill's direct manner in dealing with the tragedy of life is always colored with this critical passion. So it is that the old God who has ruled so long and so ill, to judge from the plays, is severely treated at times. He is even made sport of for the benefit of the groundling. In *Marco Millions* O'Neill makes Kublai say: "My hideous suspicion is that God is only an infinite, insane energy which creates and destroys without other purpose than to pass eternity in avoiding thought. Then the stupid man becomes the Perfect Incarnation of Omnipotence and the Polos are the true children of God!"

The whole spirit of this play is satirical and not too much importance should be attached to such a statement. But suppose one were, for the sake of argument only, to accept the world of Eugene O'Neill as a real world, and then ask the question, what sort of a God must have created such a world, the answer might approach the truth if it were: "A God of infinite, insane energy which creates and destroys without other purpose than to pass eternity in avoiding thought." This concept is further reinforced by direct statement from many other sources in the plays, as numerous examples already quoted bear witness. It is as though Nina (*Strange Interlude*) in her statement to Darrell summarized it when she says: "But life doesn't seem to be pretty, does it? And, after all, you aided and abetted God the Father in making this mess."

The God of O'Neill's plays may be described in the terms Coleridge applied to Iago: "Motiveless malignity." It is thus that Dion (*Great God Brown*) sees Him when reminiscing about his mother: "I remember a sweet, strange girl, with affectionate, bewildered eyes as if God had locked her in a dark closet without any explanation."

In this modern world of conflicting values, words are made meaningless by the contrasting definitions attached to them by opposing schools of thought. O'Neill

levels harsh criticism against Christianity and the organized religion through which it finds conventional
expression, but the critical thinker may discern in his
point of view the foundations of a better religion than
the one he denies. It was said of Tolstoi that the greatest fault he revealed as a Christian was that he thought
Jesus meant what he said in the Sermon on the Mount.
The same might be held for O'Neill, that he does not
deny Jesus as much as he denies what tradition has
made out of his teachings.

IV

The Pagan Way of Life

"Life is for each man a solitary cell whose walls
are mirrors. Terrified is Caligula by the faces he
makes! But I tell you to laugh in the mirror, that
seeing your life gay, you may begin to live as a
guest, and not as a condemned one." *Lazarus
Laughed*

I

EUGENE O'NEILL belongs in the liberal tradition of the
last fifty years. Like Shaw, Ibsen, Strindberg, Gorky,
Hauptmann (in his youth) and Andreyev, O'Neill is a
rebel against the Puritan way of life, but also like the
best dramatists and thinkers of modern times his rebellion is made vital and powerful by the conception of
a new life—vigorous, healthy and nobly self-sufficient.
Unlike many of the old dramatists, he does not regret
the death of old faiths and old dogmas. He has shed
the last vestiges of the tragic sorrow which followed
the realization that man had lost faith in an eternal life.
O'Neill's modernity lies in the fact that he has accepted
the scientific view of man and the world, and found
in that view a real philosophy of happiness. This happi-

ness is not the old acquiescent kind based on some far-off eternal peace, nor is it a happiness of foolish gayety expressed by innocuous and unthinking laughter. It is a joy that comes from accepting life on its own terms, fearlessly and without compromise. It is an affirmative philosophy which does not weep over the death of false gods, but rather sings with the joy of a captive, freed at last, from the tyranny of an ancient prison.

With O'Neill this has not led to the writing of comedy. Just the reverse, for there is little true comedy in any of his plays. That is exactly what we might expect, for man newly escaped from the dungeon of false hopes and narcotic dreams is still a victim of the slavery of the past. O'Neill sees this as the very essence of modern drama. He sees the potentiality of a new world in which men will recognize their human limitations, abandon all yearning for supernatural attributes, and embrace the brief span of life on this earth as good in itself. With one gesture they will throw away the curse of self-inflicted pain, and affirm the new world of joy in all things human.

In the meantime, the contrast between the old ideals and the new gives rise to a conflict that has created a milieu for tragedy such as has not existed since the days of the Greeks. The Greek tragedy grew out of the conflict between what man knew was the good life for him, and what tradition held to be the gods' opinion of the good life. The modern age is much the same as the great age of Greek criticism in this respect, and out of that conflict O'Neill has conceived his tragedies.

This has led him to embody the forces for evil in the puritanic ideal, and the forces for good in the modern affirmation of life. Life is destroyed, brought to a bitter end in most of O'Neill's plays, but it never accepts the death verdict without protest, without affirming the conviction that there is a way of life, could we but agree to accept it, that would lead to happiness. O'Neill, like Nietzsche, gives to life "a yea-saying free of reserve, an affirmation of suffering itself, of guilt, of all that is questionable and strange in existence." There is in him, as in Nietzsche, an almost savage will to power, a will to live life to its fullest with all its tragedy and sorrow, a will to face it with insult and scorn, scorn and insult flung with vengeance and hate against the brutal tyranny of the past. This is an affirmation of life even in the face of death. Character after character in his plays shows this noble defiance which is the essence of an affirmative philosophy. From Robert in *Beyond the Horizon* to Lavinia in *Mourning Becomes Electra* they are all rebels against the cruel tyranny of false ideals. The fierce will to live which was thwarted by the Puritanism of her past life could not break Lavinia's spirit. When the gods, in the Aeschylean sense, had finished their sport with her, she entered her house and accepted her doom. She did not submit in meekness and humility, but with courage and fortitude she remained defiant to the end. With a hatred that will last a lifetime, she says: "I'll never go out or see anyone! I'll have the shutters nailed closed so no sunlight can ever get in. I'll live alone with the dead, and keep their secrets, and let them hound me, until the curse is paid out and the last Mannon is let die! I know they will see to it I live for a long time! It takes the Mannons to punish themselves for being born." And her last words are: "Throw out all the flowers."

2

Ernest Renan was one of the most liberal thinkers of the nineteenth century in the field of religious thought, yet even so he often repeated the statement that "the most important act of our lives is death." As long as death was the final goal of life, this was true, and it was true for Renan even after he had liberated himself and his age from certain supernatural aspects of the old faith. Many of the greatest literary men of the early twentieth century were still the slaves of this doctrine. The gloom that casts such oppressive shadows over the works of Dreiser is due to the fact that he cannot avoid grief over the limited possibilities of this transitory life. Since it has no celestial scope, it follows, in his mind, that life is a lost cause, something to make tragedy out of, something to weep over, but life to Dreiser is not an end in itself to be justified by its very limitations. To him life must forever seek some illusion to shield it from the grim tragedy of reality. He considers this escape a futile gesture, perhaps even evil in itself, but none the less necessary to man. In *The Genius* he writes: "If I were personally to define religion I would say that it is a bandage that man has invented to protect a soul made bloody by circumstance, an envelope to pocket him from the unescapable and unstable illimitable." Like Hardy he thinks that "happiness was but the occasional episode in a general drama of pain." Neither Dreiser nor Hardy accepts this view with resignation. They rebel, but their rebellion is the tragedy that to them seems the inevitable lot of man. The evil lies in life itself and not in the social system, or religious system, or anything else that is subject to change. I do not mean to imply that Dreiser does not condemn the social system as a contributing factor, but he seems to think that if it was not this system it would be some other equally unfavorable to happiness for man. Pope's "whatever is is right" has become for Dreiser: whatever is is wrong, and it always will be wrong, for life is a fatal disease from which man cannot escape.

This particular view of life is also a part of O'Neill's world, but there is another element added which gives to it a new vitality. In the dramas of O'Neill there is a vigorous affirmation, an almost pagan defense of life itself.

Sometimes this takes the form of a dream of the past before modern industrialism destroyed the beauty and joy of a wholesome and carefree life. Paddy (*The Hairy Ape*) could remember the times when the life of a sailor was worth living. In contrast to the grimy slave's life in the stokehole, he pictures the bold, free life of the old-fashioned sailing ship:

Oh, the clean skins of them, and the clear eyes, the straight backs and full chests of them! Brave men they was, and bold men surely! We'd be sailing out, bound down round the Horn maybe. We'd be making sail in the dawn, with a fair breeze, singing a chanty song wid no care to it. And astern the land would be sinking low and dying out, but we'd give it no heed but a laugh, and never a look behind. For the day that was, was enough, for we was free men—and I'm thinking 'tis only slaves do be giving heed to the day that's gone or the day to come—until they're old like me. Oh, to be scudding south again wid the power of the Trade Wind driving her on steady through the nights and the days! Full sail on her! Nights and days! Nights when the foam of the wake would be flaming wid fire, when the sky'd be blazing and winking wid stars. Or the full of the moon maybe. Then you'd see her driving through the gray night, her sails stretching aloft all silver and white, not a sound on the deck, the lot of us dreaming dreams, till you'd believe 'twas no real ship at all you was on but a ghost ship like the *Flying Dutchman* they say does be roaming the seas forevermore widout touching a port. And there was the days, too. A warm sun on the clean decks.

And so it goes on, a prose poem in praise of a life that possessed real values, a life that was at peace with itself and the world in which it lived. This reminiscent world of Paddy's is gone, and in its place is the world of the coal hole and the blazing furnaces of the ocean liner. Yank calls Paddy's dream world "crazy tripe" and "a dope dream" and "hittin' de pipe of de past,

dat's what he's doin'.'" But the day is to come for Yank
when he will realize that the modern world is not for
him, and that in spite of all his boasting he does not
"belong." He does not "belong" because the gospel of
profits has won its final triumph over the gospel of life.
Life has lost its value, because the old religion of death
has found a powerful ally in the modern industrialism.
It does not therefore follow that in life itself there is no
potentiality for perfect adaptation to the world. The
day was and it may be again when man will cease to
weep for the day that is spent, cease to worry over the
day that is to come. He will live in the beauty of the
present, and glory in each moment, ceasing the futile
task of carrying ashes into the mountain, and instead
he will carry fire into the valleys. And in the valley he,
like Zarathustra, will "create new values" and "freedom for new creating."

The Great God Brown seethes with criticism of the
world of Puritan ideals. William A. Brown, architect, is
the embodiment of all that makes for the prosperous
successful business man. Profits have become his ideal,
and for profits he will sell his little, shriveled life soul;
he will sell the lives of men; he will imprison free
spirits; he will do all that is mean, niggardly and vicious; worst of all, he will do it in the name of virtue,
prosperity, religion, politics, or any other term that may
be used interchangeably to describe his befuddled conception of human values. To the casual eye with vision
darkened by the smoked glasses of temporary aims
and material prosperity, Mr. William A. Brown is not a

bad man. He may be described in the satirical words which Russell uses in defining the "good" man:

> He has a wholesome horror of wrongdoing, and realizes that it is our painful duty to castigate Sin. He has a still greater horror of wrong thinking, and considers it the business of the authorities to safeguard the young against those who question the wisdom of the views generally accepted by middle-aged successful citizens. Apart from his professional duties, at which he is assiduous, he spends much time in good works: he may encourage patriotism and military training; he may promote industry, sobriety, and virtue among wage-earners and their children by seeing to it that failures in these respects receive due punishment; he may be a trustee of a university and prevent an ill-judged respect for learning from allowing the employment of professors with subversive ideas. Above all, of course, his "morals," in the narrow sense, must be irreproachable. (Bertrand Russell, *Skeptical Essays*, p. 113.)

And such are the "good" of the world for whom the free and independent must slave for the right to live. To them the followers of liberty must bend the knee, and, in a supplicant spirit, ask for permission to live. These practical ones have the virtue of being sincere in the development of their limited plans, and on the basis of their sincerity they rule with self-given virtue over those who would live a free life unhampered by the successes of the clay-footed idols of the market place.

Opposed to the success of Brown is the fiery spirit of

Dion. He seems to be one who has turned away from life, but in reality he has only turned away from the rabble, because "he hated to share with them fountain, flame and fruit."

"And many a one who hath gone into the wilderness and suffered thirst with beasts of prey, disliked only to sit at the cistern with filthy camel-drivers." (*Zarathustra* p. 109.) Dion is one of those rare spirits who believe that the virtue of life lies in the living of it, and therefore he is subject to the indignity of the slave morality of those who know not what life is.

> But his thirst doth not persuade him to become like those comfortable ones: for where there are oases, there are also idols.

> Hungry, fierce, lonesome, God-forsaken: so doth the lion-will wish itself.

> Free from the happiness of slaves, redeemed from Deities and adorations, fearless and fear-inspiring, grand and lonesome. (*Ibid.*)

And such is the spirit of Dion who would "spit on this city of shopmen," the city which is the world of William A. Brown. Between his wife and his friend, Brown, he is beaten and thwarted. He cries out for life and is given a job, as though the beginning and end of all good things was to work for Mr. Brown. Dion's criticism is pointed when he says to Cybel, "Is that the only answer—to pin my soul into every vacant diaper?"

Cybel, the prostitute, is nearer to the real truth of life than Brown, for she at least has a vision of what life could be, as is shown by her expression of it to Dion: "Life's all right, if you let it alone."

The gospel of resignation and obedience was hateful to Dion, was bitter poison to his love of happiness and beauty. Brown did not even know what he had done, for he did not know nor understand that the spirit of a poet may be imprisoned, starved and tortured, but it cannot be broken. It does not submit, nor does it ever cease to curse its foolish jailer. When Brown rebuked Dion by calling him "positively evil," Dion replied:

> DION. When Pan was forbidden the light and warmth of the sun he grew sensitive and self-conscious and proud and revengeful—and became Prince of Darkness.
> BROWN. You don't fit the rôle of Pan, Dion. It sounds to me like Bacchus, alias the Demon Rum, doing the talking. Go home. Be a good scout. It's all well enough celebrating design being accepted but—

And Dion's answer expresses his pent-up hatred of all that Mr. Brown stands for as a man and childish thinker. In the following speech of Dion is found the full condemnation of the Brown ideal and by implication the true value of life is expressed, the value which comes from accepting the limitations of the human animal and creating happiness and beauty out of them alone.

DION. I've been the brains! I've been the design! I've
designed even his success—drunk and laughing at him
—laughing at his career! Not proud! Sick! Sick of myself and him! Designing and getting drunk! Saving
my woman and children! Ha! And this cathedral is
my masterpiece! It will make Brown the most emi-
nent architect in this state of God's Country. I put a
lot into it—what was left of my life! It's one vivid
blasphemy from sidewalk to the tips of its spires!—but
so concealed that the fools will never know. They'll
kneel and worship the ironic Silenus who tells them
the best good is never to be born! Well, blasphemy is
faith, isn't it? In self-preservation the devil must believe! But Mr. Brown, the Great Brown, has no faith!
He couldn't design a cathedral without it looking like
the First Supernatural Bank! He only believes in the
immortality of the moral belly!

The limitations of Mr. Brown, in so far as they are
the limitations of man, and an expression of the narrow, unsocial and crudely life-denying Puritanism,
must be surpassed. Dion in his struggle against the
forces of real evil represented in the practical good of
Mr. Brown becomes one of the great despisers.

From the first scene, in which Dion is compelled to
wear a mask in order that Margaret may recognize
him, to the end of his life, he is at war with a conventional false world in which the true and real values of
life are buried under a deep coating of false ideals of
speech, conduct and truth. Dion's way of life, like that

of O'Neill, seems to involve a contradiction. On the one hand he strives for a noble, free and beautiful existence, and on the other he scorns all that the world describes as its true ideal. Dion spits with contempt upon the golden rule: love thy neighbor as thyself. Is it not impossible to conceive of Dion as an ideal character, when he denies what all other men seem to call the good? He says, "Fear thy neighbor as thyself!" He is repelled by all that passes for the good in the world of conventional thought. It needs but a little scrutiny to realize that his rebellion is not against the ideals themselves, but against the swinish disregard for them that permits a lip worship so hypocritical that it does not even know that it is false. He rebels against the practice that makes it possible for man to say on Sunday, with seeming reverence: "Sell whatsoever thou hast, and give to the poor, and thou shalt have treasure in heaven: and come, take up the Cross, and follow me," and then on Monday by his actions he really says: buy cheap and sell dear, cut wages, work the help long hours, fire the old who have outlasted their usefulness, be a good capitalist, be successful, make money, and above all win the praise and adulation of fools who will worship at the shrine of Gold, or the shrine of the Great God Brown. Thus it comes to pass that those who live what they preach are not the enemies of Dion, but it is those who do not even know that there is a meaning to the ideal, or that there is a life apart from that which is measured by the profits, and the windy honors that profits bring in their wake like a pestilent

cloud of vapors. From this hateful life, Dion turns to
life that is free from contamination, a life that is puri-
fied by its biological limitations. Thus Dion loves Margaret, but he does not know who his wife is. He listens
with rapture to Cybel, the prostitute:

> CYBEL. Oh, God, sometimes the truth hits me such a
> sock between the eyes I can see the stars!—and then
> I'm so damn sorry for the lot of you, every damn
> mother's son-of-a-gun of you, that I'd like to run out
> naked into the street and love the whole mob to death
> like I was bringing you all a new brand of dope that'd
> make you forget everything that ever was for good!
> But they wouldn't see me, any more than they see each
> other. And they keep right on moving along and dying
> without my help anyway.
> DION. You've given me strength to die.
> CYBEL. You may be important but your life's not.
> There's millions of it born every second. Life can cost
> too much even for a sucker to afford it—like everything
> else. And it's not sacred—only the you inside is. The
> rest is earth.

Cybel represents the affirmative life, the life that
is of the earth, and apart from man's imposed and
erroneous ideas of moral values, is the real good of life.
She has accepted life as a value in itself. She has said
that the value of life lies in the act of living and not in
the act of denying that which gives meaning to existence. In O'Neill's own words she "is an incarnation of
Cybele, the Earth Mother doomed to segregation as a
pariah in a world of unnatural laws, but patronized

by her segregators, who are thus themselves the first victims of their laws." (Clark, *Modern Amer. Writers,* p. 160.) Man with his "unnatural laws" has renounced life, and out of the froth of his renunciation, he has mixed a witch's potion for himself. Having once drunk the fatal brew, he is no longer true to the mother who bore him, but instead he has become a monster with a divided allegiance. He has become something that must be surpassed, if he is ever to be happy again. He must listen to the strong, fresh voice of Zarathustra: "Remain true to the earth, my brethren, with the power of your virtue! Let your bestowing love and your knowledge be devoted to the meaning of the earth." O'Neill, like Nietzsche, finds the true life in the scrap that the moralist has thrown away. He counsels against the pale shadows of asceticism, and holds that man must go back to life for meaning, back to the earth, giving to the earth a meaning, a human meaning.

The Great God Brown is a dramatization of the struggle that has grown out of the false values that the moralist has taken for reality. It is a dramatization of one of the most ancient themes of tragedy: Hebraism and Hellenism, duty and pleasure, negation and affirmation, or, as in this play, St. Anthony and Dionysus. A quotation from O'Neill will help to make it clear and also keep one reminded that back of his dramatic action lies an interpretation of life. He writes:

> I had hoped the names chosen for my people would give a strong hint of this . . . Dion Anthony—Dionysus

and St. Anthony—the creative pagan acceptance of life, fighting eternal war with the masochistic, life-denying spirit of Christianity as represented by St. Anthony—the whole struggle resulting in this modern day in mutual exhaustion—creative joy in life for life's sake frustrated, rendered abortive, distorted by morality from Pan into Satan, into a Mephistopheles mocking himself in order to feel alive; Christianity, once heroic in martyrs for its intense faith, now pleading weakly for intense belief in anything, even Godhead itself. (In the play it is Cybele, the pagan Earth Mother, who makes the assertion with authority: 'Our Father, Who Art!' to the dying Brown, as it is she who tries to inspire Dion Anthony with her certainty in life for its own sake. (Clark, *Mod. Amer. Writers,* p. 160.)

Dion is man in the grip of a force he cannot control. Dion is the true man, "the supersensitive painter-poet" —all that man might have been or could be—but he is also man tangled in a witch's web. Standing guard over him is William A. Brown who believes only in the gods that make a great noise. O'Neill says of him:

Brown is the visionless demigod of our new materialistic myth—a Success—building his life of exterior things, inwardly empty and resourceless, an uncreative creature of superficial preordained social grooves, a by-product forced aside into slack waters by the deep main current of life-desire. (Clark, *op. cit.,* p. 161.)

This one, with filth at the bottom of his soul, tried to wring Dion's secret from him, as he always tries to destroy that which is beautiful, for even though he cannot recognize beauty, still he senses something that is an enemy to his clay-footed idols. Brown cannot gain his wish, but he can torture Dion until despair forces him to pass his mask on to him. In the dumb depth of his fatuous soul, he was fool enough to will his own destruction. Even as a child he had tried to steal Dion's genius, and failing in that to destroy Dion. Now his power has given him what he wanted, but as life's abject slave he did not know that he was willing his final annihilation. A pompous wind bag of success, he succumbed to the reality of life, as our whole civilization must, if it does not learn that the way of the painter-poet Dion is a surer guide to life than the banker-business man Brown.

Dion once knew a way to the good life, but the fixed ideals of a misguided conception of life's purpose made it impossible to live as he would have lived in a world that recognized beauty and happiness as the highest goal towards which life can aim. In order to live his life to himself, he was forced to wear a mask and to play a double rôle of business man and artist; self-tortured conformer and lover of freedom. In Dion, O'Neill has given us the ancient tragedy of the conflict between what man desires and what he gets from life. And the reason man gets a stone when he asks for bread is, as Nietzsche puts it: "A necessary result of the view that mankind does not follow the right road of its own accord, that it is by no means divinely ruled, but rather, that it is precisely under the cover of its most sacred values that the tendency to negation, corruption and decadence has exerted such seductive power." (*Ecce Homo* Mod. Lit. Ed. p. 90.)

3

The Great God Brown is an introduction to *Lazarus Laughed*. In Lazarus the great contradiction of desiring one thing and living another is resolved into one all-possessing affirmative attitude. Lazarus is a Nietzschean Yea-sayer. In him all opposites are resolved into a new unity. As is said of Zarathustra, so it may be said of Lazarus: "In him all oppositions are resolved into a new unity. The loftiest and the basest powers of human nature, the sweetest, the lightest, and the most terrible, stream from one source with an eternal certainty. Before him, no one knew what was height, or depth; still less did they know what was truth." Like Zarathustra, Lazarus is a dancer who put on "This crown of the laugher, this rose-garland crown: to you my brethren do I cast this crown! Laughing have I consecrated; ye higher men, *learn,* I pray you—to laugh!" (*Zarathustra,* p. 295.) Lazarus teaches man to unlearn "the sorrow-sighing, and all the populace-sadness! Oh, how sad the buffoons of the populace seem to me today." (*Ibid* p. 294.) Lazarus is man become spiritually of age. He has been through the abysm of terrible thoughts, and has embraced all into his system of values. He has learned to give "the everlasting Yea to all things, 'the

tremendous and unlimited saying of Yea and Amen . . .
Into every abyss do I hear the benediction of my yea to
Life'."

To the greedy questions of the soulless ones, Lazarus
answered:

> There is only life! Death is dead! Fear is no more!
> There is only life! There is only laughter! *And Lazarus
> begins to laugh, softly at first—a laugh so full of a com-
> plete acceptance of life, a profound assertion of joy in
> living, so devoid of all self-consciousness or fear, that it is
> like a great bird song triumphant in depths of sky, proud
> and powerful, infectious with love, casting on the listener
> an enthralling spell.*

Lazarus has achieved that which was not possible to
Dion. He has separated himself from the horrible slavery of St. Anthony, and has become the pure Diony-
sian, the affirmer of life. Fear, death, punishment, torture, tyranny, all these vile companions of St. Anthony,
the officers in the army that has held man a slave to
false ideals and perverted his happiness into a selfish
sadistic creed, all these are left behind. Lazarus faces
forward into a new world that rests upon the will to
live, which means the will to happiness—freed from
the tyranny of the past, the fear of death.

The meaning of "there is no death" is not a mere
mystical phrase. It is a generalization of the meaning of
life, for life is in itself a contradiction of death, and to
him who lives for the sake of living, death can hold no
terrors. The chorus in *Lazarus Laughed* chants:

Men call life death, and fear it.
They hide from it in horror.
Their lives are spent in hiding.
Their fear becomes their living.
They worship life as death!

LAZARUS. And here the song of Lazarus' life grew
pitiful. 'Men must learn to live,' it mourned. 'Before
their fear invented death they knew, but now they
have forgotten. They must be taught to laugh again!'
and Lazarus answered 'Yes!'

Again the famous speech of General Mannon comes
to mind to clarify Lazarus' meaning: "That's always
been the Mannons' way of thinking. They went to the
white meeting-house on Sabbaths and meditated on
death. Life was a dying. Being born was starting to
die. Death was being born."

Lazarus has taken the affirmative way of life. Death
to the lover of life is dead. And fear is dead. And all the
haunting shadows of the slaves of terror and death are
dead. And Lazarus' laugh is a "blood-stirring call to
that ultimate attainment in which all prepossession
with self is lost in an ecstatic affirmation of Life."

In this play there is no hesitation or compromise.
Lazarus has found out the truth; he knows the true
way of life, and he speaks out, urging all to follow him.
Here is O'Neill as no mere destructive critic, not that
he ever is *merely* anything except to those who have no
understanding. He affirms the life of freedom in every
sense of the word. He condemns the modern mechanized, industrialized civilization, because it stifles all that

springs from freedom, and in doing that it destroys all that is fundamental to the good life. Lazarus speaks:

> Out with you! Out into the woods! Upon the hills! Cities are prisons wherein man locks himself from life. Out with you under the sky! Are the stars too pure for your sick passions? Is the warm earth smelling of night too desirous of love for your pale introspective lusts? Out! Let laughter be your new clean lust and sanity! So far man has only learned to snicker meanly at his neighbor! Let a laughing away of self be your new right to live forever!

Here is the *will to be* expressed directly, the will to be free and happy. All the temporary and practical ideals of Brown, and all that Brown stands for are swept aside in one fine poetic gesture. All that makes life an unnecessary tragedy of hate, jealousy, selfishness, fear, puritanical bigotry and sexual depravity are swept aside. All these hindrances to the good life which are the earmarks of what we call civilization are condemned. The arraignment of our civilization for its weakness, cowardice and tragic failure is a theme in this play as it is in almost every play that O'Neill has written, and therein lies most of his strength, for a civilization that offers as the final culmination of its ideals such a spectacle as the recent World War is rotten to the core. To the nostrils of the poet and all sensitive men it stinks with the filth of the charnel house. It is a civilization of lies which were it not for the traditional belief that human beings are rational would

appear like the civilization of an over-grown mad-
house. Not only do the people torture themselves to the
point of destruction during the periods of their wars,
but during peace times—those rare intervals, those
strange interludes—they systematically deny themselves
the pleasure and freedom that might be possible for
them. Like the Orthodox Priest in *Lazarus Laughed*,
they cry out against joy and laughter, saying with him:
"It is a foul sin in the sight of Jehovah." He
lives upon the torture and the conviction of sin, and
knows only too well that, if you take from man the
fear of sin, you take from him the fear of death.
Neither the Priest nor Caligula can rule after a philosophy of life has supplanted a philosophy of death.
When the open sky, the stars, the sunshine and the
song of the birds are man's shrine, and not the white
sepulcher, then he will no longer be a slave to the religion of death. He will then be free from morality as
Nietzsche defines it: "Morality is the idiosyncrasy of
decadents, actuated by a desire *to avenge themselves
successfully upon life.*" The morality of self-renuncia-
tion which is essentially the morality of degeneration
will exist for them no more, and they will laugh with
the freedom of Dionysiac laughter.

Lazarus Laughed is the expression of O'Neill's philosophy of the "good life." By use of masks, dancing,
chorus and unique stage grouping, together with the
purely fantastic idea of Lazarus back from the grave, he
sets forth his theory of human values. He sweeps away
the values that have grown out of traditional belief, and

like Nietzsche he begins by rejecting the gospel of renunciation. This gospel, he holds, has done more to
pervert man and deprive him of happiness than any
other doctrine. This gospel has developed the bad conscience, and with Nietzsche he would say, "Believe me,
my friends: the sting of conscience teacheth one to
sting."

Lazarus is plain and outspoken to his followers on
this point. He berates them for their low ideals and
their inability to live up to the high ideal of freedom
and happiness. Too long have they lived as the slaves
of a philosophy of death to be able to realize that there
is a life worth living here and now on this earth. He
says to them:

> You Laugh, but your laughter is guilty! It laughs a
> hyena laughter, spotted, howling its hungry fear of life!
> That day I returned did I not tell you your fear was no
> more, that there is no death? You believed then—for a
> moment! You laughed—discordantly, hoarsely, but with
> a groping toward joy. What! Have you so soon forgot-
> ten, that now your laughter curses life again as of old?
> That is your tragedy! You forget! You forget the God
> in you! You wish to forget! Remembrance would imply
> the high duty to live as a son of God—generously!—
> with love!—with pride!—with laughter! This is too
> glorious a victory for you, too terrible a loneliness! Easier
> to forget, to become only a man, the son of woman, to
> hide from life against her breast, to whimper your fear
> to her resigned heart and be comforted by her resigna-
> tion! To live by denying life!

Here is an expression of the good life that should not seem strange to Americans who have long listened to the brave language of Walt Whitman. Like Whitman, O'Neill rebels against the narrow limitations of a religion of denial. Whitman and O'Neill are alike in that they are both impressed with the good things of the earth that lie wasted because man, as the slave of a false system, has labeled the beautiful as ugly and the good as bad. Having once called the very forces by which they became men by the name of evil, they go sadly on "Nailing man's soul to the cross of their fear," and then worshiping blindly at the cross that they themselves have made. Man's "loneliness is but the fear of life." It is a terror that has grown out of his desire to make himself into a god, by the road of suffering, when all the time he was a god by the way of happiness, but he could not believe in himself.

Lazarus is not a mere mystical dreamer. There is as a basis for his system a hard logic of reality. It asks the simple question: Is man here to live or to die? That he will eventually die is certain, but is that the important thing, or is it important that he live? If he chooses as Lazarus does to hold that life is an end in itself, then death is indeed no more. From moment to moment, from day to day life is in itself the only good. Make life itself the goal, and the power that all tyrants in all ages have used to enslave man is destroyed at a single blow. Caligula was charmed by the beauty of Lazarus' philosophy, but he could not accept it, for it took away from him the only instrument of power in his posses-

sion, man's fear of death. He knew that if his people
did not fear death, if they did not deny themselves the
right to happiness, he would have no power over them.
The power of the tyrant, no matter where he is or what
the form of his tyranny may be, dissolves like a wrack
in the wind when the fear of death and the renuncia-
tory philosophy embodied in that fear is swept away.
And to the practical question, "What must man do to
be saved?" Lazarus has an answer. This answer is
strong and clear, and none the less plain, because it is
couched in the form of poetry, and limited to the exigencies of a particular dramatic form. Let an age hun-
gry for an answer to the meaning of life ponder well
these words of the poet:

> LAZARUS. Eye to eye with the Fear of Death, did they
> not laugh with scorn? "Death to old Death," they
> laughed! "Once as squirming specks we crept from
> the tides of the sea. Now we return to the sea! Once
> as quivering flecks of rhythm we beat down from the
> sun. Now we reënter the sun! Cast aside is our pitiable
> pretense, our immortal egohood, the holy lantern be-
> hind which cringed our Fear of the Dark! Flung off is
> that impudent insult to life's nobility which gibbers:
> 'I, this Jew, this Roman, this noble or this slave, must
> survive in my pettiness forever!' Away with such cow-
> ardice of spirit! We will to die! We will to change!
> Laughing we lived with our gift, now with laughter
> give we back that gift to become again the Essence of
> the Giver! Dying we laugh with the Infinite. We are
> the Giver and the Gift! Laughing, we will our own
> annihilation! Laughing, we give our lives for Life's

sake!'" This must Man will as his end and his new beginning! He must conceive and desire his own passing as a mood of eternal laughter and cry with pride, "Take back, O God, and accept in turn a gift from me, my grateful blessing for Your gift—and see, O God, now I am laughing with You! I am Your laughter—and You are mine!"

This is the affirmative way of life, which accepts life on its own terms—the only way in which it is possible, or ever has been possible, to create beauty and happiness in the world. It is the Pagan way of life, but more too, for O'Neill is a modern, and as a modern his philosophy is the result of a new scientific interpretation of man. By a process of evolution man has risen to the point where he can know his past and understand some of the complex forces that have made him what he is. But if he does not learn to use that knowledge for the creation of happiness, if he persists in using it as a means to enslave the spirit, then he is as surely doomed to annihilation as if he had never risen above his ancient arboreal ancestors. He must look to a new life in which he will seek the fulfillment of his hope by making the simple assumption that there is validity in the hopes themselves. He must abandon his old way of regarding his hopes and desires as essentially evil, for in following such reasoning he devotes his whole energy to depriving himself of the happiness that might be possible to him.

As Lazarus puts it, men are too preoccupied with

death and eternal life to face the reality of this life. He says to Tiberius, who wants hope for himself:

> What is—you? But there is hope for Man! Love is Man's hope—love for his life on earth, a noble love above suspicion and distrust! Hitherto Man has always suspected his life, and in revenge and self-torture his love has been faithless! He has even betrayed Eternity, his mother, with his slave he calls Immortal Soul! Hope for you, Tiberius Caesar? Then dare to love Eternity without your fear desiring to possess her! Be brave enough to be possessed!

Here is the essence of a positive philosophy to set over against the negation of life's values. O'Neill writes with the passion of an inspired poet, as he urges man to abandon the narrow selfishness of his personal ambition which leads to fear, distrust and greed, and in their place to substitute a noble love of life, a love above suspicion, self-torture and revenge. Accept life for what it is, and make it noble within its limitations. This is no mere fantastic dream of an impractical poet, nor is it a fairy tale told by Lazarus. This is the burning truth of a new philosophy that is struggling for recognition in a civilization that totters on the very brink of its grave. It is a new concept of life that carries the fragrance of a spring breeze to chase away the decaying odors of a long winter. It is no light doctrine with which modern civilization can dally at will and discard at its leisure. Western civilization is sick to the heart. It must listen to its new prophets or it will die, and in the play of

Lazarus Laughed and in many of his other works, O'Neill has dramatized the inner urge for happiness and the good life by setting it in conflict with the old. In doing this he has given expression to the profound sense of impending doom that hangs over all of us. With Russia in the lead and the rest of the Western world fighting to escape collapse, it is apparent that the old conception of man's life as a stage of durance vile in the eternal panorama is rapidly passing away. What will be the new order if it comes? And if it does not come we are doomed like Tiberius to "a long insomnia of memories and regrets and the ghosts of dreams one has poisoned to death passing with white bodies spotted by the leprous fingers of one's lusts." There will be "Death dancing round me in the darkness, prancing to the drum beat of my heart!"

I do not mean to imply that O'Neill looks to Communistic Russia or to any other political reform as the final answer, although he might very well hold that in so far as Russia has recognized that man's first problem and his only problem is to make this life happy, she has made the first and most important step. But O'Neill's business is not that of political scientist. His task is to give dramatic reality to the deeper, inner, universal struggle of man to free himself from the invisible forces that bind him like Ixion to the wheel of his discontent. This O'Neill has done over and over again, but nowhere more vividly than in the particular play under discussion. Tiberius says: "I do not understand." The answer is clear and pointed:

LAZARUS. Men are too cowardly to understand! And so the worms of their little fears eat them and grow fat and terrible and become their jealous gods they must appease with lies!

Tiberius remains unconvinced, and replies that Lazarus' words are meaningless and that "Life is a sickness." To this Lazarus answers:

LAZARUS. So say the race of men, whose lives are long dyings! They evade their fear of death by becoming so sick of life that by the time death comes they are too lifeless to fear it! Their disease triumphs over death —a noble victory of resignation! 'We are sick,' they say, 'therefore there is no God in us, therefore there is no God!' Oh, if men would but interpret that first cry of man fresh from the womb as the laughter of one who even then says to his heart, 'It is my pride as God to become Man. Then let it be my pride as Man to recreate the God in me!'

And here is O'Neill's answer to those who, like Tiberius, "find nothing in life that merits pride." They find nothing because by means of a systematic philosophy of resignation they have perverted the impulses that lead to life and happiness into impulses that lead to pain and death. O'Neill, like Nietzsche, inveighs with fiery scorn against the institutions that have deprived man of discovering the transcendent glory of what it means to be human. Death, sanctified by religion, has created the fear of life and deprived man of the really human aspect of living, and thereby made

him into a creature that slinks from imaginary shadows and blinks with unseeing eyes at the sunshine.
Cringing before the inevitable, there are yet times when
a false courage moves them, and then in rage they
grasp their swords and "slash at ghosts in the dark.
Men, those haunted heroes!"

What they have not learned, and what they must
learn, is to recognize that their whole glory lies in their
humanity, and not in their imagined supernatural qualities. In their eternal struggle to make themselves into
little gods, they have lost their real power to be the
gods that they are. They must learn. Listen to Lazarus:

> LAZARUS. But as dust, you are eternal change, and
> everlasting growth, and a high note of laughter soar-
> ing through chaos from the deep heart of God! Be
> proud, O Dust! Then you may love the stars as equals!
> And then perhaps you may be brave enough to love
> even your fellow men without fear of their vengeance!

Here is the language of a new teacher come to preach
the gospel of a new way of life, a way out of the chaos
and despair of this disillusioned, modern world.
O'Neill has a way of life, and he knows where he is
going, all adverse comment to the contrary. The fact
that he puts it in the imaginative language of poetic or
prose drama makes it none the less clear to those who
have learned the art of imaginative symbols that must
always remain the poetry of expressive language. Lazarus is conceived by O'Neill as a teacher, and many
times he speaks of himself as one who is sent to teach.

Even in the grave his instruction came to him in the form of a voice which told him,

> Men must learn to live. . . . Before their fear invented death they knew, but now they have forgotten. They must be taught to laugh again!

And by being taught to laugh, O'Neill means they must be taught to regain the pure joy in living as an end in itself. He means that there was a time in man's development when he did not live for the benefit of buying cheap and selling dear, there was a time when he did not set up ideals that were unnatural and superhuman, and then crucify himself upon the cross of his own invention. Lazarus urges man to come down from the cross, to abandon his self-made torture rack, and in the sunshine of his brief existence make the most of such transitory beauty as life itself affords. He must recognize the fundamental cowardice of his position, and in courage face each day as his last, but not as the last of pain but as the last of joy and happiness. That it is the last is not the important point, the thing that counts is that this day, this moment, is life. *This* is what we have, and what we *have not* is but a figment of the imagination, is only food for terror-stricken minds, is the consolation which does not console. Those who have been taught that the world is a torture chamber and man a helpless victim must learn a new prayer, one which does not say, "Thy will be done," but one which says, "MY will be to laughter in life."

4

The vigorous expression of a positive conception of the "good life" is not limited to *Lazarus Laughed,* although it does get the most direct expression in this play. This fact arises out of the conception of Lazarus as a teacher, a leader, a prophet of the good life. He is one who has lived life and learned its secret. Thus his dramatic purpose in the play demands that he reveal the new conception of life. The audience is at one with the actors in the play as they ask, "What did you find beyond there, Lazarus?" And all alike hang with listening ears upon the answer, "O Curious Greedy Ones, is not one world in which you know not how to live enough for you?" And with these words, he establishes himself as their teacher, a position he holds throughout the play.

The reader who is thoroughly familiar with the work of O'Neill will realize that it is common for O'Neill's characters to partake of this rôle of teacher or leader. In no other play is it quite so direct, but character after character leaps over the boundary of speech necessary to the action of the play and passes judgment on life's values. This tendency has often led critics to condemn the looseness of his dramatic construction, and at the same time it has made O'Neill America's greatest dramatist. While the critic carps at the digressions, the audience listens with intense emotion for an answer to life's meaning. Character after character in his plays struggles against an unfriendly world, not for economic security, nor for wealth, nor power, but for peace, happiness, and, above all, understanding. Robert in *Beyond the Horizon* was a helpless victim of the poverty that gradually overcame him on his poorly managed farm, but it was not the poverty that made his life seem tragic to him, nor to the audience that watches him. His tragedy was that he never learned what lay beyond the horizon. To him life was a quest for beauty and truth, a quest that he was never able to pursue. As death comes he says: "I can hear the old voices calling me." The voices that speak of a better life, of a new world in which man may be happy because he will be free.

In *All God's Chillun Got Wings, The Hairy Ape, Anna Christie, Strange Interlude,* as in nearly all his plays, O'Neill's characters are struggling against the chains that bind them to a perverted social system. It is against the injustice of this system that they rebel so fiercely, and it is by this system that they are destroyed. To all of them there is a good life to which they aspire, but the shackles of the past are too strong for them, and in the end they are defeated, but they are never resigned to their defeat. Resignation is the philosophy of those who find life too strong for them, or those who have no vision of a better life on earth than that which the past has sanctified in misery and blood. O'Neill's characters are not of this class. They look forward to a new world freed from the unnecessary cruelty of a vicious social system and a negative conception of life. Like Cape in *Welded,* they say,

WOMAN. It's funny, aint it?

CAPE. You mean—life?

WOMAN. Sure. You got to laugh, aint you? You got to loin to like it!

CAPE. Yes! That's exactly it! That goes deeper than wisdom. To learn to love life—to accept it and be exalted—that's the one faith left to us!

Marco Millions is an excellent example of the same theme. Marco was in search of wealth, the temporary ideal of Western civilization. In O'Neill's treatment of this fatuous ass, Marco, there arises a clear conception of what he values in life. Marco is contrasted with Kublai and all of Marco's struggles to make profits and promote order end in creating pain, suffering and misery. He gains wealth, but he does not learn the meaning of love. The more he labors the greater becomes his outward display. Decorations, honors, wealth manifest themselves in brilliant display, but with each added worldly honor, with each acquisition of new power he grows correspondingly empty of real feeling, thought and understanding. In the end he achieves his great ambition and returns to his home town wealthy, and honored by the mob, but as empty of real love and knowledge as a bass drum.

This play, like so many of O'Neill's, is a condemnation of the ideals of our Western civilization. In contrast to Marco there is the wisdom of the East represented in the person of Kublai. It might be held that Kublai, as compared with Lazarus, is an exponent of resignation, which has always been the philosophy of the East. But O'Neill has given Kublai a quality which is not of the East; he has made him affirm life as a good in itself, and thus, in so far as he does so, he is a brother to Lazarus and an exponent of the theme that life's value lies in the art of complete living. "Be proud of life" is the essence of his teaching, a statement that would not be foreign to the ears of Lazarus.

It does not follow that because O'Neill has a very definite conception of what would constitute the good life that he is therefore an optimist. Quite the reverse. The more deeply man believes in the possibility of an ideal life, the more deeply must he feel the tragedy of life as it is. Like Hamlet, O'Neill is impressed with the "unweeded garden," and like him he knows that "the world is out of joint."

In this chapter I have stressed the fact that O'Neill does envision a new world where the "good life" would be the ideal, but this does not imply that he believes man will ever attain it. The obstacles to human happiness may be divided into two classes: first, those that grow out of the traditional social structure, and second, those that are inherent in the nature of man himself. Both of these hindrances to happiness are present in the plays of O'Neill, and in the last analysis it may be that the latter is more powerful than the former. A moment's contemplation will make it apparent that the fundamental difference between the two classes is that the first seems amenable to change and correction, while the second is constant and immutable.

The easy philosophy of the Communist holds that

the latter class of circumstances which lead to unhappiness grows out of the former. The Communist says change the social environment and you change man. If that were true then there would be reason to hope for some ultimate far-off event of peace and joy on earth. O'Neill is too soundly pessimistic to be beguiled by so facile a solution. To him there is something fundamentally tragic in life itself.

But this belongs to another chapter and I mention it here only in justice to O'Neill and as a warning to the reader that in spite of O'Neill's conception of a positive value in life, a value that arises out of doing rather than not doing certain things, still he is no optimist.

He is rather a man in sympathy with Kublai, and if he ever found occasion to pray, he would not refuse to obey Kublai who asked himself the question:

KUBLAI. Sovereign of the World? Then I command the world to pray! In silence! Prayer is beyond words! Contemplate the eternal life of Life! Pray thus! In silence—for one concentrated moment—be proud of life! Know in your heart that the living of life can be noble! Know that the dying of death can be noble! Be exalted by life! Be inspired by death! Be humbly proud! Be proudly grateful! Be immortal because life is immortal. Contain the harmony of womb and grave within you! Possess life as a lover—then sleep requited in the arms of death! If you awake, love again! If you sleep on, rest in peace! Who knows which? What does it matter? It is nobler not to know!

V

The Relativity of Good and Evil

DION. We communicate in code—when neither
has the other's key. *The Great God Brown*

I

The Web is the title of O'Neill's first play. It is a brief
one-act drama in which a prostitute tries to shield her
criminal lover from the clutches of the law. She fails,
and the ending is tragic. The significant point to consider is that in his very first dramatic effort, O'Neill
concerned himself with the problem of morality—or in
a broader sense, with the concept of human values.
Good and evil in conflict, good and evil in relation to
society, and hence, considered from a relative point of
view, it provides the theme for his first play. This
theme was to grow and expand into large proportions
in O'Neill's later work culminating, at last, in *Strange
Interlude*.

With a skill unsurpassed in modern drama, O'Neill
has succeeded in generalizing his theme to such an extent that no matter how fantastic his particular subject
may appear at first glance, closer study of the subject

always reveals that the particular develops into the universal, and the figures that move in somber tragedy on the stage are playing out their parts against the background of the whole social order of our modern world.

O'Neill does not leave us in doubt on this point. There are even critics who have gone so far as to hold that he has been too anxious to emphasize the social complex in relation to the individual problem of the particular dramatic situation of a particular play. This criticism does not appear sound to me, since it is only through the effective generalization that the particular achieves universal significance and becomes meaningful art. But if O'Neill makes the transition from the particular to the general in a forced and unskillful manner so that the machinery of his technique squeaks, making one conscious of the method rather than the theme, that would be a real cause for objection. This objection might very well be made against some of the early one-act plays. But how pointless it would be to impugn a man's work on the basis of the technique in his first attempts at shaping his ideas into an art form. If the discussion of his technique in *The Web* were pertinent, its remarkable effectiveness in revealing a relative concept of good and evil would be far more to the point.

The leading character in *The Web* is Rose Thomas, a prostitute. She is the prototype of several prostitutes that appear in the plays of O'Neill, and like all of her sisterhood portrayed by O'Neill, she is more sinned against than sinning. In choosing Rose Thomas for his first heroine, O'Neill made his first confession of faith, in that he definitely threw overboard conventional morality and conventional stage tradition. It must not be forgotten that in 1914 the American public was much nearer to the pure, noble, simple-minded woman tradition of Hern and his imitators than they were to Shaw, Ibsen or Galsworthy. These Europeans were not yet the leaders of dramatic excellence in America.

O'Neill wrote for himself, not for any audience that he could hope to attract. With the courage of defiance that is the charm of youth, he proceeded to make his drama an expression of human values that were directly contradictory to herd morality, and sharply opposed to the conventions of the drama, which was his particular artistic medium. This courage, which was no doubt inspired by a spirit of youthful rebellion as much as by a desire to face the gods of Mrs. Grundy, was later to stand him in good stead. He never has abandoned, and he never will, his conception of what is good subject matter for art in order to please the appetite of low tastes, or the persuasive mendacity of those who carry bags of gold. If O'Neill had accomplished nothing else for the American drama, we, as Americans might still be proud beyond words that at last we had produced an artist who was free, fearless, independent, and militantly defiant of that greedy immorality of the market place where the buyers and sellers think that all the world will bow in submission. O'Neill has not nor will he ever make concessions to such false idols.

Thus it is important to notice *The Web*. In the first place, the title itself is symbolic. Man is involved in a

web of circumstance, a web that is not of his own weav-
ing. Yet when the meshes of the web entangle him and
bring him to disaster, society which unconsciously set
this trap, holds him responsible. In the play Tim Morgan, a yeggman, is trapped as a victim of love, hate,
jealousy and commercial crime. But unlike the romantic criminal hero, O'Neill has provided no escape
for him. He is not to be released on the ground that he
was essentially a sweet young man who robbed to save
a dying mother, or to bring food to a starving baby. He
is a real criminal, but it is made perfectly plain by the
author that this criminal is a product of the pure and
the self-righteous who deal bravely and crassly in the
market place, smugly ignorant or unregardful of the
evils their very success engenders. Bad as Tim Morgan
is, the social system in its giantlike strength and power
is still more to be condemned.

The case of Rose Thomas is still more to the point.
She is a prostitute, abhorred and condemned. Like Tim
she did not choose her lot of her own free will. The
forces that made Tim a criminal made her a prostitute,
supported in her trade by those who condemn her. This
is not news and O'Neill, even in youth, knew that it
was not, but it must not be forgotten that it *was* news
to the American stage. It was the breath of fresh life,
the spirit of truth, sympathy and understanding come
to create a moral tone of high quality in the decadent
sentimentalism of smug and vicious purity that stalked
in false pride beyond the footlights. It was not merely
an example from which the knowing might, by the

grace of God, infer that the author had faint doubts
about conventional concepts of good and evil. It was
direct, vigorous and outspoken. When Rose is given an
opportunity, she tells how the "good" people treated
her. She lets her audience know that she understands
well enough why she is a prostitute dying of consumption. It is not due to her wickedness, but due to a corrupt social system that cares not a farthing for those
whom it destroys in making the false grandeur of
which it boasts. She condemns in plain words those
who made her what she is, saying:

> ROSE. They—all the good people—they got me where
> I am and they are goin' to keep me there. Reform?
> Take it from me it can't be done. They won't let yuh
> do it, and that's Gawd's truth.

This play is important because it foreshadows
O'Neill's interest in the problem of good and evil rather
than because of its intrinsic value. The same may be
said of the other early one-act plays. *Warnings* also deals
with an ethical problem. James Knapp, a ship's wire-
less operator, is informed by his home doctor, while he
is in port, that he is rapidly losing his hearing. He
knows that he should tell his commanding officer and
resign, but goaded by his wife, the financial needs of
his large family, and the social complex as a whole, he
commits the crime of going out with his ship. The ship
is wrecked because he loses his hearing, and when his
condition is discovered he shoots himself.

As in *The Web,* this play emphasizes that man's

right or wrong actions are dependent upon the demands of the social system. It dramatizes the tragic illogicality of a social order that creates an evil and then with unseeing virtue condemns the product of its own creation. With O'Neill it is not a problem of the individual good or evil of James Knapp, but it is the evil of a society built upon false ideals. It is the conflict between what society prides itself upon being and what it really is.

The symbolic title *Fog* suggests a deeper implication than that which appears on the surface of the situation presented in this one-act play. The fog that envelops a life-boat in which there is a man of business, a poet, a Polish peasant woman, and a dead child is symbolic of the helplessness of man adrift on the sea of life. This O'Neill makes even more emphatic by revealing in the dialogue between the man of business and the poet, that the man of business, who is a power in ruling the world, has a mental outlook enveloped in a deeper fog than that which surrounds the drifting life-boat. This man of business is the prototype of many characters in later plays, just as the poet is the type of the O'Neill hero. Ethical and social ideals are more important in this play than the characters themselves or the action of the play, which is almost negligible in quantity.

The fifth play *Recklessness* raises a moral problem that concerns love, sex and marriage. A prosperous "good" man discovers that his wife and his chauffeur are in love with each other. He quickly and effectively works a little trick that leads to the chauffeur's death.

When his wife learns of her lover's death, and knows that her husband was responsible, she commits suicide. Jealousy, hate, false pride, a prudish morality, and, most of all, no respect for individual liberty are the causes of the state of affairs presented in this play.

These five plays have been mentioned in some detail not because of their intrinsic merit as dramas, although considered in their relation to the author's youth they have some dramatic excellence, but because they are important to this study in a different way. They show quite plainly that from the very beginning O'Neill sought to combine two things: dramatic value with socially significant human action. It seems clear that he sought a medium in drama for the interpretation of serious problems of the modern world. This is a dangerous statement, for it might seem to imply that O'Neill was primarily a professor of ethics or a social reformer who happened to use the stage as a convenient medium. Such a thesis would be nonsense. He was, first of all, a dramatist, but he was and is a dramatist who wills to make his dramas deal with problems that are of eternal interest to man, problems that move the audience deeply because they reveal life tangled in the web of tragic dilemma. The early one-act plays are an indication of the attitude of the artist—not a measure of his mature skill.*

* The five plays of the *Thirst* volume are now definitely repudiated, and will never be reprinted with the author's permission. (Clark, *Eugene O'Neill*, p. 66.)

2

In O'Neill's plays the "good" is never a fixed quantity to which an action may be referred, measured and evaluated. The "good" is never the same. It changes with changing actions, is relative to each new situation. This accounts for the fact that many people have been unable to see any good at all in such plays as *Anna Christie, Desire Under the Elms* and *Strange Interlude*. Some of O'Neill's plays have been successfully suppressed in one locality and highly praised in another. In Los Angeles one part of the population was so outraged by *Desire Under the Elms* that suppression of the play was effected for a brief period, but after a court trial the ban was lifted and the play went on again, to the great joy of those who found it a highly moral and entertaining play.

This conflict of opinion arises out of the fact that O'Neill is modern in his approach to ethical problems, and since he is a dramatist who deals with human situations that involve prejudices and passions that are bedded deep in the experiences of the race, it is to be expected that there would be protest. The protest arises because of an essential conflict in the conception of the good. O'Neill stands at the gate of a new world revealing the doctrines of a new ethics. His dramas deal with men and women in actions that are common enough, and everyone who is not totally blinded by prejudice knows that they are common, but that is not the ground upon which the objection to the dramatist arises. The protest comes from those who, while they admit the reality of the world represented, condemn the author. They feel that he has reversed his values, giving reward to the wicked and punishment to the good. Or worse still, they say that his plays are without moral judgment; that he does not punish at all, or that he punishes indiscriminately.

This state of affairs arises out of a misunderstanding of the modern world. O'Neill's plays are developed from the point of view of a naturalistic ethics. Those who find fault with his moral attitude judge him from the vantage ground of a traditional ethics that is standardized and absolute. This is so simple that it should be self-evident, yet it is anything but that. In spite of the fact that from the days of *Sister Carrie* to the present our best modern literature in America has been emphasizing a relative, naturalistic morality, the majority of the people in many communities, like Boston for instance, still stand firm in the sinister shadows of the absolute. The absolute point of view holds that life is lived for some good end, some ulterior purpose. Consequently no act can be judged on its face value, but must be referred to a preconceived standard. If it violates this standard, then it is evil and as such must be condemned. When an author fails to make a clear judgment against such an act, he is looked upon as evil. Even among liberals there has been protest against the morality of many situations in O'Neill's plays because it is one thing to be liberal in speech, but quite a different thing to be liberal in practice.

O'Neill has achieved a naturalistic ideal of liberty and applied it with consistency and courage in his drama. His ethics are not of the Kantian order which refer actions to a preconceived ideal of an absolute good. Nor are his ethics to be classed with the book-keeping school of the utilitarians. His ethics are naturalistic. He holds that good and evil are ever changing qualities. The good is new every morning. It changes with every situation and changes with every individual. It arises not out of a fixed law sanctified by tradition and religion. He holds that the conception of the good may be and is a guide to choice, but it is not a final goal or standard by which all actions may be judged. But he goes even further in that he condemns a fixed standard as destructive of life, holding that in the last analysis it will lead to false pride, arrogant and cruel behavior, hypocrisy and a destructive fanaticism. O'Neill not only sets up a modern ethical concept, but he condemns the old as vicious and evil.

Until the reader is willing and able to grasp this conflict in ethical theory, he is not in a position to judge of the ethical problems in O'Neill's plays. That he should not be aware of the issue and yet ready and willing to pass judgment is not strange, for most people know as little about ethical theory as they know about the function of the endocrine glands, but in the latter case they have been encouraged to withhold judgment until the evidence is discovered, while in the former they have been taught a rule and encouraged to apply it even to the point of inflicting pain and death upon the helpless victims who have disobeyed.

Before entering upon a definite discussion of O'Neill's ethics as revealed in his plays, the reader should be reminded that the above discussion does not imply that O'Neill has made the final discovery of truth, and that now we can all fall down before him as a god. All that it does mean is that O'Neill belongs in theory as well as in fact to the new world that was born in the days of the industrial revolution, and this new world has through the development of experimental methods in the natural and the social sciences arrived at new concepts of what is good and what is evil just as surely as it has arrived at a new conception of the heritage of man and the age and structure of the world in which he lives. O'Neill does not stand alone. He belongs in a critical tradition that began with Ibsen and Strindberg. But he has carried the naturalistic view beyond his predecessors and has in many ways made the problems of right and wrong conduct more dramatic than they did. If this statement is true, and it might be questioned if taken too absolutely, then O'Neill's superiority lies in the fact that he does not see the relative standard as a sure solution to man's search for happiness. In contrast to Ibsen who often gives the impression that there is a right way of settling life's problems, O'Neill is inclined to a wise skepticism. He is more clearly a product of the modern complex and as such he sees the essence of life as a continual change,

growth, development. In that sense he is an evolutionist
in theory as he is also in his practice as an artist. The
traditional view has perverted the doctrine of evolution
into being evolution towards some fixed goal, but
O'Neill looks upon evolution as change, change which
will bring new social orders and new ethical problems.
In his world there is no final accounting, no last settle-
ment possible. There is only struggle and conflict and
temporary solutions. But as was emphasized in a fore-
going chapter, the value of life lies in this struggle itself. Nothing is settled, sealed and carefully put away.
All is change; all action leads to new complications and
presumably to new solutions. The world of O'Neill is
not static, and hence it is not easy to grasp for the one
who will bring to his task only the worn-out traditions
of a dead past.

3

Anna Christie presents a group of characters who by
the mysterious working of uncontrolled circumstances
were forced into a situation where the old ethical standards failed to solve their problem. Under the stress of
an emotional crisis they finally arrived at the beginning
of a new concept of right and wrong, but not until they
had almost destroyed themselves in the attempt. Before
the events which open the play on the stage the lives
of the two men, Burke and Chris, had moved in the
secure orbit of fixed creeds. They were the products
of a past age of fixed ethical values. In the shelter of

their creed they knew what was good and what was bad, and as their creed was fixed by tradition so like-wise was their conduct, for they held that one mode of behavior may be good for a man and bad for a woman.

In this practice they would have had the respect of all "good" people and do have it, had O'Neill not put their belief to the crucial test. "Good" people every-where in the world sympathize with Burke and Chris. They may refuse to admit this verbally, but the ver-balization of beliefs means very little as compared to practice. The real test of what a man believes is what he does, not what he says. If what people say were the test of belief, Western civilization would be Christian, but since the real belief is practice, our civilization is founded upon a brutal and systematized robbery which glorifies exploitation, wealth and power.

It is clear that the product of such a civilization, re-inforced by an ethics that makes some far-off goal the object of living, will be narrow, greedy, selfish and, above all, ready to condemn those who violate the creed. Chris, the father, and Burke, the lover, are typi-cally Christian in their avowed faith. This does not mean that they were good Christians, for if they had been, they would have imitated the behavior of Christ in passing judgment on their fellow sufferers in this world of sorrow. But they were practicing Christians and in the whole Western world they would pass for such without protest by the great majority of their fel-lows in the faith.

Before the implication of this problem is definitely

applied to O'Neill's play, it would be well to examine a little further into the past lives of Chris and Burke. Chris had been bred to the seas. His family had all been sailors and as sailors they had suffered the penalties of their occupation. The evil of the sailor's life had impressed itself deeply upon Chris, and true to the style of the man who has no other knowledge of ethics than that of a fixed creed he condemns it as evil, without considering the necessity of varying his practice. In this he has a million brothers in behavior, but also typical is his attitude to his family. Since he cannot rule himself according to the demands of his standard of goodness, he resolves to rule the lives that biology and tradition have given into his power.

He localizes evil in the trade of the sailor, and in order to protect his daughter, he decides to leave her on a farm in Minnesota. As he puts it: "Ay tank it's ·better Anna live on farm, den she don't know dat ole davil, sea, she don't know fader like me." Here he makes the fatal generalization on the basis of a preconceived idea of the good as something that is fixed and absolute.

When the play opens we know that his theory has been a failure, that Anna has been the victim of bitter experiences which for a time forced her into the trade of the prostitute. Then begins a new series of events: ironical and tragic. The audience is "in on the secret," and observes with tense sympathy and divided allegiance the old man and his "noble" faith in his daughter, the daughter, skeptical and bitter, gradually waking to a new life and new ideals, gradually re-defining life and its values. She has accepted by the force of circumstances a relative ethics; she knows by her experience that the good is new for each new day and the evil of her past life and its false hopes are destroyed. Health, fresh air, sunshine and moonlight, the sea and quiet develop new values and new hopes. She tolerates the fanatical falseness of her father's creed, hoping that he may remain ignorant of her past, a past which her present has now in a measure superseded. New experiences have created for her new values and fulfilled ambitions for herself that were stifled and suppressed by the stern exigencies of her past. She has, without clearly understanding the problem, arrived at a relative conception of ethics. She has reached the place in her practice of living where she discovers that life is not ruled by a code nor limited in its expression to the confines of a fixed creed. She knows it is a mixture of good and evil, a struggle in which values that make for the good life must arise out of experience and may not be imposed by the authority of a creed from the outside. The resentment she had first felt for her past has largely left her, and instead she now faces the future and the possibility of happiness.

At this point Mat Burke appears, a sailor like her father, whose physical equipment is of the highest order, but who, also like her father, has a preconceived idea of what is right and what is wrong in behavior. It is important at this point to note that Mat Burke considers the violation of chastity for men and women

alike a sin. But this is only the verbal truth. In reality
for men it is a sin that may be committed, for women
it is a sin that must be eternally condemned. Why
should this be? Two reasons are clear. In the first place,
nothing eases the conscience of a crime like condemning the same crime in others, or finding that in others
it is so far more vicious and heinous that in you it seems
almost no crime at all. There is nothing like finding a
deep sin in a neighbor which may be used as a means
to the rationalization of your own. This is a practice
followed by Mat and common to all human behavior
which is not aware of a rationalistic ethics and possessed of a willingness to practice it at any cost, even
putting it to the crucial test. The second reason also has
a definite ethical import. Mat spoke of marriage to
Anna and won from her the statement: "I ain't never
loved a man in my life before, you can always believe
that—no matter what happens." And Mat replies, giving clear evidence of how he evaluates life: "Sure I do
be believing ivery word you iver said or iver will say.
And 'tis you and me will be having a grand, beautiful
life together to the end of our days!" In the last remark he reveals that his conception of the good
life with Anna is the result of a preconceived idea, a
fixed concept that was originally foisted upon him by
a dead theory of ethics, and was later reaffirmed and
encrusted into an idol by the necessity of rationalizing
his own behavior. The startling fact that comes out
here is that he is not accepting Anna as a human being
with past experiences, with a power to live and suffer.

He is accepting her as an institution, as an ideal that was created and fixed by an immutable law of life. Anna is looked upon as an end, a goal, a something beyond the reality of life, which is a struggle, pain, change and potential of every shade of variation from ugliness to beauty, from pain to happiness.

Anna knows this and is driven to defiance. She behaves as a human being with rights of her own, to the consternation of both her lover and her father. When Anna says, "Only don't forget what you said a minute ago about it not mattering to you what other reason I got so long as I wasn't married to no one else.", Mat replies, "That's my word, and I'll stick to it!" Mat meant what he said, because he had not seen Anna as a woman. He had thought of her only as an institution, perfect as his creed was perfect, and as an instrument which should make up to him for all that he had failed to be himself. Armored in the ethical theory of Kant, and trained in Christian swordsmanship he faced the battle of love in a realistic world with the courage that only the ignorant can have. His armor proved to be of the same material as Don Quixote's helmet, and his sword was brittle glass.

Anna knew this even before she told of her past experience, and took the opportunity to tell her two men, fighting to possess her each in his own way, just what she thought of them. She laughs at Mat's statement, knowing how ignorant he is of her, as well as of himself, and then she says:

The Relativity of Good and Evil   131

First thing is, I want to tell you two guys something.
You was going on 's if one of you had got to own me.
But nobody owns me, see?—'cepting myself. I'll do what
I please and no man, I don't give a hoot who he is, can
tell me what to do! I ain't asking either of you for a
living. I can make it myself—one way or other.

She tells of her past life with a courage born of despair, knowing beforehand just what Mat will think,
realizing with that keen insight which is born of experience and reason that he will condemn because he
has never in his life accepted an ethical theory based
upon reality. Not that she herself has a reasoned and
philosophical ethics, but by experience she has learned
that good and evil are not fixed quantities. She told
them that "Being on the sea had changed me and made
me feel different about things, 's if all I'd been through
wasn't me and didn't count and was yust like it never
happened." It made her think about life in a new way,
creating for her new values: relative, realistic, capable
of new potentialities for happiness.

The shadow of a faint hope which led her to face
the truth of her past rather than live a life of lies and
deception did not flicker long. Mat rises in his self-
righteous rage to condemn her. His first reaction is to
call her "a slut" and move to kill her. Her answer is
simple, "Go ahead! I'll be thankful to you, honest. I'm
sick of the whole game." Then follows Mat's statement
which needs to be quoted in full, since it sets forth the
ethics of the dead past which is at war with the living
good of the present as revealed in Anna. Mat, who had

been but a moment before speaking of love and family
to Anna, now shouts:

> Though I do be thinking I'd have a good right to
> smash your skull like a rotten egg. Was there iver a
> woman in the world had the rottenness in her that you
> have, and was there iver a man the like of me was made
> the fool of the world, and me thinking thoughts about
> you, and having great love for you, and dreaming
> dreams of the fine life we'd have when we'd be wedded!
> Yerra, God help me! I'm destroyed entirely and my
> heart is broken in bits! I'm asking God Himself, was it
> for this He'd have me roaming the earth since I was a
> lad only, to come to black shame in the end, where I'd
> be giving a power of love to a woman is the same as
> others you'd meet in any hooker-shanty in port, with red
> gowns on them and paint on their grinning mugs, would
> be sleeping with any man for a dollar or two.

He prolongs his cursing to extreme ends, and finally
when he reaches the excess of self-pity he concludes by
saying to Anna:

> You've destroyed me this day and may you lie awake
> in the long nights, tormented with thoughts of Mat
> Burke and the great wrong you've done him!

The truth, which Mat did not realize, was not that
Anna had destroyed him, but that he was destroyed by
a traditional ethical belief which allowed for no read-
justment to the problems of reality. Anna was his salvation, only he did not know it, nor would he know it

until he traveled the hard road back, unlearning and throwing away the false doctrine of values upon which he had built his shabby morality, a morality that almost made him into a murderer the first time it was put to the crucial test.

When Anna says, "You been doing the same thing all your life, picking up a new girl in every port. How're you any better than I was?", Mat avoids the question, by saying, "Is it no shame you have at all?" This reply indicates that he did not understand her position and subsequent development reveals that he may never understand.

Which leads to the conclusion. Mat does not work to a new and better understanding of the problem involved in his relations with Anna. He forgives her and they patch up a truce. But in his forgiveness he invokes the law of his essentially corrupt morality. He brings to bear upon his problem a bit of old magic as ludicrous and outworn as the snake's skull and swamp water of the Negro magician. He makes Anna swear to the truth of her statement on a cross given him by his mother. He stands before Anna conscious of having met with the first real tragedy of his life and brags about the power of this cross, saying: "I'm telling you there's great power in it, and 'tis great bad luck it's saved me from." He is not capable of accepting Anna as a human being. He must forever try to make her something she is not, something he thinks she should be. He does not realize that one human being does not have the right to forgive another; that forgiveness is part of a slave morality which has no real value when put to the test of behavior.

Chris unconsciously sums up the whole confused, irrational, tragic behavior of all the characters involved when he says: "Fog, fog, fog, all bloody time. You can't see vhere you vas going, no."

This is the theme of the play. None of them knows where he is going. The worst thing in their lives is not their experiences with the physical structure of their world, tragic as that has been for Anna and all of them; the worst thing is that they do not know how to use that experience as a means to a new and a better life. They are ruined by an outworn ethical theory which uses absolute standards to measure the most variable quantity that exists in the world—human experience.

O'Neill has given an effective dramatic interpretation of a situation that has sweeping implications for our modern world. He has made it possible to see clearly that more fatal than the misfortunes of experience is the tragedy of being incapable of reconciling these misfortunes to a sensible and a realistic theory of ethics.

4

The reader who is familiar with all of O'Neill's plays will realize that the question of conflict between theory and practice of the good life as so far discussed is present in all of his plays in one form or another. The theme of happiness destroyed by wrong ideas is woven into the network of O'Neill's philosophy. That is one reason why the tragedy of life impresses him so much more than any other aspect of living.

The way in which an evil morality, a perverse set of ideas, complicates unavoidable sorrow is revealed in *The First Man*. Curtis Jayson's wife died in giving birth to a child, which was a double tragedy to her husband, for his happiness and his work were centered in his friendship with his wife. But the worst thing of all was that his family and friends wrongfully accused her of immorality, poisoned the relationship between Curtis and his best friend, and embittered Curtis' life.

The situation does not make for an especially strong play, but the problem of life depraved by narrow, puritanical and vicious morality is clear enough. The "good" people whose goodness consisted in outward obedience to a fixed creed do evil rather than good. This is the theme of the play. The audience which lives for the moment under the sway of the dramatist condemns such pious and hypocritical virtue as is represented by the family of Curtis, but it cannot forget that there is a social order just off the stage which is motivated to action by the same vicious thought as is represented by the ones who condemned Curtis Jayson's wife. To them the family is good and Jayson and his wife are evil. They have no real evidence, but it is the nature of the great majority to repudiate evidence, or not even to recognize what constitutes evidence. Evidence would deprive them of the pleasure which they derive from castigating sin. To the great majority

Jayson's family are good people. Jayson they regard as viciously negligent, and his wife as a sinner. Thus in their obedience to a fixed ethical theory they have exactly reversed the good and the evil. This is all the more apparent in this play, for neither Jayson nor his wife had violated conventional morality. His wife had been suspected, and to be under suspicion is tantamount to guilt with the majority. When Curtis leaves his family abject because he seems to be departing without a word of farewell, his reply is direct: "Yes, I'm going without a word—because I can't find the fitting one. Be thankful I can't."

The same theme is expressed in *Welded*. Eleanor and Cape were desperately in love with each other, but the happiness and beauty which should have been the fruit of this love was turned to bitterness and gall. When one begins to inquire into the reasons for a situation that would seem strange and monstrous were it not that experience has made the horror of such tragedies commonplace, one realizes that their self-inflicted torture resulted from a wrong theory of ethics. On the face of it this appears to be too easy as a solution. "Can life," it is asked, "be reduced to theories of ethics?" The answer can be as simple as the question; human behavior does not spring full grown and un-caused into the world any more than an automobile does. That its causes are far more difficult of analysis than the causes which produce the automobile, does not imply that they are absent. Hence to say that Cape and Eleanor destroyed their happiness because of a vicious ethics is essentially true, but just what all the factors were that made up their lives and created their ethics would be as hard to explain as to explain life itself.

Cape cannot accept his wife for what she is. Like Burke he is hampered by a set of ideas which makes him condemn that which the free expression of himself as a human being wants to love. He knows that in her past she has not been a chaste woman. Tradition, which he has overcome rationally, still lingers in his behavior, leading him to torture himself and her with vile suspicions and petty jealousy. Jealousy, suspicion and hatred are all the children of an ethical theory that fixes an absolute as a standard of behavior. If Cape could have accepted a naturalistic ethics which above all things recognizes the right of the individual to his own life as long as it does not endanger to an unbearable degree the freedom and happiness of others, he would not have driven both himself and his wife to despair.

Eleanor is much wiser than her husband and tries to make him see her and her life in the light of a more rational theory. She speaks words very similar to those of Anna when Anna was accused because of her past. In defense of herself she is compelled to admit that had she lied, she might have avoided all this futile struggle. Thus she puts the "moral" Cape into the position of inspiring falsehood in his pursuit of truth. Eleanor calls him a "mean hypocrite." He replies:

CAPE *(stung—bitingly)* Don't act moral indignation! What else could I have thought? When we first fell in love, you confessed frankly you had had lovers—not John but others—

ELEANOR *(brokenly—with mingled grief and rage)* I was an idiot! I should have lied to you! But I thought you'd understand—that I'd been searching for something—that I needed love—something I found in you! I tried to make you see—the truth—that those experiences had only made me appreciate you all the more when I found you! I told you how little these men had meant to me, that in the state of mind I had been in they had no significance either one way or the other, and that such an attitude is possible for a woman without her being low. I thought you understood. But you didn't, you're not big enough for that!

Barrett Clark calls this, "the most deliberately and exclusively intellectual of all the plays. It is a work of hard surfaces; the study of a man and woman hopelessly linked together by bonds of passion." (p. 136.) And further on in his discussion he adds: "O'Neill makes his play less a spectacle of life than a philosophic disquisition. . . . I seek men and women and find only a pair of animated abstractions." (p. 140.) "Bonds of passion" instead of freedom and happiness resulted from a false understanding of human rights, and the prejudices of a life ruled by a traditional ethics.

5

Strange Interlude is a fine example of a play which involves the condemnation of an old ethical theory and the definite implication of a new one to take its place. The criticism of an absolute ethics, based upon a fixed standard and accepted as universal, is in this play direct and severe. There is left no room for quibbling on that score. As a consequence it is no wonder at all that many people should have felt that the play was immoral and subversive of ethical standards. And in so far as they expressed this feeling they were stating the truth. The only thing to remember in this connection is that there is more than one standard of ethics, and from the naturalistic point of view standards in so far as they reflect something that is fixed and universal no longer exist. What does exist is variable human behavior that is good or bad in relation to the individual and his group.

A quick review of *Strange Interlude* brings out the fact that many of the great commandments incorporated in Christian ethics are violated. If these commandments are used as a standard of judgment, *Strange Interlude* is subversive of the good life, for it cannot be said that violation of these standards leads to unhappiness and punishment for such wrongdoing. The reverse is true. Such happiness and successful living as Nina achieves come through the violation of fixed standards. Obedience to these standards did not bring happiness, nor peace, nor anything that makes for the good life.

The best way in which to approach this question is to analyze in turn several commandments and observe what happens to them in the play. The warning that the name of God should not be taken in vain is violated throughout the play. This passes almost without notice, since it is common among men to use the name of God indiscriminately and without reverence.

The second law questioned is "Honor thy father and mother." The very opening of the play is a direct violation of this commandment. And it should be noted that to all outward appearances Nina's father was a fine, gentle, kindly old man, a scholar who lived in "a cosy cultured retreat, sedulously built as a sanctuary where, secure with the culture of the past at his back," he could view the present "safely from a distance, as a superior with condescending disdain, pity, and even amusement." In this secluded retreat the old professor of Greek with a New England background of ethics and an intellectual training in the literature and thought of ancient Athens felt secure and comfortable. There were no new books in his library. There was nothing about him to suggest that he understood the problems of the modern world, nor that he had made any effort to realize that the life of his daughter might involve the consideration of ethical standards different from those that he believed—no matter how falsely—had served his New England forebears so well. He was "most liberal—even radical—in his tolerant understanding of the manners and morals of Greece and Imperial Rome!" Yet with all his understanding he did not know his own daughter, and when a problem arose involving her happiness and future, he referred to his New England past not to his intellectual training and forced a decision for her which led to the tragic consequences which are revealed in the play.

The situation is plain. Professor Leeds apparently was a man who had obeyed *The Commandments,* yet in so doing he had neglected the reality of his daughter's life and in obeying the law he brought misery upon himself and in a sense ruined her whole life.

When she discovers just what he had done in persuading her lover against marriage before his departure for the war where he was killed, she turns against her father, despising him for the very principles that motivated his behavior. She does not honor her father. She loathes him and all that he stands for, since it is through him and his commandments that she has lost Gordon, love, and the chance to have become a mother to a child of Gordon's. In so far as she had honored her father in the past, she now pays the penalty in sorrow and despair. This commandment is violated, but more than that it is condemned as a universal principle.

It should be remembered that it is not only Nina who does not honor her father, but that Marsden who does honor his mother has by obedience to this principle made himself a slave to her selfish love and instead of being good and free and happy his life is that of a weakling who shuns reality. In honoring his mother he has become "an old maid who seduces himself in his novels."

Sam Evans has a profound respect for his mother and the memory of his father, but that is only because he has been kept in the dark about them. He does not know that his father came from a family of lunatics, and that he married his mother without telling her the truth about his family.

Thou shalt not commit adultery. But in *Strange Interlude* adultery becomes not a sin but a necessity. In the very beginning of the events that lead to the tragic circumstances of this story Nina might have been saved had she violated the moral law of chastity. Nina's opinion on the subject is direct and clear. She believes that instead of being good because she obeyed tradition she is in reality evil. She feels that her greatest sin is that she reverenced a tradition to such an extent that she violated the urge to life, love and happiness. Deluding herself by saying that her lover would come back and marry her, she remained chaste and lost her one chance to have a child by him. Her resentment flares up against her father and the ideals he had so uncritically followed all his days, and her tongue blossoms into speech:

> NINA. I'm still Gordon's silly virgin! And Gordon is muddy ashes! And I've lost my happiness forever! All that last night I knew he wanted me. I knew it was only the honorable code-bound Gordon, who kept commanding from his brain, no, you mustn't, you must respect her, you must wait till you have a marriage license!

If this outburst against chastity and sexual purity as an absolute guide stood alone in the play, alone and unsupported by further evidence, it would scarcely be justifiable to emphasize its importance in discussing the ethics of Eugene O'Neill. But it does not stand alone. It expresses a point of view that runs like a theme throughout the play. The whole play is an expression of rebellion against a world that lives by absolute standards. These standards are clothed in the vesture of nobility, but when critically examined prove to be the source of pain and suffering. They lure the weary into their proffered shelter, and as the unwary recline in their arms they are destroyed. They lead to death not life.

O'Neill makes this very plain in the character of Sam's mother. She married Mr. Evans without knowing of the insanity in his family. When she learned of it she agreed with her husband that they should never have children, but their resolve was not enough, and one day Mrs. Evans knew that she was to become a mother. She knew that her husband's fear of what might happen to their child would destroy the peace of mind so essential to his health. Under the stress of this fear she faced the reality of what absolute standards mean. She told Nina:

MRS. EVANS. I remember when I was carrying Sam, sometimes I'd forget I was a wife, I'd only remember the child in me. And then I used to wish I'd gone out deliberate in our first year, without my husband knowing, and picked a man, a healthy male to breed by, same's we do with stock, to give the man I loved a healthy child. And if I didn't love the other man nor him me where would be the harm? Then God

would whisper: 'It'd be a sin, adultery, the worst sin!'
But after He'd gone I'd argue back again to myself,
then we'd have a healthy child, I needn't be afraid!
And maybe my husband would feel without ever
knowing how he felt it, that I wasn't afraid and that
child wasn't cursed and so he needn't fear and I could
save him. But I was too afraid of God then to have
ever done it!

This is a bald statement of the ethics involved, but
taken in the context of the play it does not seem too
direct. As is always the case with O'Neill, his dramatic
setting is so intense that it will carry the heaviest load
of philosophic discourse without losing for a moment
the dramatic intensity. Mrs. Evans has learned by bitter
experience that if "there is peace in the green fields of
Eden . . . you got to die to find out!" Her standard had
changed from one of obedience to a fixed moral principle to one of relative values in which life to its fullest
is the only point of reference. "Being happy, that's the
nearest we can ever come to knowing what's good!
Being happy, that's good! The rest is just talk." She
learned from her experience that obedience to the
moral law led to death, that violation of it might
have brought peace and well-being. Her sin of obedience led to her own unhappiness and now it confronts
the happiness of Nina. So determined is Mrs. Evans on
this point that she urges Nina to have an abortion, and
then deliberately choose a healthy father for her child
without letting her husband know anything about it.
Her whole theme is: "Whatever you can do to make

him happy is good—is good, Nina! I don't care what!
You got to have a healthy baby—sometime—so's you
can both be happy! It's your rightful duty!"

Here is a complete reversal of standards. Violation of
two of the fixed Commandments, on the grounds that
man is born to live for life's sake—not to die for it.
Mrs. Evans obeyed the ancient law and her reward was
a life of terrible suffering, a life never free for a single
day from the haunting specter of fear. Nina took the
new path, and in spite of all the unhappiness she suffered, the impartial judge must admit that her life was
a dream world of happiness compared with that of
Mrs. Evans.

6

It would be possible to continue the analysis of
Strange Interlude in the relation to the Ten Commandments and to find that in a greater or less degree all
of them have been violated in this play. Since more
emotion than intelligence is attached to this particular
form of traditional ethics it must be remembered that
O'Neill did *not* set out to develop a thesis in which he
tried to prove that the way to happiness is systematically
to violate the Ten Commandments. That would reduce
him to the last extremity of the absurd. But *Strange
Interlude* is a play which deals with ethical values. To
deny this would be to deny its central theme, that of
a group of characters struggling for a successful orien-

tation of their lives in a world of social and moral chaos not of their own making.

In the process of making this needed adjustment they violate tradition and in the process of this change O'Neill takes tradition to task and by simplification sets forth a new conception of behavior. The ethics which he defends has grown out of the modern world of scientific discovery. It is an ethics that is not related to the impassioned mysteries of the past, but is a product of modern science, including chemistry, biology, astronomy—the whole scientific interpretation of the world in which we live today. O'Neill assumes that man lives for this life here on earth and not for a life hereafter. This leads him to examine behavior in the light of experience, and the consequences attendant upon human acts in relation to each other. In the final analysis this point of view produces a naturalistic ethics.

An examination of such an attitude in the light of modern ethical theory will bear out the conclusion that O'Neill is dealing with a criticism of life which, while it is at variance with traditonal thought, is in harmony with the best of present-day critical ethics. All that O'Neill is insisting upon is that behavior in obedience to a fixed creed denies the first principle of a rational conception of conduct, and instead of leading to the good life may just as often lead to evil. He holds that good and evil are not to be defined in the abstract, but must be analyzed in relation to specific acts of human beings in a definite social complex. Like John Dewey in *Human Nature and Conduct* he holds that "Since morals is concerned with conduct, it grows out of specific empirical facts." Like Dewey he believes that most ethical theories have neglected or "refused to admit this idea. For Christendom as a whole, morality has been connected with supernatural commands, rewards and penalties." O'Neill has emphasized the fallacy of such a point of view, by treating it realistically, by testing it in relation to actual human behavior.

The following paragraph from Dewey may help to explain the real basis upon which O'Neill's ethics are founded. In harmony with Dewey, he holds that:

> It is the first business of mind to be 'realistic,' to see things 'as they are.' If, for example, biology can give us knowledge of the causes of competency and incompetency, strength and weakness, that knowledge is all to the good. A non-sentimental morals will seek for all the instruction natural science can give concerning the biological conditions and consequences of inferiority and superiority. But knowledge of facts does not entail conformity and acquiescence. The contrary is the case. Perception of things as they are is but a stage in the process of making them different. They have already begun to be different in being known, for by that fact they enter into a different context, a context of foresight and judgment of better and worse. A false psychology of a separate realm of consciousness is the only reason this fact is not generally acknowledged. Morality resides not in perception of fact, but in the *use* made of its perception. It is a monstrous assumption that its sole use is to utter benedictions upon fact and its offspring. It is the part of intelligence to tell when to use the fact to conform and

perpetuate, and when to use it to vary conditions and consequences. (*Human Nature and Conduct,* p. 298ff.)

The implications of a naturalistic ethics do not lead to absolute standards nor do they convey the necessity of final solutions. In *Strange Interlude* as in nearly all O'Neill plays there is no final solution. He refuses his audience the comfortable satisfaction that arises out of finality. He sees life as an ever-changing struggle, and in his plays there is always a world of complex and unresolved behavior that carries on beyond the ending. He makes very few definite solutions, because in his world all values are relative and life is an unceasing stream of experience.

VI

Determinism, Fatalism and Free Will

"We do what we must—and sand covers our bodies
and our deeds." *The Fountain*
"We're never free—except to do what we have to
do." *All God's Chillun Got Wings*

I

A RELATIVE standard in ethics implies a kinship with
determinism. The cosmic searchings of the nineteenth
century into the structure of the universe and, particularly, into the grim history of man's origin and development emphasized the importance of a causal chain.
This, in time, led to a deterministic philosophy of
which modern relativity in ethics is the inevitable logical consequence. O'Neill in following this trend in
modern thought is part of the main current of contemporary life. His virtue lies in the perfect manner in
which he gives artistic expression to the new world in
which we live. An important aspect of this new world
is philosophic determinism. To understand O'Neill's
relation to this point of view is of primary importance
since much of what he has to say hinges upon this
concept. The whole tragic import of his plays is often

missed unless the reader is aware of O'Neill's tradition, a tradition which is as genuine and as vital to our world today as was the religious and philosophic tradition of ancient Athens to the dramas of Aeschylus and Euripides.

Since the deterministic view of life is a direct contradiction of free will, a word of explanation may lead to a clear exposition of O'Neill's position as a determinist. As far as contemporary literature is concerned, free will may be disposed of with a gesture. Determinism plays the rôle of Hamlet in the drama of modern life, while free will has fallen from its high estate to the point where it barely stumbles through the part assigned to Osric, a character from the noblest of all plays that only the constant reader of *Hamlet* ever remembers. It is not strange that free will should have so insignificant a place in contemporary literature, for the whole tendency of modern science is to seek the causes that will explain the phenomena of life. The inevitable result of modern thought, or evolution, beginning with Darwin, would tend to question freedom of choice. Darwin explained man on the basis of the struggle for existence and natural selection. In his doctrine there was only one loophole where free will might enter in and that was in his account of accidental variation, but even if accidental variation were to be accounted for on the grounds of a free choice, it would mean little or nothing as far as man's hope for himself is concerned. The only grounds for hope would be that the evidence would tend to prove that variation in species was systematic, advantageous, and always promoted finer adjustment of the individual to his environment. But such is not the case. Variation seems to be truly unpurposeful, since it is a detriment to the variant as often as it is advantageous. In fact there are probably thousands of variations that are detrimental or of negligible value to one which makes for improvement.

Contemporary literature in its attempt to deal with man in his modern physical and intellectual environment finds no room for a free will, nor any grounds for assuming an action as undetermined by the whole complex of that environment. This has led to a new theory of tragedy which is perhaps more implicitly than consciously a part in the philosophy of most modern dramatists. O'Neill, however, knows what he is doing and understands the theory upon which he bases his work, as will be clear later in the analysis of his notes to *Mourning Becomes Electra*.

In O'Neill's plays free will is a negligible quantity, for his tragedies are not the result of an uncaused free choice. Nor is the element of fatalism in its historic sense a factor in his drama. This may best be explained by a brief consideration of what tragedy is from a fatalistic point of view. Like the determinist the fatalist holds that man is the victim of circumstances over which he has no control. No matter what happens to the fatalist he assumes that it was prearranged for him by a power outside the world (God or spirits), and, furthermore, he believes that power to be a conscious force which acts arbitrarily and has a prevision of the end which it achieves. The fatalist is also in one sense of the word a free-willist. He believes that in most cases he is at liberty to behave as he desires, but in the major experience of life he thinks that an outside power has intervened to pass judgment or grant reward. This is a type of accident at variance with modern thought, for it places the cause in the hands of an arbitrary supernatural force which has no direct connection with the laws of physics, biology, economics or social behavior patterns. These are the real forces in modern tragedy, and they make the fundamental distinction between classical and modern, between fatalism and determinism.

2

In analyzing the fatalistic point of view in contrast to determination as it is revealed in the works of O'Neill, no better example of a fatalistic play could be chosen than the *Oedipus Tyrannus* of Sophocles. The play opens with Oedipus as king happily married to Jocasta. There is only one thing that causes him sorrow, and that is the evil which has fallen upon his people. A messenger, who has been sent to the oracle, returns to tell the king that this evil is due to the fact that the murderer of the former king, Laius, lives in the city unpunished for his crime. It is then revealed that Oedipus had fled from his native city in order to escape a prophecy that he would one day be guilty of murdering his own father and marrying his own mother. But his wife Jocasta, who was the widow of the dead Laius, tells him not to worry, for mortals give false prophecies. She relates how it had once been told to King Laius that his own son should kill him, but it did not come to pass "for he fell, by strangers, murdered, for so fame reports, by robbers, in the place where three ways meet." The next development in the story comes when the queen reveals to the king that by her former marriage she had given birth to a child with deformed feet. The only reasonable course open to her was to dispose of this child by the conventional method of exposure to the elements. Consequently she gave her baby to an old shepherd and asked him to see that her wishes were carried out.

From this point the story moves rapidly to a climax. A shepherd appears who tells Oedipus the people from whom he had fled in order to avoid the decree of the Fates were not his parents, but that he, the shepherd, had received Oedipus from another shepherd. This man is now sent for and it is revealed that Oedipus is the son of Jocasta, for the old shepherd confesses that he did not expose the child given him by the queen. Thus the cycle is complete. Oedipus unwittingly killed his father, and equally without his knowledge married his own mother. His mother kills herself while the king plucks his own eyes out in order that he may no longer look upon the hateful world which has made sport of his hopes and his virtues. As the king appears with his bleeding eyes, the chorus is moved to cry:

> What power malignant heaped
> On thy poor head such complicated woe?

And again the chorus speaks to point the meaning of the play:

> Let mortals hence be taught to look beyond
> The present time, nor dare to say, a man
> Till the last decisive hour
> Shall close his life without the taste of woe.

From this account of the story it is plain that nothing that Oedipus could have done for himself would have averted his doom. This fact would not in itself distinguish Oedipus from a character such as Lavinia in *Mourning Becomes Electra*. The difference lies not in the ill which befalls the character but in the means by which it is brought about. In the case of Oedipus the tragedy was superimposed from the outside. It cut across the current of his life instead of growing out of it. There was nothing in the nature of the life of Oedipus to warrant the judgment that was executed upon him. It did not grow out of his experience, nor was it the result of hereditary faults, nor did it come from the immediate circumstances of his environment. It comes out of a clear sky because some capricious God willed it so. Oedipus himself says, "This must be the work of some malignant power." No other explanation seemed possible to him, for all his life he had sought goodness, honor and beauty. He had lived a virtuous life, happiest when he served his state and his people. There was nothing in his life to account for the injustice which befell him, except that it was the expression of "some malignant power."

The view of the world represented by fatalism is purposive, even teleological in that there is a plan which involves a prevision of a goal. This preconceived end may be one of misfortune for the individual as it was in the case of Oedipus, but it likewise holds a potentiality for the opposite. In all cases it works through experience, but it does not arise in experience or events that are primarily of this world. It thus follows that it involves the concept of anthropomorphic beings who rule arbitrarily over the destinies of men. It is primitive faith as opposed to modern science. Its value must be purely aesthetic to the modern thinker, and it can no longer serve as a guide to the contemporary artist.

O'Neill has not failed to realize this, but he has also realized that the ancients were essentially true to the nature of the world in emphasizing the helplessness of man in his struggle with the forces of life. From this realization has grown his deep appreciation of the Greek point of view both in ethics and in technique, but his solution has been in the direction of determinism as opposed to fatalism.

3

The determinist also holds that man is the victim of circumstance, but in this case there are no outside powers. To the determinist there is no conscious purpose in the universe, and there is no prevision of an end either good or bad. According to this view man is what he is because of his heredity and environment, and every action has its definite cause which, in its turn, was caused until the whole of man's life is an endless chain of causes and effects. From the determinist's point of view freedom is a myth, because everything has its sufficient reason for being; a man is free to do that which he has to do, which simply means, that he is free to be the product of the forces that made him what he is.

This view of man has characterized the most significant and the best of modern literature since the days of Ibsen in Norway and Hardy in England. Since it is of primary importance to realize the application of this theory to modern drama, and especially to O'Neill, it will be worth while to draw examples to illustrate the point before coming to the analysis of O'Neill's own plays.

Ibsen's *Ghosts* is a case in point. The principal character is Oswald. Oswald has this in common with Oedipus that he was a victim of powers over which he had no control, but in his case the forces that molded his life lay in the complex of experience; they flowed in his blood stream, and they were not, as in the case of Oedipus, imposed from the outside as the expression of the will of capricious and untrustworthy gods. The story is simple. Oswald's mother was compelled by her parents to marry Chamberlain Alving, because of the wealth and social position such a marriage might make

possible. Her youth and her training left her no re-
course but to obey her parents' wishes. After the marriage she was horrified by her husband's grossness,
vulgarity and sensuality. By training she knew of only
one thing to do when in trouble and that was to go
to her pastor for advice. She visited Pastor Manders for
whom she had a feeling almost of love, but Pastor
Manders was the victim of a code. He had repeated
the commandments of his Bible so often that, even
though he may have doubted them, any question relative to morals brought from him a conditioned re-
sponse. He was not a bad man. That is, he meant well
—but as far as assistance to Mrs. Alving was concerned
the church might as well have provided an automatic
slot machine into which a person in distress could drop
a nickel expecting it to grind out advice and consolation. The answer for Mrs. Alving was that she should
return to her lord and master, and in all things be
obedient to him. This she did, with the result that a
son was born who became the victim of circumstances
before which he was impotent. He had the taint of
hereditary syphilis, and at the end of the play he is
kept insanely babbling, "Mother, give me the sun. The
sun. The sun."

From birth to insanity Oswald was bound as it were
in a net of steel from which neither natural nor supernatural power could free him. With Oedipus he has
this in common: that his doom was sealed before he
was born. The difference lies in this: that in the case
of the king, a supernatural being decided what the end

should be without any known reference to the past. In the case of Oswald there was a chain of experience, or a definite sequence of cause and effect which moved inexorably to a fixed end. The point of view of the fatalist is primitive in that it is based upon a world of magic, a world in which miracles can occur because there is no hard and fast relationship of cause and effect between man's experiences and the rest of the world. Determinism is modern in that it is a philosophy of life that grows out of an understanding of life as an integral part of the universe, and not as something that is specially created and thus capable of miraculous behavior. From this scientific point of view the behavior of man is no more mysterious than the behavior of the atmosphere that encircles our globe. In each case there may be many aspects of behavior that are unknown, but the assumption of science is that should they ever be fully explained there will be nothing that does not fit into the scheme of what we already know. In other words, from the modern point of view, the world of miraculous accidents exists no more.

The question of why this tragedy befell Oswald is answered by referring it to the endless chain of experiences that composed the physical and social environment of his life—and of any life. This answer is an evasion if one seeks absolute truth, but as has already been established, absolutes in ethics are as dead as those who first established them as theories applicable to the explanations of human behavior.

4

O'Neill's strength as a dramatist is emphasized by his deterministic philosophy. It makes his tragedies logically sound, and emotionally convincing. But it also tends to limit his appeal to those who have some realization of what has happened to Western civilization in the last century. To those who still cling to a dualistic philosophy and insist upon a free will, O'Neill must seem to force his characters to an end that is not inevitable. From the free-will point of view it is always possible to say: Why did this character not do something else? From a deterministic point of view the answer is simple: He could do nothing else. Hardy expresses it when he describes the forces which controlled the life of Jude:

A compelling arm of extraordinary muscular power seized hold of him—something which had nothing in common with the spirits and influences that had moved him hitherto. This seemed to care little for his reason and his will, nothing for his so-called elevated intentions, and moved him along, as a violent schoolmaster a schoolboy he has seized by the collar, in a direction which tended towards the embrace of a woman for whom he had no respect, and whose life had nothing in common with his own except locality. *(Jude the Obscure.)*

Somerset Maugham expresses the same idea over and over again in his novel *Of Human Bondage.* His lead-

ing character is "as though he were a leaf in the wind."
He says:

> I act as though I were a free agent. But when action is
> performed it is clear that all the forces of the universe
> from all eternity conspired to cause it, and nothing I
> could do could have prevented it. It was inevitable.

In another passage the character is described in these
words:

> He acted as though he were a machine driven by two
> forces of his environment and his personality; his reason
> was someone looking on, observing the facts but power-
> less to interfere.

Galsworthy in the *Forsyte Saga* uses almost identical
terminology in describing the importance of Old
Jolyon:

> There he sat in the gloomy comfort of the room, a
> puppet in the power of great forces that cared nothing
> for family or class or creed, but moved machine-like,
> with dread processes to inscrutable ends.

Which all harmonizes very well with Anatole France's
characteristic generalization, "Men seemed to him more
like beans in the trough of a coffee-mill."

If one turns from these statements of the deterministic position to the analysis of characters and plots in
the contemporary novel or drama of Europe and
America, he finds that in the larger aspects as well as

the minor details the same thing holds true. Galsworthy's dramas provide endless examples. Consider the case of Falder in *Justice* or that of Matt Denant in *Escape*. In America, Dreiser's great studies of human tragedy have consistently emphasized the deterministic point of view. From *Sister Carrie* to *An American Tragedy,* he has developed his characters and his plots within the web of a deterministic philosophy. Dreiser states his theme when he says of Clyde Griffiths' father that he was "the product of an environment and a religious theory."

But even before Dreiser, Mark Twain had written this doctrine into *The Mysterious Stranger*. Satan gives a fantastic, but none the less real, account of determinism in his explanation to the boys who are his listeners:

> Among you boys you have a game: you push a brick, it knocks its neighbor over, the neighbor knocks over the next brick—and so on till all the row is prostrate. That is human life. A child's first act knocks over the initial brick, and the rest will follow inexorably. If you could see into the future, as I can, you would see everything that was going to happen to that creature, for nothing can change the order of its life after the first event has determined it. That is, nothing will change it, because each act unfailingly begets an act, that act begets another, and so on to the end, and the seer can look forward down the line and see just when each act is to have birth, from cradle to grave.

Does God order the career?

Foreordain it? No. The man's circumstances and environment order it. His first act determines the second
and all that follow after.

*   *   *   *

Yes. Now, then, no man ever does drop a link—the
thing has never happened! Even when he is trying to
make up his mind as to whether he will do a thing or
not, that itself is a link, an act, and has its proper place
in his chain; and when he finally decides an act, that
also was the thing which he was absolutely certain to do.
You see, now, that a man will never drop a link in his
chain. He cannot. If he made up his mind to try, that
project would itself be an unavoidable link—a thought
bound to occur to him at that precise moment, and made
certain by the first act of his babyhood.

This interpretation of man's life is the inevitable out-
come of nineteenth-century empirical philosophy. It has
changed the whole concept of our world. Mrs. White-
field in *Man and Superman* sums it up very well when
she says:

It's a very queer world. It used to be so straightforward and simple; and now nobody seems to think and
feel as they ought. Nothing has been right since that
speech that Professor Tyndall made at Belfast.

5

O'Neill belongs in this tradition. He has never treated
his characters as free agents. Even in his very earliest

plays, he developed his men and women against a background of social and biological forces, thus giving a deep and a universal significance to his themes. When Rose (*The Web*) went to a doctor about her health:

> ROSE. He told me I had the 'con' and had it bad. He said the only hope fur me was to git out in the country, sleep in the open air, and eat a lot of good food. He might as well 'uv told me to go to Heaven and I told him so.

And in the end she is described as *crushed by the ironic life force.* The point I wish to make is not that this is a great play, but that when O'Neill began interpreting life through the medium of the drama, he emphasized heredity and environment as the great tragic forces which held man in their grasp. Man might will, desire, have good intentions and noble aspirations, but if these forces that controlled his destiny were adverse, all of his dreams would come to nothing.

In *Gold* Captain Bartlett is developed as a man obsessed with a single idea which holds him in its power as effectively as if he were bound in a cage of steel. He didn't want to be a bad man; he didn't want to commit murder. What he really wanted was to be a good father to his children and a kind husband to his wife. But circumstance in the form of poverty, the sea and stories of buried treasure had developed in him the fatal hope for gold—easy gold. Because of this romantic passion for gold, he becomes a murderer and following that a haunted, fear-stricken spirit, the victim of two conflicting desires: one, the wish to set right, in as far as is possible, his great crime, and the other, a will to believe in the reality of his buried treasure. When his wife suspects his crime she urges him to confess, to free his conscience and be again the man he would like to be. He listens to her and for a moment he is almost able to yield to the impulse set up in him by her plea. Then the old obsession reasserts itself. The thought of his gold comes back and he answers:

> CAPTAIN BARTLETT. Confess and let someone steal the gold! Ye'd make an old woman o' me, would ye, Sarah?—an old, Sunday go-to-meetin' woman snivelin' and prayin' to God for pardon?

The obsession dominates him to the end. It is this obsession that gives unity to the structure, emphasis to the theme, and to the story the plausibility that makes it convincing. A further analysis of Captain Bartlett is clearly sketched into the plot, which accounts for his original passion for gold, making his character seem fully rounded and understandable in the light of ordinary experience. He is a logical product of his environment and his heredity. There were no supernatural forces that guided his life to its sad end. The powers that worked through his life were those that all may understand, who realize that once born into this world certain definite causes operate to determine a course of action.

This may be more clearly illustrated in the case of *Anna Christie,* for in that play the author has definitely created characters whose desires were in direct variance to their actions. In this play O'Neill has revealed the real conflict between what man desires in this life and what he gets. Anna was a normal child with normal physical characteristics and aspirations. Her first great disadvantage was that she did not have the protection and care that parents usually give their children. This handicap was made worse by a physical beauty that under different conditions might have been to her a real advantage.

Her father in his ignorance had sent her to live with her cousins, and it was one of them who first led her astray, not with her consent. She reviews her past from a deterministic point of view when she says:

> ANNA. It wasn't none of my fault. I hated him worse'n hell and he knew it. But he was big and strong.
>
> *   *   *   *
>
> That was why I run away from the farm. That was what made me get a yob as a nurse girl in St. Paul. And you think that was a nice yob for a girl, too, don't you? *(Sarcastically)* With all them nice inland fellers yust looking for a chance to marry me, I s'pose. Marry me? What a chance! They wasn't looking for marrying. I'm owning up to everything fair and square. I was caged in, I tell you—yust like in yail—taking care of other people's kids—listening to 'em bawling and crying day and night—when I wanted to be out—and I was lonesome—lonesome as hell! *(With a sudden weariness in her voice)* So I give up finally. What was the use?

This is her past history from her own life, a history that belies a free will, and emphasizes the forces of experience, environment that broke her spirit for the time being, and made a girl who wished for a happy life into a prostitute. Praise or blame are alike futile. As O'Neill tells the story it becomes as ludicrous to blame Anna for what she did as it would be to blame a child for getting itself born. The moralist who still lives in the world of ethical absolutes might say that she should have resisted. But again that is futile. She did resist, but her strength was not equal to the forces that opposed her. To the moralist it would be fair to answer by asking him: If you saw a man throw a child to its death from a high building would you blame the child because it did not have sufficient strength to resist its enemy? The reply here would be self-evident, because the antagonist is easily defined. In the case of Anna the antagonist is an intangible force, but no less sinister or powerful. Anna describes it when she says: "I was caged in—yust like being in yail."

The only reason Anna's past does not carry complete conviction to every reader arises because there are still people who are unfamiliar with the trend of modern thought, and also because we all tend to rely upon belief sanctioned by tradition, for that requires no individual intellectual effort. Determinism lacks this sanction, and a character developed without this tradition must for a time seem strange, even unreal, to those who have not grasped the author's full implication. Our intellectual tradition has emphasized freedom, a

freedom that has in modern times become understandable only as a rationalization of desire. We no longer
blame a person who develops a case of spotted fever
although we cannot isolate the cause. Social sickness is
no more uncaused than physical sickness, but is often
more difficult to diagnose.

O'Neill has taken the modern deterministic point of
view, and against the background of intangible forces
reveals the tragedy of Anna's struggle for life. The
story gives no opportunity for praise or blame. There
is nothing to forgive; there is everything to be endured.
Anna sums it all up for her father:

> ANNA. There ain't nothing to forgive, anyway. It ain't
> your fault, and it ain't mine, and it ain't his neither.
> We're all poor nuts, and things happen, and we yust
> get mixed in wrong, that's all.

6

The Long Voyage Home combines the two aspects
of determinism with great clarity. In its simplicity and
directness it is a perfect one-act play. Olson is a stocky
middle-aged Swede whose life as a sailor has kept him
from visiting his home for more than ten years. He
has often been urged by his mother to come back home,
and at the end of every voyage his intentions have been
to do so. Companionship with his sailor friends, the
traditional celebrations of the sailors after reaching port
at the end of a voyage, the temptation to get drunk—

all these things have been stronger than his will to overcome them and go home. After every voyage these powers have dominated his behavior leading to the necessity to ship out again.

Time has passed, and Olson realizes that if he is ever to see his mother again he must do it now. Thus he refuses to drink with his comrades, knowing that if he becomes intoxicated, it will be the same old story over again. This is the assertion of his will in triumph over the desires that formerly held sway. The new power to resist the usual shore temptation is clearly determined by the age of his mother, his brother's offer of a place on the farm, and his temporary nausea for the sailor's life. A new combination of forces leads him to achieve that which at other times seemed impossible. His own review of his past and the new plan states the case:

OLSON. I write back always I come soon; and I mean all time to go back home at end of voyage. But I come ashore, I take one drink, I take many drinks, I get drunk, I spend all money, I have to ship away for other voyage. So dis time I say to myself: Don't drink one drink, Ollie, or, sure, you don't get home. And I want go home dis time. I feel homesick for farm and to see my people again. Yust like little boy, I feel homesick. Dat's why I don't drink noting tonight but dis—belly-wash! You know, Miss Freda, my mother get very old, and I want see her. She might die and I would never—

His ability to turn away from his past becomes as much a matter of pure determinism as was his former inability to do so. He is a victim of forces over which he has no control. At this point when it seems as though he will be free to follow the new set of desires, he falls a victim to forces that lie not in his character, but in the world outside himself. The saloon-keeper gives him knockout drops in his soft-drink, robs him of his money, and has him carried aboard a particularly ill-favored boat that is sailing for a voyage around Cape Horn. He is shanghaied. His will which seemed for once to have harmonized perfectly with his desire is thwarted by physical force. His destiny once more became something other than he wished. The determinism of this experience is easily perceived, but O'Neill has made it clear that when compared with the past and judged by the results, he was as much a victim of himself at the end of all the previous voyages as he was the victim of the saloon-keeper and a drug in this particular episode. Each time he went back to the sea. Each time he failed to go home. His whole life was made up of willingness to follow one course of action and being compelled to pursue its opposite.

In *Ile,* another play of the sea, the same ironic fate pursues the characters of the Captain and his wife. His wife was losing her mind because of the loneliness, the terrible strain of waiting month after month for the ice to break, and the whales to come so that her husband could get his cargo of whale oil. She pleads

with him to take her home, to give up the stupid waiting. Captain Keeney realizes her condition, and for a
time his love for her almost overcomes his tradition as
the Captain of a whaling ship. He loves her more than
his cargo of oil, but the laws of his past experience are
stronger than his will to give in to his wife's desires.
It is as though he were held in the grasp of invisible
hands. He cries out: "I got to git it in spite of all Hell,
and by God, I ain't agoin' home till I do git it!"

He had always brought home a full load. He had
won a reputation that became a causal chain in his life,
and now when he would gladly have sacrificed for his
wife, he finds his imagination picturing the sneers and
jokes of other captains in his home port, laughing at
him for failing at last to get his load of oil. This his
wife calls, "a stupid, stubborn reason," but it is powerful enough to keep Captain Keeney at his task and to
drive his wife to insanity.

7

The effectiveness of O'Neill's tragedies arises out of
this consistent application of the deterministic principle. It gives clearness and almost classic tone to his
dramas. O'Neill has given an objective, artistic interpretation to the deterministic principles of modern
science, or at least to the science that has dominated the
thought of our modern world up to the days of Ed-
dington and Jeans.

It is a deterministic philosophy that makes *The Em-*

peror Jones convincing. With relentless imagination
O'Neill has followed through the life history of his
strange Emperor. As long as Jones held sway from his
throne, no power could touch him. His past, for all
that appearances might reveal, could have been that of
genuine nobility. He acts the part, and the social environment is in perfect harmony. Gradually a sinister
note of rebellion trembles faintly through his realm.
His work is over, and with his gain secured he plans
to leave.

It is only when he enters the dark forest that his past,
the irrevocable past which he has so long concealed,
begins to assert itself. No iron law enforced by physical
power could have been more relentless than was Emperor Jones' past. His social heritage of slave tradition,
the debasing work of the Negro as the white man's
servant, his crimes, his childhood superstitions, including his biological heritage—all these forces which he
thought were forgotten reasserted their power over
him. They were transmuted into the beatings of his
heart by the native tom tom as it echoed in the depth
of the forest. With perfect regularity, these forces of
heredity and environment crowd in upon the consciousness of the Emperor until he loses his regal nature
and tears away the trappings of his assumed grandeur.
One by one they disappear, and as he becomes more
and more naked, he becomes more and more a Negro
criminal tortured by primitive fears of the dark. In
the end he loses the battle, conquered, but not by the
physical strength of the natives, for they did not even

change their position. All they did while Jones circled wildly through the forest was to beat their drums. He was destroyed by the forces of his past. It was not the natives that barred his way to freedom; it was the "strong medicine" of his Negro heritage.

8

Strange Interlude illustrates the same principles of determinism. Each character considered in the light of his desires proves to be driven by forces that are stronger than those desires to an end that is the opposite of his hopes and his ambition. Professor Leeds wanted his daughter to be happy, but he was held in the vise-like grip of New England tradition which made it impossible for him to give Nina the freedom of action necessary to her well-being. The cultural pattern of his life made him strangely unfitted for an adviser to a young woman at the most crucial moment of her life. He referred her appeal for love in its fullest sense to the narrow principles of his Puritan faith—not because he believed implicitly in this doctrine, but because tradition made him helpless and unable to act in any other way.

Not only was he bound by the cultural pattern of his place and time, but he was also the victim of a selfish love for his daughter which blocked every effort that he might have made to give her the freedom which his reason convinced him was her right. This theme, which gets its fullest expression in *Mourning Becomes*

Electra, is present here. Professor Leeds was in love with his daughter, and no matter how much he might try to make himself believe that she should live her own life, he could never admit her right to any lover other than himself. This was the power that ruled his action, and its effectiveness was all the more complete because he would not recognize its presence. It was not Gordon that he hated; it was Nina's lover come to take his place, to force him into the position of father, which made him use every device he could invent to keep her to himself.

Under the stress of emotion he suddenly loses control of himself and when Nina says, "It's too late for lies," he replies:

> PROFESSOR LEEDS. Let us say that I *persuaded* myself it was for your sake. That may be true. You are young. You think one can live with truth. Very well. It is also true I was jealous of Gordon. I was alone and I wanted to keep your love. I hated him as one hates a thief one may not accuse nor punish. I did my best to prevent your marriage. I was glad when he died. There. Is that what you wish me to say?

Professor Leeds followed the only course that was possible for him even though it led to an end that meant the defeat of the thing he wished to achieve. As an aid to his desire to delude himself and conceal from himself his real motives, he used Marsden as a foil. He was willing to believe that he could tolerate Marsden, for subconsciously he knew that Marsden was in love with his own mother. His situation is the same as that of the professor, the only difference being mother-son instead of father-daughter love. Marsden had always believed himself in love with Nina, but this was only a disguise for his real love for his mother. His work as a novelist, his friendships, his travels, every major act of his life was referred back to his mother for justification and approval. She was the dominating influence in his life, governing all of his important decisions. Marsden was free to do the things he had to do, the things that were determined by his complex relationship with his mother. In neither his case nor that of Professor Leeds is there any suggestion of overt relationship, for tradition would not permit that, but the chains that bound their actions were none the less unbreakable. The prison in which they lived was securely barred. The only unique thing about it was that for the most part they refused to admit its existence. They lived in the belief that they were free, while every major act of their lives emphasized the fact that they were imprisoned.

The life of Nina follows the same deterministic pattern. She was bound by a convention that she hated and despised when she permitted Gordon to leave for the war without becoming her lover in the fullest sense. The dire consequences of this one act determines the tragedy which follows. It becomes convincing only when one realizes that Nina was the victim of circumstances that transcended her control. The death of her lover led to a violent nervous disturbance which manifested itself in a will to sexual expression. There is no freedom in this except the freedom that an undammed stream has to flow down hill. Nina behaved as the forces that dominated her life compelled her to act.

From her days as a nurse to the end of the play she is dominated by her tragic love for Gordon. When happiness seems for a moment possible to her, it is blighted by the sad history of her husband's past as revealed to her by Mrs. Evans. The deterministic principle is easily apparent in this episode, though no more real than in any other situation in the play. It is of no avail to appeal to justice, foresight, intelligence or virtue, for no matter what may be said for or against Nina the simple and terrible truth remains that when she visited her mother-in-law, she discovered that she was pregnant with a child whose ancestors had been insane. Her will to love a baby, her desire to make her husband happy, and every other aspiration for a good life were thwarted in a single moment when she became aware of certain biological factors that were not within the scope of her control.

At this particular point it may be said that she exerted her will by defeating the purposes of nature. She destroyed the life within her in order that she might not bring forth a baby doomed to insanity. A moment's consideration is sufficient to sum up the evidence that led to this act. O'Neill has given it in the powerful scene between Nina and Mrs. Evans. The revelation in the upstairs room precipitated the action just as clearly as if some individual with the power had taken Nina prisoner, forced her to take an anaesthetic and then performed the operation.

O'Neill has made his characters the victims of circumstances over which they have no control. They move in a world of dark and sinister forces, which govern the destinies of men and women helpless and impotent before the workings of these unpredictable powers. This does not mean that his characters are weaklings whose lives are pathetic but not tragic. Just the reverse is true. It is the great character whose life becomes significant when it struggles against the inevitable. Darrell, Nina and Marsden are all rebels against the despotism of facts as these facts move slowly and inexorably to enmesh and destroy their hopes and their happiness. It is their defiant struggle against these facts that lends dignity to their lives, and it is at this point that their universality becomes apparent. Thus strife with adversity is a parallel to the life of all those who do not gracefully or supinely accept the inevitable. The development of character in O'Neill's dramas is always typical and in a sense universal in that it is the common lot of man to feel the heavy power of those circumstances over which he has no control and against which his spirit rebels in bitterness and pain.

With age comes reconciliation, but not peace. The fire of protest burns low; exhaustion leads man to submit without protest, for he has learned that his rebellion is a cry in the night to which the only answer is the faint echo of his protest. So in *Strange Interlude* the intensity of the flame dies slowly to a mere glowing ember. Marsden summarizes:

> MARSDEN. So let's you and me forget the whole dis-
> tressing episode, regard it as an interlude, of trial and
> preparation, say, in which our souls have been scraped
> clean of impure flesh and made worthy to bleach in
> peace.
> NINA. Strange Interlude! Yes, our lives are merely
> strange dark interludes in the electrical display of God
> the Father!

9

One of the first questions O'Neill asked himself when he began searching for a modern manner of treating the ancient Electra story is published in his notes:

> Is it possible to get modern psychological approxima-
> tion of Greek sense of fate into such a play, which an
> intelligent audience of today, possessed by no belief in
> gods or supernatural retribution, could accept and be
> moved by?—(Notes to *Mourning Becomes Electra* #1.)

His answer, as it may be inferred from the play, is that determinism is the modern substitute for the Greek sense of fate. In spite of the protest that has been made against O'Neill's assumption that the modern intelligent audience is essentially skeptical of supernatural retribution, it remains a plain fact that as far as its attitude towards art is concerned O'Neill's assumption is a fact. No intelligent audience today will be satisfied by supernatural retribution. The Greek gods are dead as far as the theater is concerned, and O'Neill in recognizing this fact at the outset faced his problem squarely. He saw that the Electra theme which could be handled with such convincing argument by the Greeks, because the Fates could bear the heavy burden of responsibility, must be treated by a far subtler psychological method if it were to appear valid to a modern audience.

The next step in his argument was to arrive at an interpretation of his characters in the light of modern science which would give living reality to the poetic, but primitive, Greek Fates. That man is the victim of powers he cannot control is clearly stated in the Greek drama, but the modern explanation of what these powers are and how they work is far more complex than the solution offered by the Greeks.

O'Neill's answer was to treat his characters from the point of view of philosophic determinism. In working out the behavior of Orin, he cannot rely upon Fates, Furies or Gods; he must find the cause elsewhere. For these supernatural powers he substitutes "Puritan conviction of man born to sin and punishment—Orestes' furies within him, his conscience—" (Notes to *Mourning Becomes Electra* #5) This is followed up in the development of Abe Mannon by using "sexual frustration by his Puritan sense of guilt turning love to lust." For the awful sense of fate in the Greek drama, he substitutes "a psychological fate" (Note #16). This conception of the problem is followed in a later note by a clear statement of the deterministic principle.

> The unavoidable entire melodramatic action must be felt as working out of psychic fate from past—thereby attain tragic significance—or else!—a hell of a problem, a modern tragic interpretation of classic fate without benefit of gods—for it must, before everything, remain modern psychological play—fate springing out of the family—" (Note #16.)

Every detail of the play is built up on this deterministic principle. As Lavinia says to Seth: "There's no rest in this house which Grandfather built as a temple of Hate and Death." This is a fact that Seth understood, for he had already said, "There's been evil in that house since it was first built in hate—and it's kept growin' there ever since, as what's happened there has proved." But in this play it is not a supernatural power acting arbitrarily with a vision of the end desired that causes evil to flourish in the House of Mannon. Abe Mannon destroyed his house and built a new one because his brother ran away with Marie Brantôme, a servant girl in the house. Love, jealousy, hate and a puritanic conscience were the moving factors that laid the foundations for the tragic end of the Mannon family. The motivating forces are inward, psychological, complex, but not supernatural.

Marie Brantôme became the type loved by the Mannons. David won her away from his brother Abe, who then forced David into poverty which ended in suicide.

Abe and David were not the only ones in the family who had been attracted to Marie. Abe's son Ezra had also loved her.

> SETH. He was only a boy then, but he was crazy about her, too, like a youngster would be. His mother was stern with him, while Marie, she made a fuss over him and petted him.
> LAVINIA. Father, too!
> SETH. Ayeh—but he hated her worse than anyone when it got found out she was his uncle David's fancy woman.

Ezra hated Marie Brantôme, but when he married, the influence of his early love determined the type of woman that he chose for his wife. Marie had made "a fuss over him and petted him," and determined for him what his future destiny should be. Without his will and all unconscious of the powers at work, the child's mind and tastes were formed in the direction of a destiny he could not foresee and that he would have fled from in terror could he have known its tragic implications. Brant, the son of Marie, gives the clue to the deterministic chain. In speaking to Lavinia he says:

> BRANT. You're so like your mother in some ways. Your face is the dead image of hers. And look at your hair. You won't meet hair like yours and hers again in a month of Sundays. I only know of one other woman who had it. You'll think it strange when I tell you. It was my mother.

*   *   *   *

Yes, she had beautiful hair like your mother's, that
hung down to her knees, and big, deep, sad eyes that
were blue as the Caribbean Sea!

In an earlier passage Christine is described as having
"deep-set eyes, of a dark violet hue."

O'Neill makes it clear that it was Christine's likeness
to Marie that determined Ezra's falling in love, and it
was the peculiar movement and vital grace of her body
that inspired his passion. Seth emphasizes this quality
in his description of Marie:

SETH. Marie? She was always laughin' and singin'—
frisky and full of life—with something free and wild
about her like an animile. Purty she was, too! . . .
Hair just the color of your Maw's and yourn she had.

Compare this with the author's description of Christine
and the fatal similarity is complete. "She has a fine,
voluptuous figure and she moves with a flowing animal grace."

When old Abe Mannon brought Marie Brantôme
into his house as a servant he started a chain of events
that moved with dread certainty to the destruction of
the Mannon family. O'Neill has not rested all of his
argument upon so slight a chain of evidence, but has
given his family history validity and power by revealing the social complex of New England Puritan heritage as the fit medium for nurturing this particular
series of events.

The house which Lavinia recognized as a "temple of

hate and death" was to Christine equally horrible in form and spirit.

> CHRISTINE. Each time I come back after being away it appears more like a sepulchre! The "whited" one of the Bible—pagan temple front stuck like a mask on Puritan gray ugliness! It's just like old Abe Mannon to build such a monstrosity—as a temple for his hatred.

The house becomes a symbol of the conflict between love and the moral code. This particular moral code determines how the Mannons shall act in relation to each other, to the community, and to the state. It fixes the mask which passes for virtue to the casual observer. But underneath the exterior calm there surges a deep, fiery, passionate life which may for a time be suppressed but is never subdued.

It is these two forces in conflict that feed the flame of fury which springs from the fatal likeness of the Mannon women to Marie Brantôme. It makes possible the love and the hatred that spread their deadly virus throughout their lives and determined their tragic destruction.

O'Neill emphasizes the similarity among the men as well. Orin looks like his father and Brant also bears the family resemblance inherited from his father, the grand uncle of Orin. This makes the circle complete. Brant is attracted to Christine, because she resembles his mother, and he hates Ezra just as Orin hates his father, for he also is in love with his mother. The same thing holds for Lavinia and accounts for her love for Brant which turns to hatred when her affections are spurned. Orin recognized this, as is revealed by his comment on Lavinia's brief love affair in San Francisco.

ORIN. Wilkins reminded you of Brant—
LAVINIA. No!
ORIN. And that's why you suddenly discarded mourning in Frisco and bought new clothes—in Mother's colors!

It is by a close adherence to determinism that O'Neill achieves a tragic parallel to the Greek Electra theme. He cannot pass the responsibility for the behavior of his characters into the custody of capricious gods. He must make his audience realize that there is a sufficient and a human reason for their behavior. This he has done by accounting for the family's past history, following along the deterministic practice of Ibsen, where there is a fine parallel in *Rosmersholm*. O'Neill did not model after this play, but the technique of accounting for the behavior of the characters is similar—because Ibsen like O'Neill was a determinist. This method has given the needed modern interpretation to make the Electra story convincing to a contemporary audience. When the play is over, all the characters are accounted for, in that every action is explained in relation to social, physical and psychological forces that dominated their lives.

Dudley Nichols' fine introductory essay to the Mod-

ern Library edition of *The Emperor Jones* recognized
this deterministic aspect of O'Neill long ago. He wrote:

> While his imaginative world and spiritual potency
> bear many points of resemblance to those of Aeschylus,
> Sophocles and Euripides, it is his likeness with the latter
> one would linger on. In O'Neill as in Euripides fate, the
> prime motive of ancient tragedy, is no longer felt as a
> capricious external power but as the inevitable outcome
> of character and the unavoidable condition of life. Tragic
> pathos is refined to a sense of universal human fellow-
> ship in frailty and suffering. And the dramatic interest
> of Euripides the rebel lay in the thought and experience
> of the ordinary individual. He completely shifted the
> tragic situation from a conflict between man and the
> divine laws of the Universe to man's inner soul.

The world of O'Neill as revealed in the sum total of
his works is a world in which free will has been reduced
to necessity. The behavior of the men and women who
live in this world is not free behavior, that is, it is not
unaccounted for and unrelated to the forces which
determine it. This gives tragic beauty to O'Neill's interpretation of life, but it also implies ethical consequences. In a deterministic world free from the traditional hopes of an Arabian Nights psychology, it may
be possible to analyze the causes of human conduct.
The moral dogma of praise and blame will perish and
in their place may come understanding and a new
moral order. It is this implied hope that lends a warm
vitality to the plays; it gives the reader a sense of

power, or at least it offers an interpretation of life that is a challenge, something more than a supine hope. It is only when life is recognized as deterministic that it will be possible to act and plan to make it better, or even to conceive what may be meant by better. O'Neill has revealed the forces that work through the lives of his characters, and by this method he has achieved a fair modicum of artistic reality which helps to make his plays intellectual as well as aesthetic in their appeal.

VII

Social Implications

SECOND VOICE. The child was diseased at
birth, stricken with a hereditary ill that only
the most vital men are able to shake off.
FIRST VOICE. You mean?
SECOND VOICE. I mean poverty—the most
deadly and prevalent of all diseases. *Fog.*

I

A PLAY which resolves itself into an argument against
capitalism or against anything else loses its value as art
even though sympathy for the author's point of view
may be quite universal. The opposite is likewise true. A
work of art which is divorced from man's struggle
with an unfriendly and an unmoral universe loses the
most abiding appeal that art can have for man.
O'Neill's tremendous success as a dramatist depends to
a great extent upon the fact that he has had something
to say about the modern social order that has been
worth saying. His technique and his form have been
admirable vehicles for an interpretation of the conflict
which arises out of the circumstances of the world in
which we live.

186

In *Fog,* an early one-act play, O'Neill's point of view is clearly stated. It is more of an argument than a play, but for the purpose of understanding O'Neill's philosophy it has real value. The poor workmanship of the young artist is often the key to understanding the implication of the mature work. In O'Neill's early plays his point of view is clear. *Fog* is symbolic of the state of mind of the business man who is adrift in a boat with a poet, a woman and a dead child. When the business man expresses concern over the child's death, the poet replies by giving a lecture on social injustice which surrounds the lives of the poor. He says:

> What chance had that poor child? Naturally sickly and weak from underfeeding, transplanted to the stinking room of a tenement or the filthy hovel of a mining village, what glowing opportunities did life hold out that death should not be regarded as a blessing for him? I mean if he possessed the ordinary amount of ability and intelligence—considering him as the average child of ignorant Polish immigrants. Surely his prospects of ever becoming anything but a beast of burden were not bright, were they?

The business man answers with a doubtful negative, which implies that he thinks there should be some way out. He expresses the usual vague hope of those who find it hard to face reality. The poet then pushes the problem still further by asking an embarrassing question:

If you could bring him back to life, would you do so?
Could you conscientiously drag him away from that fine
sleep of his to face what he would have to face? Leaving
the joy you would give his mother out of the question,
would you do it for him individually?

The implications of these questions are very general.
They apply not only to the dead child in the boat, but
to millions of unfortunate victims of our industrial system. It is as though O'Neill had said: "If you were
God would you not prevent this monstrous abortion
called the living poor?" What right have we to permit
life to be born that exists only for slavery or worse than
slavery—a life of neglect and suffering to end in a
charity bread line, and a pauper's grave? The poet is
explicit, and defines his terms:

I mean poverty—the most deadly and prevalent of all
diseases.

The business man is irritated by such a statement and
tries to escape by asserting that he is "not responsible
for the way the world is run." And the poet replies,
"But you are responsible," continuing:

I mean supposing we—the self-satisfied, successful members of society—are responsible for the injustice· visited upon the heads of our less fortunate "brothers-in-
Christ" because of our shameful indifference to it. We
see misery all around us and we do not care. We do
nothing to prevent it. Are we not then, in part at least,
responsible for it? Have you ever thought of that?

O'Neill has thought a great deal about that and has given his answer in many different plays. It is because he has thought of man in relation to his social system that his plays have become something more than a moment's entertainment. It is not man as an individual alone that concerns O'Neill; it is man in a social order, tortured, starved, disillusioned, thwarted and driven to disaster by the forces of a system which cares nothing for the general welfare of society. Man moves across the stage of an O'Neill play not as a free and detached individual, not merely as an individual in relation to a few characters who are associated with him in the immediate drama which makes the play, but he treats man against a rich background of social forces. Beyond the backdrop, before the beginning of the play, and beyond the ending lies a definite social system that is as important to an appreciation of the play as is the action which takes place on the stage in the presence of the audience. It is the skill with which the dramatist has made his audience aware of this larger significance of his theme that lends to O'Neill's drama its rich, sympathetic tone. It is the social implication that makes his play have a life in the mind of the audience after it has left the theater and scattered to the quiet of individual thought.

2

In the early one-act plays this is stated in direct speech; but as his technique developed, O'Neill made the background more implicit than explicit, which is exactly as it should be. But O'Neill like all great dramatists is not afraid of the direct criticism which, from a technical point of view, may be considered as a digression. No man ever made more digressions to generalize about life and its tragic lot than did Shakespeare or Goethe. They had something to say and they would say it no matter what the consequences might be. O'Neill is far more restrained than any of his predecessors in the drama, even than his modern contemporaries, but that he is concerned with the problem of man in relation to the present social order is apparent in all of his plays. Even those that use an historical background come under this classification. The social implication of the greed for empire is boldly set forth in *The Fountain,* and the direct criticism of modern business ideals is the whole theme of *Marco Millions.* In such a purely fantastic drama as *The Emperor Jones,* O'Neill does not permit us to forget the social implication. When Brutus Jones lost his nerve in the forest, the grim shadows of his past came to haunt him. And what were they? Slavery, crime, penitentiaries, the whole vicious, illogical structure of our modern industrial world, which goad the poverty-stricken day and night to commit crime, and then when it is committed, punishes the criminal it has helped to make—punishes without reference to the causes that inspired the crime. Jones escaped the direct punishment, but he could not escape the deep scars left by a vicious system. In the pantomime of the prison scene and at the auc-

tion mart our social order as well as the character of
Jones is clearly revealed.

But in the plays mentioned above, the social criticism
supplies only a rich background. It is in *Anna Christie,
Strange Interlude, The Hairy Ape* and *All God's Chillun Got Wings* that the modern social order is directly,
and in some cases, bitterly criticized.

3

In *The Hairy Ape* O'Neill presents a problem that
has broader implications than the immediate success
or failure of Yank. Yank becomes aware of the fact that
he does not "belong." He finds out that while he has
been doing his work the world has been gradually but
quite rapidly revolutionized by machinery, a revolution that has not carried him with it. He finds that a
new world which disregards human rights and aspirations has left him stranded. The one thing which made
his life endurable was that he felt that he "belonged,"
that he was a necessary, vital and human part of a social order. But one day he awoke to the fact that he
counted for nothing as an individual. If he could have
reasoned it out clearly, he would have known that as
soon as a machine known as an automatic stoker could
be invented, he would be thrown overboard. He would
have known that the progress of invention is for the
benefit of those who exploit the workers and not for
the good of society as a whole. And this is not Yank's
problem alone, but the problem of our whole social sys-

tem. There are literally millions of men and women
who are blood relations of Yank in this modern industrial world. Like Yank they have grown up in the faith
that they "belonged," that they were a necessary and
respected part of a social order, but they have lived to
find out that they are nothing of the kind. As they
walk up and down the world looking for work only to
be turned away with a brutal word; as they stand in
thousands of bread lines to receive food not much better
than slop that charity flings them; as they shiver from
cold, and see their loved ones die from want, consoled
only by the fact that they, too, will soon be dead, they
come to the realization that they do not belong. They
see an abundance of food, clothing and shelter lavishly
wasted on every hand, but nothing is offered them.
They taste only the food that has been allowed to rot,
because of a system which does not or cannot change its
ideals. They stand on the sidewalks of the world, desolate, abandoned, even hated and despised for being
something they did not ask to be. They are forced to
listen to the empty talk which flows like a garbage-
choked river from the vacuous minds of the protected
ones. Like Yank they must listen as he listened one
bright Sunday morning on Fifth Avenue while the fat
ones came past him talking of the church service in the
following manner.

> Dear Doctor Caiaphas! He is so sincere!
> What was the sermon? I dozed off.
> About the radicals, my dear—and the false doctrines
> that are being preached.

We must organize a hundred per cent American bazaar.

And let everyone contribute one one-hundredth per cent of their income tax.

What an original idea!

We can devote the proceeds to rehabilitating the veil of the temple.

But that has been done so many times.

Nothing could reflect more clearly than does this scene the utter bankruptcy of the modern system to deal with the problem that confronts Yank and millions of others. The system has evolved beyond control and each day the gap between Yank and his needs grows wider.

Yank tries desperately to cope with the problem and for his pains is thrown into jail where a fellow prisoner makes a plain and direct criticism of the social order by reading a senator's puerile defense of a system that offers imprisonment or starvation as its only answer to social injustice. This speech, quoted in full, shows the extent to which O'Neill introduces a direct approach to the social problem. Thus spoke Senator Queen as reported in the *Sunday Times:*

> There is a menace existing in this country today which threatens the vitals of our fair Republic—as foul a menace against the very life-blood of the American Eagle as was the foul conspiracy of Catiline against the eagles of ancient Rome! I refer to that devil's brew of rascals, jailbirds, murderers and cutthroats who libel all honest workingmen by calling themselves the Industrial Work-

ers of the World; but in the light of their nefarious plots, I call them the Industrial *Wreckers* of the World. This fiendish organization is a foul ulcer on the fair body of our Democracy—Like Cato I say to this Senate, the I. W. W. must be destroyed! For they represent an ever-present dagger pointed at the heart of the greatest nation the world has ever known, where all men are born free and equal, with equal opportunities to all, where the Founding Fathers have guaranteed to each one happiness, where Truth, Honor, Liberty, Justice, and the Brotherhood of Man are a religion absorbed with one's mother milk, taught at our father's knee, sealed, signed, and stamped upon in the glorious Constitution of these United States. . . .

They plot with fire in one hand and dynamite in the other. They stop not before murder to gain their ends, nor at the outraging of defenseless womanhood. They would tear down society, put the lowest scum in the seats of the mighty, turn Almighty God's revealed plan for the world topsy-turvy, and make of our sweet and lovely civilization a shambles, a desolation where man, God's masterpiece, would soon degenerate back to the ape!

Literature of all types during the last sixty years has dealt with social problems. Social protest has been the moving spirit in literature since the days of Zola. In *The Hairy Ape* O'Neill reveals himself in sympathy with this tradition, with the one difference that he is not dealing with the condemnation of a particular political order. His problem is the deeper one of the psychological implications of the machine age. His predecessors might have shown how Yank lost his job and finally through starvation was led to crime to support himself and family, or some similar theme. But it should be remembered that Yank's problem was not loss of work. He could have had all the work he wanted. Furthermore, O'Neill does not appeal to the emotions by having Yank lose a sweetheart, mother, or children. Yank is alone as far as any family connections are concerned. It is not work that Yank is seeking. What Yank wants is to know that he "belongs." He wants to find out what it is that has happened to the world which separates him from the realization that what he is doing is a necessary and a fitting part of the life of the world.

In pursuit of the answer to this problem he receives blows and insults—no insult greater than that which is expressed in the typical speech of the senator who attributes to the workers all the sins of which he and his class are guilty. The real danger to modern civilization is the stupidity and timidity of the ruling classes. Therein lies the real drama of this play. It is not that Yank as an individual moves the audience very deeply. He is neither charming nor likeable, nor capable of arousing deep emotion as a person. Had O'Neill meant this play to be the tragedy of Yank, he would have made him a more likeable character. But Yank is more than an individual. He is a symbol of the deep protest that rises like a wave against the whole structure of modern civilization. He is man crying out against a system which has not only exploited man's body but his spirit as well. The play is not a protest against low wages and unemployment as is the case in the traditional social drama, Hauptmann's *The Weavers,* for example, but it is a condemnation of the whole structure of machine civilization, a civilization which succeeds only when it destroys the psychological well-being of those who make it possible. It is this which gives the play universality and enlists the sympathy and understanding of the audience. It is a play which might be called by any of the many titles of books that describe the disintegration of modern civilization; it is a part of the *Decline of the West.*

Because of its deep psychological and philosophical implication *The Hairy Ape* cannot be classed with a type of social drama which solves a problem and points a way out. The sickness of the machine age is not wholly a problem of relating production and consumption. It goes much deeper than that. The whole concept of life, of man's relation to the world, of his place in it is involved. Yank was not concerned about distribution —vitally important as that is—he wanted to be a creative part of the social structure, and no man working in the stoke-hole of a liner, or making the two hundred and fifty-sixth part of a shoe in regulation eight-hour shifts can ever "belong" in the same sense that man belonged as a creative worker in the eighteenth century. Yank is a protest against the mordant success of the machine age.

O'Neill makes this clear as Yank moves from one defeat to another striving vainly to find some answer to

his problem. In prison he heard of the I. W. W.s and
thought to find among them an answer. They threw
him into the street, just as the Communists of today
would deny him a place. The Communists would not
accept Yank, because Yank is an individualist not a
party man. What he wants is to be a creative worker
proud of what he as an individual has created.

Yank's speech after he has been thrown from the
I. W. W.'s headquarters is an explicit summary of the
whole situation. O'Neill shows that wages, distribution,
shorter hours and all the rest of it is no solution. Yank
in the pose of "The Thinker" reviews the whole situation, ending by admitting that his greatest crime was
that of being born. Yank speaks, referring first to the
men who threw him out into the street:

YANK *(Bitterly)* So dem boids don't tink I belong,
neider. Aw, to hell wit 'em! Dey're in de wrong pew
—de same old bull—soapboxes and Salvation Army—
no guts! Cut out an hour offen de job a day and make
me happy! Gimme a dollar more a day and make me
happy! Tree square a day, and cauliflowers in de front
yard—ekal rights—a woman and kids—a lousy vote—
and I'm all fixed for Jesus, huh? Aw, hell! What does
dat get yuh? Dis ting's in your inside, but it ain't your
belly. Feedin' your face—sinkers and coffee—dat don't
touch it. It's way down—at de bottom. Yuh can't grab
it, and yuh can't stop it. It moves, and everything
moves. It stops and de whole woild stops. Dat's me
now—I don't tick, see?—I'm a busted Ingersoll, dat's
what. Steel was me, and I owned de woild. Now I

ain't steel, and de woild owns me. Aw, Hell! I can't
see—it's all dark, get me? It's all wrong! Say, youse
up dere, Man in de Moon, yuh look so wise, gimme de
answer, huh? Slip me de inside dope, de information
right from de stable—where do I get off at, huh?

A POLICEMAN *(Who has come up the street in time
to hear this last—with grim humor)* You'll get off at
the station, you boob, if you don't get up out of that
and keep movin'.

YANK *(Looking up at him—with a hard, bitter laugh)*
Sure! Lock me up! Put me in a cage! Dat's de on'y
answer yuh know. G'wan, lock me up!

POLICEMAN. What you been doin'?

YANK. Enough to gimme life for! I was born, see?
Sure, dat's de charge. Write it in de blotter. I was
born, get me!

POLICEMAN. God pity your old woman! But I've no
time for kidding. You're soused. I'd run you in but it's
too long a walk to the station. Come on now, get up,
or I'll fan your ears with this club. Beat it now!

YANK. Say, where do I go from here?

POLICEMAN. Go to hell.

A careful reading of Yank's analysis makes further
comment unnecessary. The machine age has done
something to man that wages, food, home, family,
shorter hours and a "lousy vote" won't remedy. As the
machine created wealth it destroyed the joy of living,
the only thing that wealth is good for. O'Neill has presented the paradox of modern civilization with great
insight into its fundamental tragedy. Like Yank we

all say, "where do we go from here," and the answer is "Hell."

4

The importance of O'Neill as a social critic lies in the fact that he emphasizes the psychological aspect of the modern social order. He points out the disease of our acquisitive society. He does not merely stress the fact that workers are exploited to create wealth for the few, but shows how in our modern machine-made world they are deprived of the sense of harmony and mental well-being that comes from doing something that seems important and necessary. Man's work is a necessary part of his personality; it is an extension of his ego; it makes him feel that he is a necessary part of the life of the world in which he lives. Modern industry tends to destroy this psychological counterpart of work, and in so far as it does, it leaves the worker a nervous, irritable and dissatisfied misfit. Yank was such a worker, and at the same time, conscious of the thing he had lost. He didn't want a job simply because it would be a means to earning a living; he wanted a job in which he could live.

In *All God's Chillun Got Wings* this problem is carried out still further and applied to one of the great problems of social inequality in modern America. The American Negro is technically free, but psychologically he is still in bondage. I don't want to give the impression that he is not also in economic bondage, as, indeed, we all are, but that may be taken for granted. O'Neill has not overlooked that, but he has turned to the more subtle and dangerous kind of slavery for his dramatic materials. The serfs of the Middle Ages were economic slaves, but they belonged to a system and were recognized as important individuals in that system. In the terms of Yank, they "belonged." The modern worker does not belong. He is a number on a tin badge, not a unified and significant personality.

Jim Harris the principal character of *All God's Chillun Got Wings* is a Negro whose problem is to "belong." It is the story of Yank over again from a different angle. Like Yank, Jim's trouble is not primarily economic. He seems to have the means of a livelihood. It is not a problem of physical starvation but of psychological persecution. This persecution leads Jim to feel that only through marrying a white girl can he win the position in life that he craves and that is necessary to his happiness.

The love of Ella, the white girl, and Jim, the Negro, is genuine, but in the end it is destroyed, or it destroys them. The social pressure of a society that cannot overcome its race prejudice makes Jim a failure and drives Ella to insanity. It may well be argued that the Negro needs economic security, but beyond that, then what? Jim tried it and failed. He failed because the social system denied him something that he wanted more than wages and votes, it denied him the right to belong.

O'Neill has selected the material out of which the

modern Negro's tragedy is perpetuated beyond the termination of his physical slavery. He has arraigned the deep and powerful prejudices of American civilization before the bar of true justice, and he has convicted our civilization of enforcing a slavery as gross, disgusting and deadly as any that our forefathers supported before the days of the Civil War. Because modern American civilization is steeped in the prejudices of its past injustice to the Negro, it is now a slave to its own sins. In order to escape the opprobrium of an economic slavery, it has changed the terms but kept the facts as they were. O'Neill is not so naïve as to believe that this is the result of a conscious program. Few significant social attitudes are. But it is none the less deadly.

After seventeen years of struggle Jim Harris finally abandons his program. He was generous, sincere, kind hearted, brave and very able as a student. These qualities might have made a white man successful, but because Jim was a Negro, he failed. Even his marriage failed, and his white wife, in spite of herself, turned against him. White supremacy is maintained at the price of social injustice to the Negro. O'Neill has made the personal story of Jim Harris and Ella Downey into a drama of great social importance for America. He has gone beyond the problem of economic slavery to the greater dangers of psychological bondage, and through the tragic love of these two characters has written an indictment of one important phase of American civilization.

The self-righteous recognized the indictment, and

acted, as only "good" people can, with vicious hatred
and destructive power. A brief quotation from *The
Provincetown* reveals how "Virtue" tried to deal with
a play that should have been welcomed for its deep,
sympathetic understanding of an American tragedy:

> The fact that it dealt with a marriage between a Negro
> and a white girl, and that the wife at one point in the
> action kisses her husband's hand, had been avidly seized
> upon. Ku Kluxers, Citizen Fixits and Southern Gentle-
> women, most of whom did not trouble to read the play
> (which had been published in the *American Mercury*)
> were goaded into action. Facts were enlarged and dis-
> torted, and expressions of opinion from pastors in Missis-
> sippi, from Colonels of the Confederate Army, from
> champions of Nordic integrity in Iowa, were printed
> and reprinted from one end of the country to the
> other. A picture of Mary Blair, who was to play the
> wife, was syndicated hundreds of times with the caption
> 'White Actress Kisses Negro's Hand,' and a harmless
> little paragraph by Irvin S. Cobb about how 'All God's
> Chillun' would need their wings in Paducah, Kentucky,
> where he came from, echoed and reëchoed in print like
> a thunderbolt of the demigod Authority. The envelopes
> from the clipping bureau grew larger and larger until
> great boxes began to arrive. The office soon gave up the
> gargantuan task of pasting clippings into the press book
> and began stuffing them into shoe boxes and storing
> them in the back of the most remote closet in the theater.
> In the final totaling it was found that the press-clipping
> bill exceeded the cost of the scenery.

5

Marco Millions is an excellent study in the social concept of the Western business ideal. Marco serves as a symbol for big business. Although the play deals with Marco Polo and Kublai Khan, one has no difficulty in recognizing him as a good American business man whose ideal of life is to buy cheap and sell dear. O'Neill has given to this play a touch of light satire which makes his criticism of modern society all the more penetrating.

O'Neill shows how Marco began his career as a normal child with an idealistic attitude towards life. He was romantic in love, sensitive to beauty, generous in his relations to other people, and unmaterialistic. But under the training of his father and his uncle he gradually lost the gentle sweetness of his character and assumed the character of the stereotyped business man. This means more than simply the occupation of trading. Trading for profit in itself seems innocent enough. An uncritical thinker might even hold that a man could pursue the ideal of profit and at the same time maintain a certain personal integrity, love of beauty, generosity and creative imagination.

It is on this point that the significance of O'Neill's play turns. For he seems to hold that the profit motive is at the root of the evil in Western civilization. The profit motive destroys that which is best and noblest in man, making him into a beast who is capable of no great passions and no real love of the beautiful and the good. Under the deadly influence of this practical ideal, he becomes an excellent judge of quantity, and believes that quantity is synonymous with quality.

The limitation of this concept leads to others even more destructive. It leads to a narrow selfish bigotry which finds expression in condemning every point of view that does not harmonize with the desire for bigger and better profits. Maffeo expresses it well when he says "All Mahometans are crazy." To the rulers of our Western world all theories which run counter to the profit seeking motive are considered manifestations of insanity. When Maffeo saw a dervish dancer, he was deeply moved, but not by the art of the performer, but by the thought that "If we had him in Venice we could make a mint of money exhibiting him."

Trade with profit is this man's ideal. He will endure any hardship, work long hours, endanger his health and his life for profit. He pursues profit with the passionate intensity of a fanatic. As Maffeo puts it: "Any climate is healthy where trade is brisk." He knows no leisure, for his mind is forever stewing in the stink of his profits. He is tortured by new visions of greater incomes wherever he goes. Only that which is innocuous can give him pleasure. Thus Marco liked the theater, that is, he liked to go to a play that did not rise above his belly's needs. His excellence as a dramatic critic has been copied by that New Yorker who wrote "Evening Becomes Intolerable".* He and Marco are blood brothers. Marco summarizes:

* J. George Frederick in *Vanity Fair*, Jan. 1932.

There's nothing better than to sit down in a good seat
at a good play after a good day's work in which you
know you've accomplished something, and after you've
had a good dinner, and just take it easy and enjoy a
good wholesome thrill or a good laugh and get your
mind off serious things until it's time to go to bed.

Marco is the perfect business man. "He has memo-
rized everything and learned nothing." His capacity for
experiencing life is limited to his trade. His greatest
thrill is a balance in his favor on the day's business. As
Kublai says of him: "He has not even a mortal soul; he
has only an acquisitive instinct." This leads him to deal
with all human values in the terms of profit and loss in
the market place.

One of Kublai's counsellors described Marco's ex-
ploits as mayor of Yang-Chau, saying:

> I talked recently with a poet who had fled from there
> in horror. Yang-Chau used to have a soul, he said. Now
> it has a brand new Court House. And another, a man
> of wide culture, told me, our Christian mayor is exter-
> minating our pleasures and our rats as if they were twin
> breeds of vermin!

Marco Millions is a satire on the modern business
man. If it were no more than that it might be amusing,
but it would scarcely be very important in the study of
O'Neill's criticism of life. He chose Marco Polo as his
principal character because through him and his ex-
ploits he could contrast the East and the West.
Through him he could picture the mordant disintegra-

tion of Western civilization as it undermines all things beautiful and good in its pursuit of profits. This play, then, is a further indictment of the whole system of Western ideals. Marco is the ruler of the Western world, and with Marco in power, how long can it last? That is what O'Neill asks, and from what the world looks like today it might well be said that his question is of vital importance. While economists and bankers worry over Communism and a new system of distribution, O'Neill points to the whole philosophical conception of life which dominates our world and indicates where the real cause of disaster lies. Life is the only justification for living, and life is not measured by mechanical inventions and profits in dollars and cents.

The following rather lengthy quotation summarizes the business ideal of the Western world, and by implication reveals the thoroughness of O'Neill's indictment of the prevailing ideals:

> MARCO. My tax scheme, Your Majesty, that got such wonderful results is simplicity itself. I simply reversed the old system. For one thing I found they had a high tax on excess profits. Imagine a profit being excess! Why, it isn't humanly possible! I repealed it. And I repealed the tax on luxuries. I found out the great majority in Yang-Chau couldn't afford luxuries. The tax wasn't democratic enough to make it pay! I crossed it off and I wrote on the statute books a law that taxes every necessity in life, a law that hits every man's pocket equally, be he beggar or banker! And I got results!

CHU-YIN. In beggars?

KUBLAI. I have received a petition from the inhabi-
tants of Yang-Chau enumerating over three thousand
cases of your gross abuse of power!

MARCO. Oh, so they've sent that vile slander to you,
have they? That's the work of a mere handful of
radicals—

KUBLAI. Five hundred thousand names are signed to
it. Half a million citizens accuse you of endeavoring
to stamp out their ancient culture.

MARCO. What! Why, I even had a law passed that
anyone caught interfering with culture would be subject to a fine! It was Section One of a blanket statute
that every citizen must be happy or go to jail. I found
it was the unhappy ones who were always making
trouble and getting discontented. You see, here's the
way I figure it; if a man's good, he's happy—and if he
isn't happy, it's a sure sign he's no good to himself or
anyone else and he better be put where he can't do
harm.

6

The world revealed by Eugene O'Neill is tragic because it is without intelligent social organization. Ignorance, brutality, selfishness, greed and hatred are the
dominant forces in this world of O'Neill. The multitude of men and women who pass by in the imagination as one tries to vision the sum total of life that
O'Neill has presented in his plays is a sorry lot. Here
by the roadside lies a young man coughing his lungs
out as he cries for the beauty which lies beyond the

horizon; here is a girl tortured into committing a murder; another passes with a fixed look of dry-eyed sorrow that is just breaking into insanity over her lover killed in war; a handsome Negro passes with the sorrow of hopeless despair furrowing every line of his face; in a narrow room another breaks under the strain of life as his fevered imagination turns gilded trinkets into gold; in the cold seas of the north a woman goes mad from loneliness; in a beautiful New England home starved and misguided love brings endless tragedy; and so one could go on with the enumeration.

And what has turned potential happiness for these human beings into sure and grim tragedy? Is it that there is something in nature that makes these hard hearts? Is it that man is doomed by his humanity to make every third thought his grave? No doubt that is partially the truth, or at least the only truth that we have tried and practiced. But O'Neill also emphasizes the fact of a social system which is destructive in itself, which thwarts every effort to achieve happiness, which puts a value on misery and pain as a good in itself, and worst of all encourages and rewards everything that is predatory and destructive, condemning beauty, well-being and happiness as a sin. O'Neill's interpretation of the world is grim and terrible. Many have called it lopsided and monstrous. There is no denying that people may feel that he over-emphasizes the gruesome, but if O'Neill is to be condemned for his interpretation of life as essentially tragic, then he may take it as an honor to be by such a device classed with Sophocles, Dante and Shakespeare among those who considered this world "an unweeded garden, where things rank and gross in nature possess it merely."

It may be that in such protest against injustice as O'Neill reveals in his social dramas lies the hope for a better world. He has given dramatic power to this particular aspect of our modern social order and by so doing has helped to make the problems real to his audience. This may disappoint those who go to the theater to rest as did Marco, but to those who go to the theater for a memorable experience, O'Neill has something to say that is worth saying.

VIII

Pessimism and Tragedy

> ROBERT. (*Speaking of the death of his daughter,
> Mary.*) Our last hope of happiness! I could
> curse God from the bottom of my soul—if there
> was a God!
> RUTH. Mary's better off—being dead.
> ROBERT. We'd all be better off, for that
> matter. *Beyond the Horizon*

I

IT IS a commonplace in O'Neill criticism to call him a
pessimist, and by some strange process of reasoning to
imply that pessimism is to be condemned in art as well
as in life. The following statement from Carl Van
Doren's *American and British Literature Since 1890* is
a restrained expression of a point of view that has been
repeated almost endlessly:

> O'Neill's view of life, it now seems clear, is of some-
> thing which unaccountably frustrates the individual
> spirit. The fault may lie in life itself, or it may lie in the
> insufficiency of given individuals; O'Neill as a play-
> wright does not decide which but proceeds to create

dumb, tortured persons who come in the end to worse than naught. (p. 106.)

While Mr. Van Doren is careful not to pass an ethical judgment, others have implied that since O'Neill is a pessimist, he is therefore false to the truth of life.

Before his position as a pessimist is analyzed, it may be well to distinguish between two types of pessimism that have flourished in the literature of the last half century. The one type sees the universe as fundamentally unfavorable to man, and at times even ruled by a conscious power bent on evil. This type of pessimism stems from Schopenhauer, Von Hartmann and the early nineteenth-century pessimists. In so far as the followers of this school, such as Andreyev and Hardy, actually imply a conscious force of evil, they are still children of the anthropomorphic world against which they so passionately rebelled. They came to look upon the old faiths as false dreams, false beliefs to be abandoned by intelligent men, but in their art they still were unable to view man in the light of an animal in a world of physical forces, but they must continue to treat him against the background of a purposeful universe. Theirs is a queer combination of medieval and modern. In the *Life of Man* Andreyev is concerned with man and eternity, writing:

Coming from the night he will return to the night. Bereft of thought, bereft of feeling, unknown to all, he will perish utterly, vanishing without trace into infinity.

This may be true, but from a realistic point of view, all that can be said is, "What of it?" As Matthew Arnold put it,

> Long fed on boundless hopes, O race of man,
> How angrily thou spurn'st all simpler fare!

And angrily does Andreyev spurn the simpler fare. The whole of his position as a pessimist may be summarized in the following quotation from the *Life of Man*.

> Look and listen, ye who have come hither for mirth and laughter. Lo, there will pass before you all the life of Man, with its dark beginning and its dark end. Hitherto non-existent, mysteriously hidden in infinite time, without thought or feeling, utterly unknown, he will mysteriously break through the barriers of non-existence and with a cry will announce the beginning of his brief life. In the night of nonexistence will blaze up a candle, lighted by an unseen hand. This is the life of Man. Behold its flame. It is the life of Man.

> *   *   *   *

> Irresistibly dragged on by time, he will tread inevitably all the steps of human life, upward to its climax and downward to its end. Limited in vision, he will not see the step to which his unsure foot is already raising him. Limited in knowledge, he will never know what the coming day or hour or moment is bringing to him. And in his blind ignorance, worn by apprehension, harassed by hopes and fears, he will complete submissively the iron round of destiny.

The pessimism of Andreyev is typical of modern literature, but not of O'Neill. O'Neill is not concerned about man's ultimate destiny, he is not disturbed by the fact that man and all his works may some day drift into the darkness of space a frozen and unseen monument to the vagaries of the creative process. His pessimism is of man in this world in which he must live and justify himself if life is to have a meaning. His pessimism is born of man, not of God or the universe. It is a pessimism that has in it some gleam of hope, for it holds that man's greatest tragedies are of his own making, and thus it is a fair presumption to hope that man may unmake them. Not that O'Neill says that he will do so; he may recognize the persistence of man's hopeless hope, but even granting all that, there is still a vast difference between the position of O'Neill and that of Schopenhauer.

In discussing this phase of O'Neill's pessimism there is a remark from Galsworthy on the subject that may help to make the definition of pessimism as it applies to the subject more clear and understandable. Galsworthy writes:

> As a man lives and thinks, so will he write. But it is certain, that to the making of good drama, as to the practice of every other art, there must be brought an almost passionate love of discipline, a white-heat of self-respect, a desire to make the truest, fairest, best thing in one's power; and that to these must be added an eye that does not flinch. Such qualities alone will bring to a

drama the selfless character which soaks it with inevitability.

The word 'pessimist' is frequently applied to the few dramatists who have been content to work in this way. It has been applied, among others, to Euripides, to Shakespeare, to Ibsen; it will be applied to many in the future. Nothing, however, is more dubious than the way in which these two words 'pessimist' and 'optimist' are used, for the optimist appears to be he who cannot bear the world as it is, and is forced by his nature to picture it as it ought to be, and the pessimist one who cannot only bear the world as it is, but loves it well enough to draw it faithfully. The true lover of the human race is surely he who can put up with it in all its forms, in vice as well as in virtue, in defeat no less than in victory; the true seer he who sees not only joy but sorrow, the true painter of human life one who blinks nothing. It may be that he is also, incidentally, its true benefactor. (L. Lewisohn, *A Modern Book of Criticism*, Mod. Lib., p. 114.)

This type of pessimism is freed from the tyranny of absolute laws and may lead man to understand that if he is to be happy in this life, he must reconcile himself to its inevitable limitations. He must realize that it is his show. He is director and actor, and if the performance is rotten he can't blame God or any other power outside himself. Nor can he be so irrational as to ask for better materials than life itself has offered him. And this I take to be a measure of O'Neill's pessimism. He does not hold that because we have lost our medieval conception of an anthropomorphic God with a Hell beneath us and a Heaven above that life is therefore and forever a hopeless tragedy. The deep and all-obliterating gloom that characterizes such a poet as James Thomson has no parallel in O'Neill. When Thomson discovered that he had been tricked into a false faith in the days of his youth, he assumed that nothing but despair could follow. The same is true of Hardy's reaction, when he discovered that "What is good for God's gardener is not good for God's birds." This fact made him sure that "Happiness is but an occasional episode in a general drama of pain." And so it was with most of the modern realists. They escaped from one doom only to make themselves another even more terrible than its predecessor. To O'Neill belongs the credit of seeing life more clearly and firmly than did many of those who were his spiritual forefathers. He deals with man's life here and now. Within the limits of this world he finds his justification for life.

But as he looks about him in the world and finds that man has striven artfully and savagely to deprive himself of such transitory happiness as is actually possible to life, surely he can not be held responsible for that, and, on the basis of his interpretation of this truth, be condemned as a pessimist who has no hope for man. His critics are continually asking him to write comedy or to be something that he is not. Why not ask Leonardo da Vinci to paint like Holbein. It would be just as reasonable. Once in answer to the question would he ever write about happiness, he answered:

Sure I'll write about happiness if I can happen to
meet up with that luxury, and find it sufficiently dramatic and in harmony with any deep rhythm in life.
But happiness is a word. What does it mean? Exalta-
tion, an intensified feeling of the significant worth of
man's being and becoming? Well, if it means that—and
not a mere smirking contentment with one's lot—I know
there is more of it in one real tragedy than in all the
happy-ending plays ever written. It's mere present-day
judgment to think of tragedy as unhappy! The Greeks
and the Elizabethans knew better. They felt the tremendous lift to it. It roused them spiritually to a deeper
understanding of life. Through it they found release
from the petty considerations of everyday existence.
They saw their lives ennobled by it. A work of art is
always happy; all else is unhappy. . . . I don't love life
because it's pretty. Prettiness is only clothes-deep. I am a
truer lover than that. I love it naked. There is beauty to
me even in its ugliness. (*Clark. op. cit.* p. 146.)

And if more than this were needed, Barrett H.
Clark's own statement which follows the quotation
adds the needed touch. He writes:

I called O'Neill an optimist before I had read these
words, and by that I meant that he was a militant apostle of Life with a capital L. He dares look upon it without passing judgment; he lays it bare to the best of his
ability as an artist and poet. (*Ibid.* p. 146.)

Man's "being and becoming" is the essence of
O'Neill's pessimism, and this is a theme that from one
point of view may be called a kind of optimism. I do

not wish to confuse the issue or to make the meaning of the two words in question any more shadowy or meaningless than they already are. It serves the understanding of O'Neill better to call him a pessimist, but with a difference. He is a pessimist who loves life; one whose love goes so deep that he cannot remain supine and unmoved by its present failure blocking its potential happiness. He loves life well enough to condemn those who shun it in fear and trembling, and to urge those who can face its reality to make the most of it.

2

The characters of his plays bear out this interpretation of his philosophy of life. Whatever else may be said of them, they do not cringe. They are above all else courageous and defiant. It is this quality in them which gives exhilaration to the grimmest tragedy of O'Neill. They may and they do go down to defeat and death, but they never ask to be forgiven. They are game to the end. Sometimes they realize the reason for their failure, as did Ponce de Leon, but they always accept it bravely. If O'Neill has given us a true picture of the world of man, then in spite of all its disaster it is still a good world in which to live, for it is peopled with men and women in whom the undying fire of rebellion is a living flame, and as long as that is true there is still hope that something may yet happen to solve the riddle of man's inherent tragedy before the final sunset and the eternal darkness settle over the world.

It is not strange that a dramatist in America who holds an affirmative view of life as strong as this should be often misunderstood and severely criticized by those who due to their inability to cope with reality must forever live in the vague shadowy hope of some "far-off divine event" which will be given freely in answer to a pious wish. To such people O'Neill is and always will be anathema. They could not understand him if they would. He stands for a life that they are afraid to see. They can accept the same thing in the Greeks or in Shakespeare, because to them tradition is a god that sanctifies all things. But when a modern poet expresses in the terms of modern life the same grim truth that the ancients perceived, the soft ones are shocked and horrified. The extent to which they go is well illustrated by an article by H. K. Kemelman in the *Bookman* for September 1932. This article goes so far as to hold that O'Neill has done nothing for the modern drama except that which is bad. Style, technique, characters, dramatic interest, plot structure, and philosophy of life are all cheap, tawdry and utterly disgusting. This essay is so unbalanced that to all those who are interested in the modern drama of America it must forever remain as an example of how amusing tradition and humanism are when they are combined in an attempt at literary criticism.

The point of view of Mr. Kemelman could scarcely have any effect upon O'Neill, nor upon those who

know what he has done to give a new lease of life to
the modern drama in America. But there have been
times when he has been sorely tried by unfair and narrow criticism of his work. So much so that once when
provoked to reply to such criticism, he wrote a letter in
defense of his work, or rather in explanation of what
the drama meant to him. In this letter quoted by Quinn
(*History of the American Drama from the Civil War
to the Present Day,* Vol. II. p. 199) O'Neill gives an
exact statement of his theory of tragedy and of what
he has done to change the Greek theory to make it fit
the modern world in which we live. Thus he writes:

> It's not in me to pose much as a "misunderstood one,"
> but it does seem discouragingly (that is, if one lacked a
> sense of ironic humor!) evident to me that most of my
> critics don't want to see what I'm trying to do or how
> I'm trying to do it, although I flatter myself that end and
> means are characteristic, individual and positive enough
> not to be mistaken for anyone's else, or for those of any
> "modern" or "pre-modern" school. To be called a "sordid
> realist" one day, a "grim pessimistic naturalist" the next,
> a "lying Moral Romanticist" the next, etc. is quite per-
> plexing—not to add the *Times* editorial that settled *De-
> sire* once and for all by calling it a "Neo-Primitive," a
> Matisse of the drama, as it were! So I'm really longing
> to explain and try and convince some sympathetic ear
> that I've tried to make myself a melting pot for all these
> methods, seeing some virtues for my ends in each of
> them, and thereby, if there is enough real fire in me,
> boil down to my own technique. But where I feel my-

self most neglected is just where I set most store by myself—as a bit of a poet, who has labored with the spoken word to evolve original rhythms of beauty where beauty apparently isn't—*Jones, Ape, God's Chillun, Desire,* etc.—and to see the transfiguring nobility of tragedy, in as near the Greek sense as one can grasp it, in seemingly the most confirmed mystic, too, for I'm always, always, trying to interpret Life in terms of lives, never just lives in terms of character. I'm always acutely conscious of the Force behind—(Fate, God, our biological past creating our present, whatever one calls it—Mystery certainly)—and of the eternal tragedy of Man in his glorious, self-destructive struggle to make the Force express him instead of being, as an animal is, an infinitesimal incident in its expression. And my profound conviction is that this is the only subject worth writing about and that it is possible—or can be—to develop a tragic expression in terms of transfigured modern values and symbols in the theatre which may to some degree bring home to members of a modern audience their ennobling identity with the tragic figures on the stage. Of course, this is very much of a dream, but where the theatre is concerned, one must have a dream and the Greek dream in tragedy is the noblest ever!

3

In this direct revelation of his conception of tragedy and his statement of what he has tried to do, O'Neill has given his readers an opportunity to understand his purpose, and if they desire it to test his intentions in relation to his practice. In the first place it must be con-

ceded that if O'Neill spoke his true meaning, and there
is not the slightest reason to suspect that he did not,
then his intentions in modern drama are of the very
highest and most noble that any artist could aspire to
achieve. He has often given ample evidence that he
does not cater to popularity. On this point he expressed
himself in a letter to the *Times* in which he said against
the charge that he had tacked a happy ending to *Anna
Christie*:

> Lastly, to those who think I deliberately distorted my
> last act because a "happy ending" would be calculated to
> make the play more of a popular success I have only this
> to say: the sad truth is that you have precedents enough
> and to spare in the history of our drama for such a sus-
> picion. But, on the other hand, you have every reason
> not to believe it of me. (*Quinn*. II. p. 177ff.)

On this point he has never failed to put popular es-
teem lower than the ideals of his art. On the second
point, that of his attempt to combine all the techniques
that are peculiarly modern and make himself a "melt-
ing pot for all these methods," he must again be praised
for his effort, even if he has not wholly succeeded. At
least it may be quite truly said that in *The Great God
Brown* he has gone further in this direction and with
greater success than any other living dramatist.

On the next point even the "humanists" would be
compelled to praise his purpose, for he claims that tragedy in the Greek sense is his idea of what tragedy
should be. With one exception, and this is important

to all careful students of O'Neill, and if properly put
might be admitted even by the humanists. Read again
the passage on "Force, Fate, God, and our biological
past." And also the line, "to make Force express him
instead of being, as an animal is, an infinitesimal incident in its expression." This is the point at which he
departs from the Greek conception, but at the same
time remains in harmony with the Greek in spirit. Fate
or God was the force that determined destiny in the
Greek drama, but in the modern world those terms
have lost their meaning except in a very theoretical
sense, and in their place has come the modern biological and psychological interpretation of man's behavior.

The real beauty in an O'Neill tragedy demands that
the spectator forget the "trailing clouds of glory" that
were his primitive psychological heritage, and look at
life as a thing good in itself—good in that it has within
itself the potentialities of happiness. Thus on this issue
as so many others that grow out of the study of O'Neill
it is necessary to keep in mind that O'Neill has as
marked a philosophical heritage as it is to remember
that he has a heritage from the stage. O'Neill's tragedies are related to the philosophy of Nietzsche in this
one respect that they are an affirmation of life; they
deal with life for the sake of living and not for the sake
of eternity. His tragedies are based on the assumption,
warranted by modern science, that the forces of nature
can be "employed in the service of the higher egoism,"
this from Nietzsche. O'Neill follows Nietzsche's idea

of the *theoretical man*. This is an idea which embodies the belief that "It can correct the world by knowledge, guide life by science, and actually confine the individual within a limited sphere of solvable problems, from which he can cheerfully say to life: 'I desire thee: it is worth while to know thee'." (*The Birth of Tragedy.* p. 287.)

The tragedy of Robert in *Beyond the Horizon* is that he lived for the "beyond," based all of his actions on that concept and lost the real life which he might have lived here. His pitiful belief that "Only through contact with suffering, Andy, will you awaken" is the tragedy that could have been avoided had he faced the reality of the life about him and said yea to it with the gusto of one who believed that it was good in itself. Instead he accepts his defeat and clings to a shadowy hope that "Only through sacrifice—the secret beyond there—" will set the crooked straight. Robert's answer to life is similar to that of Miss Gilpin's to Murray in *The Straw*.

> MURRAY. Oh, why did you give me a hopeless hope?
> MISS GILPIN. Isn't all life just that—when you think of it?

4

There is the fire of an indomitable will to life in the world of O'Neill. To grasp its full significance one must be ready to look upon life as an adventure in a grim world, or the result will be failure to comprehend his meaning. The person whose scope of criticism is limited by his ability to add up the number of times O'Neill writes "damn," or the number of murders committed in the sum total of his works, or the number of neurotic characters he introduces, may arrive at certain facts interesting in themselves, but surely a trifle strange as a measure of the artist's worth. Arithmetic must forever remain a distant cousin of the true critic.

T. K. Whipple gives us a fine account of the complexity of O'Neill's world, but in overlooking the essence of O'Neill's philosophical relation to Nietzsche, he sees this world of O'Neill's creation as "thoroughly hostile to human life." I quote the passage in full since it represents a point of view just the opposite of what to me seems the truth.

> To read O'Neill, then, or to witness his plays is to live temporarily in an intense but a simplified and impoverished world, a world narrow in range and meager in substance. Scanty to begin with, this world has been further stripped and denuded by its creator's preoccupation with primal forces only. And not only is it so to speak an emaciated skeleton world, but also one which by subordinating man and making him the helpless victim of larger forces, and by depicting him as always undergoing a spiritual defeat, is thoroughly hostile to human life. In fact, in spite of the violent forms in which life manifests itself, the ruling principle of his world is death, not life. It crushes and kills.
> Existence is a process of dehumanization. To read

O'Neill may be a salutary and bracing experience, for he is a corrective, a bitter herb, a perpetual northeast wind, and he brings us squarely face to face with one aspect of life which, though we may think it partial, we recognize as true; but we soon begin to long for a more nourishing imaginative diet—we cannot live long at a time in a world so fatal to life as his. Such are the qualities of the experience he offers us, of the world he has imagined. (T. K. Whipple *The Spokesman* p. 240.)

If one neglects the real spirit of O'Neill's tragedies then this judgment of his world might be true, but O'Neill has a great deal more to say than T. K. Whipple has been able to concede. This may be clear when one realizes that Whipple does not understand O'Neill as a thinker at all. He says,

> I hesitate to call O'Neill a thinker, for in his plays there is little sign of logical processes; but by means of intuition guided by his feeling he has arrived at understanding. If he has reasoned little about life, he has contemplated it long and hard. (*Ibid*. p. 242.)

This seems to me unfair and not adequate as an indication of what O'Neill has tried to do. The statement of his theory of tragedy is evidence that he knew where he was going and what he wanted to do, and the influence of Nietzsche points in the direction of a definite philosophical system the logic of which may be as tenuous as that of Nietzsche, but none the less exacting.

In order to understand and appreciate the life force of O'Neill's world it must be remembered that he does not think that death means the negation of living, or that the fear of death should destroy the value of life. He says yea to death with the same enthusiasm that he greets life. He does not bow before any aspect of life in humility, for life to him is its own reason for being, and not the servant of supernatural forces.

The men and women that move in the world of O'Neill are boldly defiant. They realize defeat, but scorn it—even cursing it. This world of O'Neill is a world of bitter struggle and tragic lives, but to those who accept its reality it is a world rich in experience, adventure and daring, where men and women demand that life give them some positive value. In spite of destruction which stalks on every highway in the world of O'Neill, as it does also in the world of the Greek tragedy, it is still a good world to live in, because it is a world where brave, charming, complex and interesting men and women are present at every turn. They are in a sense sick, that is, they are not fat, happy, contented and resigned to a gospel of prosperity and good business opportunities. By being sick I mean that they are civilized. They have awakened to the realization of what it means to be human. They are aware that to be human means to desire from life more than food, clothing and shelter. They yearn for happiness as the ultimate good, and when their struggle nears the end they are more defiant than submissive. Living in the world of O'Neill is not an easy task, but it is interesting. It is a world that demands courage, that is intense with experience, and that above all is not supine. It is a world in which

we are not allowed to "delude ourselves with some tawdry substitute." To O'Neill "Life doesn't end. One experience is but the birth of another."

Think over the heroes of his plays from the one-acts
to the very latest, and defiant courage is the keynote
of them all. Yank was game to the end and even when
death was upon him he faced it with the knowledge
that "I know whatever it is that comes after it can't be
no worser'n this." And Smitty's "damned from here
to eternity," reflects a spirit that is good to live
with. The same may be said of most of them, as
it might be said of all those who are "damned
from here to eternity." They may not be comfortable, but they are something that is better; they are
interesting. There is a dynamic creative force that
gives depth to the world of O'Neill. No pale meaningless shadows in this world of his. If it is at all permissi-
ble to compare O'Neill to Shakespeare it is on this
ground that he comes nearer to him than on any other.
The splendid, grim and at times terrible defiance of
the whole structure of the world which is a part of the
great characters of Shakespeare is also a part of the
characters of O'Neill's plays. Old Captain Bartlett sacrifices everything in order to maintain that wild, un-
believable dream of his. It leads to disaster; but what
of that? The spirit of his defiance makes him mean
something, just as Lear's idiotic rejection of Cordelia
gives meaning and depth to his life. Far be it from me
to say that King Lear is not more complex than Captain Bartlett, but those who are so timid and fearful

and shudder at the insanity, murder and horror in O'Neill's plays are also the ones who accept the same unbalanced life in Shakespeare and the Greeks. They never turn a hair at the multiplicity of murders in *Macbeth*. They even bow to the eye-gouging in *Lear*, but they shudder at the more plausible crimes in the works of O'Neill.

Art is an affirmation of the greatness of the human spirit, its courage, its defiance, its rebellion against the reality of its unfulfilled desire. That is the essence of Milton's Satan, and in so far as O'Neill is an artist in the conception of plot and the creation of character the same spirit is in him. The Emperor Jones is just such a character. He is pursued by the most harassing experiences that man is capable of meeting in this world, and while he is not without fear of the ghastly shadows that pursue him, always when they have pushed him far enough he defies them, and in that defiance lies his greatness and also his meaning for the audience.

The same is true of Yank—(*The Hairy Ape*). Every device of modern torture is used against him, and always he defies the forces that would crush him. His final end is no exception, for although he is killed, he never asked forgiveness from life. He was a crude, ignorant searcher for some meaning to the social structure, a meaning which he did not find, but to his glory it must be said that although he failed in the search, he did not fail as a searcher. Something of the glory of Ponce de Leon is shown in the spirit of this "Hairy Ape."

Old Ephraim Cabot is another of that strange nobility which lives in the world of O'Neill. Although
beaten and thwarted at every turn, still he did not give
up. His spirit is well expressed when he says to Abbie:
"Ye'd ought t' loved me. I'm a man. If ye'd loved me,
I'd never told no Sheriff on ye no matter what ye did,
if they was t' brile me alive!" Ephraim Cabot is over
seventy-five years old, but you know that he means
what he says. There is real spirit here. It is the spirit of
the lawless, the boldly defiant, and it doesn't fit the
obedient ones who are the "good" citizens, but in the
world of art there is not much to be said for the petty
laws that must forever govern those who have not the
strength to live alone.

Nina in *Strange Interlude* battles with the adver-
sities of circumstance to a victory that only heroic courage and great fortitude could achieve. She seeks a
higher justice than that of the law, and in spite of failures by the way her courage gives her a reality that is
artistically victorious. To those who would like life to
be comfortable and above all things nice and sweet,
Nina must seem a strange and even dangerous woman,
but to those who look upon life as an adventure in
which only those who have the courage to give it meaning are the heroes, Nina may be safely admired. The
motives which actuate her are as convincing as those
that actuated Hamlet's mother.

When the tragic issue confronted Anna, she did not
whimper. She made both her father and Mat accept her
as she was. With all of her sad past before us she is still

a creation of beauty, because she is willing to fight on in spite of obstacles that would have daunted a less courageous soul.

From these characters to Lavinia is an easy transition, for they are all of one family in that they are all rebels against the world in which they live. They are all nervous, high-strung, impetuous, and they are also determined that life shall give them more than it is willing to give. In this sense they are idealists, for they are not reconciled to the inevitable limitations of their world. In the end they discover their limitations, and accept their doom, but not quietly or without protest. Like Lavinia they may retire behind the closed doors and barred windows, but they will not do it humbly. They protest even after they have realized the futility of the struggle. This may or may not be the way of wisdom, and surely it is not the way of peace and resignation. There is no promise of a sunrise after the shadows and storms of night have passed in the world of O'Neill. He does not open a haven to the weary and heavy-laden, but for those to whom there is charm and beauty in the turbulence of life itself, this world of O'Neill is interesting and is intense. There is in it the Nietzschean will to power—the glorification of life.

5

This emphasis upon the heroic will to live, which is so apparent in O'Neill must not be emphasized to the exclusion of that genuine bitterness and heartrending despair which is the essence of all tragedy. It is in O'Neill at every turn. Nothing is more typical of this aspect of his tragedy than the manner in which the audience is led to believe in a "hopeless hope." Jayson in *The First Man* has at last achieved the success and recognition which he desired for himself, but most of all for his wife, when he discovers that his wife is pregnant and all of his plans are lost. The audience is led to hope for a solution, which, if they were cool and rational, they would know to be impossible. The truth is revealed to Jayson, and his life is ruined, a ruin that is heightened effectively, if not convincingly, by the accidental death of his wife.

In *Desire Under the Elms* young Cabot is almost on the verge of settling the tangled web of love and passion, but even as he approaches the way out, the tragedy falls swift and sharp, and all is lost.

The most striking example of this aspect of the O'Neill tragedy is that of General Mannon's return from war. It is about nine o'clock in the evening. "The light of a half moon falls on the house, giving it an unreal, detached, eerie quality." The past of the war, and the more horrible past of his unsuccessful life with Christine passes in review before the General's eyes. He has finally admitted to himself the mockery of his suppressions, evasions and puritanical illusions, and a new fire of joy and hope has sprung into being. He has arrived at the point where life for its own sake has achieved a meaning. All this he pours out to Christine in the impulsive joy and hope that has come with the slaying of the ghosts of his past. In his new philosophy there is a greater courage than was ever needed for the battlefields of war.

As all this passes before the spectator, his heart is wrung with pity and terror, for he knows that on this very night Christine is planning to murder him. It will not be amiss at this point to quote part of the General's speech:

> I came home to surrender to you—what's inside me, I love you. I loved you then, and all the years between, and I love you now. . . . I want that said! Maybe you have forgotten it. I wouldn't blame you. I guess I haven't said it or showed it much—ever. Something queer in me keeps me mum about the things I'd like most to say— keeps me hiding the things I'd like to show. Something keeps me sitting numb in my own heart—like a statue of a dead man in a town square. (*Suddenly he reaches over and takes her hand.*) I want to find what that wall is marriage put between us! You've got to help me smash it down! We have twenty good years still before us! I've been thinking of what we could do to get back to each other. I've a notion if we'd leave the children and go off on a voyage together—to the other side of the world— find some island where we could be alone a while. You'll find I have changed, Christine. I'm sick of death! I want life! Maybe you could love me now! I've got to make you love me!

Here is the cup of bitterness filled to the brim! Not only for the General but also for Christine. He talks of a new life, of his need for her help, of his hatred of death, and with every beat of the heart the shadow of his doom grows darker and heavier. There is a rapid shift of scene to his bedroom, and death comes to meet him as he stretches out his arms to embrace a new life. The General's end is not unlike that of Yank in *The Hairy Ape*. They both find that they belong only in death.

Of *The Hairy Ape*, O'Neill has written the following, which bears directly on the point under consideration:

> Yank can't go forward, and so he tries to go back. This is what his shaking hands with the gorilla meant. But he can't go back to "belonging" either. The gorilla kills him. The subject here is the same ancient one that always was and always will be the one subject for drama, and that is man and his struggle with his own fate. The struggle used to be with the gods, but is now with himself, his own past, his attempt "to belong." (Clark p. 127.)

While this was said of *The Hairy Ape* it might just as truly have been said of *Mourning Becomes Electra,* or of any O'Neill tragedy, for that matter. Fate as a power in the life of man is now ancient history; in its place stand the forces of man's "own past," or heredity and environment. It is these forces that O'Neill uses, and there is no reason why they may not be just as real to the imagination of the modern man as were the Fates to the imagination of the Greeks.

And this harmonizes with Clark's statement concerning *The Great God Brown* that "it is a dramatic paean to man's struggle to identify himself with nature."

In this struggle which partakes of eternal qualities, it is not strange that O'Neill should see bitterness and irony as important factors. They give color and aesthetic satisfaction to the spectacle that he presents. Brown in Dion's mask summarizes for himself and his audience the ironic meaning of life:

> Life is imperfect, Brothers! Men have their faults, Sister! But with a few drops of glue much may be done! A little dab of pasty resignation here and there—and even broken hearts may be repaired to do yeoman service! . . . Man is born broken. He lives by mending. The grace of God is glue!

Heroes on their way to dusty death is the ironic touch that O'Neill gives to his characters. This is no soft-hearted tragedy which ends by advising us that all is for the best. It has something of the satirical strength of Voltaire. It combines the futility of life with its paradox, that there is meaning from moment to moment and that we should get the best of experience since we are doomed to that by being here. But in the end Dion had it right. When speaking of the cathedral he designed for Brown he uttered these words:

> This cathedral is my masterpiece! . . . It's one vivid blasphemy from sidewalk to the tips of its spires!—but so concealed that the fools will never know. They'll kneel and worship the ironic Silenus who tells them the best good is never to be born.

IX

Optimism and Comedy

LAZARUS. Sometimes it is hard to laugh—even at men.

* * * *

LAZARUS. The greatness of Man is that no god can save him—until he becomes a god.

I

BARRETT CLARK called O'Neill an optimist, and by that he meant "a militant apostle of life with a capital L." What he meant is that O'Neill finds the spectacle of life fascinating. He glories in its lights and shadows, observes its strange, varicolored drama, analyzes the secret springs of its grim and beautiful passions, and transmutes its conflicts into an art form. Clark implies that O'Neill accepts life with all of its tragic defeat, and out of its chaos creates a beauty that is a good in itself. There is this affirmative value in O'Neill's pessimism, which from one point of view may be called a kind of optimism.

In a letter written March 26, 1925, O'Neill had this to say of his responsibility as a dramatist:

The poetical (in the broadest and deepest sense) vision illuminating even the most sordid and mean blind alleys of life—which I am convinced is, and is to be, my concern and justification as a dramatist . . . (Goldberg, *The Theater of Nathan*. p. 158.)

And it is and forever must be his justification, that he has accepted the world as it is, and out of its dark shadows he has created light, color, vitality and poetic beauty. That may not be optimism and it is certainly not comedy; nor will it please those who deny the existence of evil, but it is the elixir of life to those who love truth better than falsehood, and who believe that the bridge to life as it ought to be must first be anchored to life as it is. He refuses us the idle fancy of "deluding ourselves with some tawdry substitute."

As for comedy, his plays are not devoid of the comic spirit in its best sense. But it is never the carefree abandoned comedy which gayly and happily shuns the sorrows and tragedies of life. When O'Neill introduces comedy it is for the purpose of heightening the tragic atmosphere. It is that bitter, ironic kind of comedy which is the spiritual child of the grave scene in *Hamlet*. Laughter at an O'Neill play is tense and nervous. It is the forced laughter that is akin to sorrow, for it comes from the keen perception of the ironic comedy of all life. Chris and Marthy are laugh-provoking characters. There is not a scene in the play in which the character of Chris is not ridiculous to the point of being laughter-provoking, but neither is there a scene in which Chris does not also inspire tragic sorrow.

With but few exceptions comedy in O'Neill's plays flowers on the verge of the grave, and few are the moments when the sad futility of thwarted lives passing in solemn procession can be forgotten or disregarded long enough to give rise to whole-hearted laughter. There is an earnestness of purpose in all of O'Neill's work which is foreign to the spirit of comedy. Could he write in the vein of Aristophanes or Molière, comedy might serve the deeper needs of his being fully as well as tragedy, but it is clear that the critical spirit of these great masters of comedy contains an element that has so far not appeared in the works of O'Neill. They express in their comedies a note of deep and abiding bitterness that is not characteristic of O'Neill. He has greater hopes for man, a firmer belief in man's latent power to achieve real nobility than either Molière or Aristophanes. O'Neill is the product of the modern world. The whole romantic concept of man from Rousseau to the twentieth century finds its embodiment in modern thought, and it is in this modern milieu that O'Neill works. He believes that man can be saved and also that he is worth saving, but he maintains that as yet the road to the new life is perilously dark. Tragedy is a more suitable medium for the main currents of thought in the modern world. The bitter comedy of Aristophanes which makes man so ridiculous that he is worth no more than an ironic jest does not harmonize with the great drive which in the twentieth century is reshaping the whole structure of Western civilization.

It does not harmonize with the creative mind of O'Neill who is a child of his age.

To O'Neill man is noble—a being worthy of pity and sorrow, and that even in his darkest tragic moments he gives promise of a great future. O'Neill deprecates a world in which futile tragedy springs from self-inflicted tortures that grow out of living for death rather than for life. It is the dawn of a new day which inspires him. It is his genuine faith in man's ability to learn that there are better ways to live than those which man has followed in the past, which is the spur to his creative effort. In a letter (quoted in the preceding chapter) he gives emphasis to this fact when he writes,

> a work of art is always happy; all else is unhappy. . . . I don't love life because it's pretty. Prettiness is only clothes-deep. I am a truer lover than that. I love it naked. There is beauty to me even in its ugliness. (*Clark. op. cit.* p. 146ff.)

This letter not only explains why comedy has not been his characteristic medium, but it also states his reason for preferring tragedy. It is naked life that he wants. But the critic might still say that comedy need not abandon realism, and such a reply would be to the point. Hence the emphasis really belongs upon another statement in this letter: "I am a truer lover than that." He is too much a lover of life to be light-hearted or bitterly cynical—the quality needed for comedy. He still wants to save the world in spite of itself. This establishes his kinship to most of the great art of the world. The creative artist does not create for the sake of beauty alone. The passion which motivates his art lies embedded in a philosophy which embraces certain ideals of man's right to a better life. Such art is, and always must be, philosophical in its import. This is especially true of tragedy, for by its very nature it is a serious study of man's relation to the universe.

2

Tragedy has been the chief medium for O'Neill, but the comic spirit has not been absent from his plays. Nor is the method and technique of comedy outside the range of his ability. The proof of this is *Ah, Wilderness!* The action of this play moves in an atmosphere of gentle satire. The men and women in this play are not too complex, their life problems not too involved to permit of a satisfactory and happy solution.

In order to make his plot convincing to himself and his audience he had to set the scene a generation back from the present in a small town untouched by the fierce struggle of modern industrialism. This gives the whole play a genuine realistic touch. There is a gentle reminiscent quality about *Ah, Wilderness!* that is very charming. Here is revealed an aspect of American life that at present seems almost as dead as the Middle Ages. It is the atmosphere of *The Rubaiyat,* of Swinburne, of college days when college life was not too serious a business. Arthur Miller, the young man from Yale, has no doubts about his purpose in life. He knows that a Yale man is sure of his place in the sun. Fraternities, games, little affairs with women, from which he learns about life, are his most genuine interests. Not a single spark from the coming struggle for power ever illuminates the complacent depths of his mind.

He is the son of a well-to-do middle-class family in the great days of peace and prosperity that preceded the world economic and spiritual collapse. *Ah, Wilderness!* is a true historical comedy. It is a fleeting glimpse into the days that are gone forever. In that lies its very great charm to the men and women who have reached forty. The college student of today does not recognize Arthur, for today the army of the unemployed marches so near the campus that even a student at Yale must know that fraternities and football are relatively unimportant. But in its setting *Ah, Wilderness!* is perfect.

Arthur's brother, Richard, is far more serious-minded. He is the typical O'Neill character in one respect. He is described as possessing "extreme sensitiveness . . . a restless, apprehensive, defiant, shy, dreamy, self-conscious intelligence." In a different environment these are the qualities in the O'Neill hero that make for tragedy, but in the small-town scene of this play they lead to an amusing, gentle, romantic rebellion which is finally resolved in moonlight and romance.

And so it is with all the characters. They are well-meaning men and women whose problems are for the moment a trifle disturbing. The passion which flamed

in the culture of the nineties puzzles the older generation and is not very well understood by the youngsters,
but as a means to an end it serves as excellent dramatic material. Grown-up people can live again for a
moment in the days when they also quoted *The Rubaiyat* and Swinburne, dreamed in the moonlight,
made brave promises, and occasionally, at rare intervals,
saw the darker side of life in a small hotel at a back-
room bar "dimly lighted by two fly-specked globes in a
fly-specked gilt chandelier suspended from the middle
of the ceiling."

No character in the play quite discovers what it's all
about, nor does he quite solve all the problems that he
sensed as needing resolution. Nat Miller doesn't quite
succeed in telling his son just what every young man
should know. His wife doesn't make her point on her
objections to the "revolutionary" books that Richard
reads, Sid Davis and Lily Miller get no nearer to the
conclusion of their long-endured romance; Mr. Mc-
Comber is forced to recede from his stern position towards his daughter; while Richard and Muriel solve
their problem in a manner that does not promise complete harmony for the future. But it does not matter,
for there are no great problems in this play to be solved.
There are tense moments, but they are too amusing to
be taken seriously. It is good comedy from start to
finish.

Ah, Wilderness! stands as a strange interlude in the
midst of a world of tragedy. It indicates O'Neill's versa-
tility, but it does not add greatly to his interpretation

of the modern world which is the theme of this book. The imagined world of *Ah, Wilderness!* is not without its value as a contrast to the reality of the present. It tends to emphasize the darkness of today by revealing what was thought to be the light of yesterday. To the student of O'Neill the grim shadows of the past play over the easily solved complex of this romantic world of comedy. The future for Arthur and Richard will be fraught with difficulties that neither moonlight nor romance explain away. From the reading of Swinburne and *The Rubaiyat* Richard will move to Hardy, Dreiser, Thomas Mann, Faulkner, and O'Neill; from the peace of a small Connecticut town in 1906 he will move to the world conflict of 1914; from the economic security of pre-war days to the collapse following the war; from the philosophical idealism of his youth to the realistic materialism of maturity. When that day comes he may have moments of real delight in an occasional glance at his past romances, but he may also realize that as a preparation for what is to come, they give little on which to build for the future struggle.

3

To O'Neill who loves life for its potentiality as well as for its sequence of experiences, tragedy and not comedy has been the best medium for his art. In tragedy he can vent his bitterness against the self-imposed cruelty of man, and at the same time he can vision the good life as a force battling against the evil. *Mourning*

Becomes Electra is a good case in point. There is in it an element of the comic which reduces man to the ludicrous. But that is mere by-play. It is the Mannon family with its traditional beliefs, beliefs based on the puritanical heritage of American culture, that drive the family to disaster. It is this force in American life that has inspired the art of O'Neill in this play, and it is his love for a nobler and a freer life that formed his tragic theme. Even for the Mannons life was rich in potential beauty—even happiness—but the roads that led to the good life were barred to them by the white walls of the "Meeting House," the symbol of a ghostly past that survives in a culture that has changed all of its outward manifestation while it still mumbles the ritual of the ancient law. General Mannon saw it all on the night when he returned from the four years of civil war. As he sat on the steps of his house in the soft, sensuous atmosphere of night, he told of his desire for a new life, freed from the tortures of false beliefs and Puritan culture. But it was too late, as it must always be too late until society is aroused to a faith in life itself, to a life that does not measure its value in terms of death.

Since to love life means to accept it as essentially tragic is O'Neill's philosophy as an artist, his use of comedy has usually been a means to the development of tragedy. He knows life too well to believe that it does not have its comedy, but since he is concerned with the whole and not the insignificant part, comedy must be subservient to the master spirit, the guiding force, and that is tragedy. Thus he has used comedy to express the irony and tragedy of life. It does not provide a relief from the tragic intensity of a scene: it merely heightens the effect. O'Neill does not fall victim to the academic theory of "tragic relief." He knows that the best use of comedy in tragedy does not contradict the chief theme. *The Emperor Jones* begins almost as a comedy, but before many lines are spoken the ominous spirit of tragedy creeps into the atmosphere. By quick and subtle transitions the comic gives place to the tragic, and the ludicrous antics of the self-made emperor become the very substance of his tragic defeat. As he sinks deeper and deeper into the terrors of his past, as he becomes more and more the victim of his own past and the ancient racial pattern asserts itself, that which was comic becomes tragic, laughter changes to sympathy and terror. This use of comedy in this particular play is typical of O'Neill, and harmonizes with his whole conception of the purpose of his art.

In *Desire Under the Elms, Gold* and *All God's Chillun Got Wings* the same use of comedy is apparent. There are moments in all of these plays that, could they be divorced from the whole and comprehended apart from the spirit of the play, might be called comic. But in their place and properly grasped, they are an integral part of the tragic mood. Like the mad scenes from *King Lear* they are too serious to be amusing. Nothing could be more ridiculously funny than Lear's antics in the mad scenes, were it not that they are so heartrending, so profoundly and painfully sad. O'Neill has suc-

ceeded in making the ridiculous behavior of his characters almost lead his audience to laughter, and then he
turns this impulse to laugh into sympathy and understanding which make laughter impossible and heighten
the tragic note.

X

Technique

Must get more distance and perspective—more
sense of fate—more sense of the unreal behind
what we call reality which is the real reality!—
the unrealistic truth wearing the mask of lying
reality. *Mourning Becomes Electra*. Note #16

I

IN THE "ideal" theater the audience arrives fully pre-
pared for a profound aesthetic experience. Men and
women alike abandon all light-hearted chatter as soon
as they enter the auditorium. They file to their seats
without a murmur, and settle themselves into their
chairs with a tense expectant look upon their faces. All
seats are taken and everyone is in his proper stall. There
has been no talking, disturbance or quarreling with
the ushers about the correct location designated on the
ticket. The last person arrives and then after two minutes of intense silence, the lights go out and the curtains slowly part revealing the actors on the scene. The
first speech sounds with peculiar clarity upon the ears
of the expectant audience.

If this were true, the serious problem of how to in-

terest an audience and at the same time acquaint it
with the subject of the play would be more than half
solved. Since the real situation is just the reverse of
that described, it requires great skill to manipulate the
characters and the action in the opening scene. This is
a truth so obvious that it may be superfluous to mention it, but at the same time it is a quality that is rare
even in great dramatists. No one has ever written plays
in which the problem of the beginning is managed
more skillfully than in the plays of O'Neill. In the first
place he was trained to the theater from childhood. He
knows the stage intimately, and no problem in dramatic technique is too elementary to miss his notice. He
never overestimates the interest and nature of an audience. He knows that it is important at the parting of
the curtains to unify a heterogeneous group of people,
restless, talking, disorganized, concentrating on as
many different subjects as there are people. This psychological problem is further complicated by the movement and commotion of the latecomers, who are still
pushing past people already seated in order to find a
place for themselves. This situation so characteristic of
the opening of any play is managed with skillful technique by O'Neill.

Every play appeals primarily to the sense of hearing,
but aided and intensified by visual imagery. No commotion can quite obscure the setting which is revealed
as the curtains are drawn and quiet begins to settle
over the audience. But it is not enough to reveal the
scene, for action is expected and must follow immedi-

ately. If the characters begin to talk as soon as the curtain rises, then their conversation must be so unimportant that it does not matter if several of the first speeches are missed, for it is certain that they will not be heard by many people in the audience. This was managed in much of the traditional drama by the servant and his innocuous remarks. O'Neill does not use this method. To him the first scene is important from the very beginning. Thus instead of opening with conversation it always begins with some form of pantomime that is vital to the story, symbolic of the theme, and impressive in itself.

From the one-act plays to the latest work this technique of the beginning is practical. It combines action and interpretation, at the same time unifying and interesting the audience while it wastes no time in starting the serious business of revealing the theme of the play. *The Emperor Jones* provides as good a case as any for specific analysis. When the stage is revealed the pantomime is immediately tense and very dramatic. "A native Negro woman sneaks in cautiously from the entrance on the right." This action in itself is full of evil foreboding, and if it is not enough to focus the attention of the audience there is more to follow. "She hesitates beside the doorway, peering back as if in extreme dread of being discovered. Then she begins to glide noiselessly, a step at a time, toward the doorway in the rear. At this moment Smithers appears beneath the portico. . . . He sees the woman and stops to watch her suspiciously." Finally Smithers "springs forward and grabs her firmly by the shoulder. She struggles to get away, fiercely but silently." This graphic pantomime takes several minutes and is so dramatic in its character that by the time it is all carried through the audience is waiting for the words that will give meaning to the action.

This silent action serves a double purpose. It not only unifies the audience, but it arouses a questioning curiosity. This places the burden of the induction squarely on the shoulders of the audience and makes the perfect transition from the parting of the curtain to the forward-moving action of the play. When Smithers asks "What's the gaime, any'ow," he is voicing the thought of everyone in the audience. The captive one, in answering the question, tells the audience what it needs to know. This information is elaborated by the gratuitous comments of Smithers, whose speeches are explanatory but also justified by reason of his personal grudge against the Negro, Emperor Jones. Even his appearance on the stage is carefully accounted for, and is used as a means of letting the audience know that there is trouble brewing. He was not surprised at what he saw, when he entered, for, as he puts it: "There's somethin' funny goin' on. I smelled it in the air first thing I got up this mornin'."

Thus by a technique that is never forced, that is crowded with drama from the moment the set is revealed, and that gives a symbolic suggestion of the struggle that is to follow, the action begins before the opening is over, and the play is on its way. Typical of

O'Neill's opening technique is the use of song and music to accompany the pantomime. This is used effectively in such plays as *The Moon of the Caribbees,* *All God's Chillun Got Wings* and *Mourning Becomes Electra.* In the last two, particularly, it serves a double purpose of drawing the attention of the audience and at the same time of lending atmosphere that is appropriate to the play. In the Negro play it is "Only a bird in a Gilded Cage" and in the Electra it is "Shenandoah." Of this O'Neill writes in his notes: "The chanty 'Shenandoah'—use this more—as a sort of theme song —its simple sad rhythm of hopeless sea longing peculiarly significant—even the stupid words have striking meaning when considered in relation to tragic events in play." (*Mourning Becomes Electra* Note #16.)

2

The next problem in the opening of a play is the presentation of the induction. In order to notice how crudely a great dramatist may sometimes manage this matter of introducing the characters to the audience, giving enough of the past to arouse a personal interest in them, and stating the particular problem of the immediate situation, read the opening of Shakespeare's *Richard III.* Modern technique and modern stage tradition demand greater subtlety, and O'Neill has met the demand in an adequate manner. *Desire Under the Elms* provides an excellent example. Referring back to the method discussed above, in this play the audience

is summoned to attention by the appearance of one of
the characters on the porch of the house, which provides the set, and ringing a large bell. "This he swings
mechanically, awakening a deafening clangor." He
looks at the sky and says: "God! Purty!" He then "spits
on the ground with intense disgust, turns and goes back
into the house."

Next appear the men who were summoned by the
ringing of the bell. Like the one before them they also
look at the sky. This creates a warrant for the reminiscent remark that reveals something of the nature of the
man: "Eighteen years ago." The other who has been
following his own thoughts answers "What?" And the
reply is: "Jenn. My woman. She died."

The sky now becomes the inspiration for the next
speech which is a reference to gold, and leads to the
prospect of finding gold in California. This helps to
date the play, and leads to the reasonableness of the
following statement of facts that are obvious to the
two men and yet must be conveyed to the audience.
This is always the crucial moment of the induction, for
it would be quite ludicrous if the brothers were to tell
each other that they were brothers, that they had a
father, and that it was a brother of theirs who rang the
bell. Yet all these facts must be conveyed to the audience. The following speech, inspired by the reference to
California gold makes a good beginning:

Here—it's stones atop o' the ground—stones atop o'
stones—makin' stone walls—year atop o' year—him 'n'

yew 'n' me 'n' Eben—makin' stone walls fur him
to fence us in!

This speech fairly motivated, and without a single
gratuitous element, gives the name of the first character, and suggests that all three are brothers and that the
"him" must be their father. In addition the stones are
symbolic of their lives.

The next problem is to tell who "him" is. This is
done by referring to the investment that each has in the
farm, and that leads to the very natural speculation
about his two-months' absence, and the possibility, that
since he is old, he may be dead. Then follows the most
direct bit of evidence:

> Left us in the fields an evenin' like this. Hitched up
> an' druv off into the West. That's plum onnateral. He
> hain't never been off this farm 'ceptin' t' the village in
> thirty year or more, not since he married Eben's maw.

Again this information, which is not new to the
speakers, and is given here for the benefit of the audience, is justified by its nature, and by the new-sprung
desire on the part of the brothers to go to California. It
must have been a subject of comment among them
often that their father had suddenly left the farm without explanation two months ago. This being all the
more strange, since he had not taken a trip for thirty
years. It further suggests that Eben is only a half
brother, and that the father has already had two wives.
That they are the children of the same father is revealed

when Eben remarks sarcastically from the window
"Honor thy father." After a few more casual remarks
including a further reference to the sky and California
the scene ends on the same note as the beginning.

This scene allowing time for the pantomime could
be played in five minutes, yet in that brief time it has
revealed a good deal about the relationship of the three
men. It has characterized the father. It has given a
description of the setting, and revealed the dumb but
determined rebellion of the two oldest brothers, the
fiercer spirit of the younger, and the hatred as well as
the fear that all three of them feel towards their father.

3

An important aspect of O'Neill's technique is his
conscious and studied use of symbolism. This does not
imply that the audience is aware of this technique in an
unpleasant manner. It is done with care and designed
to extend the scope and meaning of the play beyond the
limited boundary of straightforward realism. It is apparent in the early plays through his use of setting that
will suggest the theme. In *Beyond the Horizon* he alter-
nates the scenes—one inside and one outside scene for
each act—by this device suggesting the conflict between
the fixed prison and the yearning for freedom. Bearing directly on this point is his own comment on the
critics:

> They have all accused me of bungling through igno-
> rance—whereas, if I had wanted to, I could have laid the

> whole play in the farm interior, and made it tight as a drum *à la* Pinero. Then, too, I should imagine the symbolism I intended to convey by the alternating scenes would be apparent even from a glance at the program. (*Clark*. p. 96ff.)

This use of a symbolic setting gives him greater flexibility and increases the imaginative quality of his drama. It is a method that has been characteristic of O'Neill from the very beginning of his work. In the early one-act plays *Fog* is a typical example. The use of the fog as symbolic of a state of mind is rather trite, but serves to indicate that impatient and passionate quality of O'Neill's imagination which has made it possible for him to push his play out beyond the limitation of the boards on which it is acted. It has thus been possible for him to liberate the drama from the narrow limitations of a temporary stage tradition and give to his plays almost as much freedom and scope as was practiced by Shakespeare. This technique which is so easily acceptable to the audience, and has grown familiar with his development, is a tribute to his inventive genius and his skill, for unlike Shakespeare, who could hang up a sign and call the scene a battlefield or the Forest of Arden, O'Neill must satisfy the audience by a suggestion of reality in combination with his symbolism.

This he does by using certain aspects of nature as a theme in such a play as *Anna Christie* where "dat ole davil, sea" in combination, at times, with the fog lends a symbolic meaning to the play. Another example is *All God's Chillun Got Wings*. Here he definitely violates strict realism in order to give immediate symbolic meaning to his play. When the curtains part the scene revealed is of three narrow streets that converge, suggesting the struggle of race conflicts that were centered in this little corner of the world. This idea is intensified by the grouping of the actors. "In the street leading left, the faces are all white; in the street leading right, all black." Next it becomes apparent that the conflict is to be limited and involves the conflict of the sexes: "On the sidewalk are eight children, four boys and four girls. Two of each sex are white, two black." By thus formalizing his set and the position of the characters, he has told the audience the theme of his story before a word is spoken. He has also generalized the particular, giving scope and significance to his drama beyond that which attaches to the individuals directly involved in the play. The movement of the people, the different quality of the laughter, and the spectacle as a whole with its attendant pantomime, typical of his method referred to in the preceding section, all contribute to the meaning and the understanding of the play.

The first act of *Marco Millions* is pure symbolism. In the prologue three great religions are represented, each being an outward symbol without inward meaning, except as a justification for such prejudices as serve the practical ends of each who professes it. This is further emphasized by the procession of the dead Queen. For the moment she represents power and the others end

their conflict by becoming slaves in her train—the train
of a dead Queen.

The six scenes of the first act symbolize the progress
of Marco Polo from the West to the East, from the
world of limited, practical values to the world of eternal values, from the world of naïve faith in human
values to the world of skeptical philosophy and relative
standards. But it marks also another progress which
could not be accomplished except by the use of symbolism. As Marco goes to the East he grows up to the
West. Thus there is a reverse action which gives this
particular act a charming complexity, and makes it an
interesting study in the conflicting ideals of East and
West, of youthful dreams and mature realities. It is
further complicated by an ironic theme, for as Marco
goes to the East to meet the great Khan he loses gradually, under the careful tutelage of his father and his
uncle, the conception of life which would make him
understand the meaning of life as reflected in the
philosophy of Kublai. By means of a series of symbolic
scenes Marco makes the transition from a sweet and
earnest youth, proud of his dreams and his hopes, and
genuine in his faith, to a shrewd business man, whose
values are profits, and whose ideals are mercenary. He
forgets his youthful love, and by this is symbolized the
loss of all that was pure and genuine in his philosophy.
The locket bearing his sweetheart's picture is stained by
a prostitute's kiss, and his poem, written to his sweetheart, is ground in the dust by a prostitute's heel, but
not until he has denied its authorship, which is a denial

of his former ideals. He ends by being a boaster, a braggart, a man who sees clearly the mote in his neighbor's eye. He has become brave and self-confident, and he has lost the power to sympathize with others; he has lost the power to be generous; he has lost the power to love; he has become a blind automaton whose life is condemned to the vicious slavery of not even knowing that he doesn't know. This complex situation is made clear, and gives dramatic emphasis, by means of symbolism, a symbolism that develops keen and penetrating satire on Western ideals with special reference to the United States in the gambling 'twenties.

This use of symbolism has lent a poetic quality to O'Neill's prose; it has universalized his theme; and it has added an emotional quality to his realism. This method has made it possible for him at any moment in his writing to depart from the orderly, logical language of prose into the psychological sequence of imaginative language. He has been able to remain true to the realism of his characters, and at the same time suggest those strange warnings, intuitions, fantastic ideas that play on the periphery of consciousness, or lie buried in the subconscious, but at times assert themselves with painful vividness. Examples of this may be found in every play. Old Cabot in *Desire Under the Elms* mixed a hard cruel sense of reality with an almost superstitious feeling for atmosphere. It seems perfectly natural to hear him say:

> It's cold in this house. It's oneasy.
> They's thin's pokin' about in the dark—in the corners.

and later he comes back to the same idea:

> Even the music can't drive it out—somethin'. Ye kin
> feel it droppin' off the elums, climbin' up the roof,
> sneakin' down the chimney, pokin' in the corners!
> They's no peace in houses, they's no rest livin' with
> folks. Somethin's always livin' with ye.

In this particular case there is added to the symbolism a quality that is almost mystical. This speech is a
soliloquy and seems to be an echo to the action that is
going on in the upstairs rooms of the house, where
Eben and Abbie are meeting over the cradle of the
baby that the old man believes is his own. Further discussion of this mystical use of coincidence follows in
the next section. At this time I wish only to emphasize
the use of symbolism to intensify and give scope to the
theme.

As O'Neill grew and developed as a dramatist he
followed faithfully his original technique. His plays
grew in scope and theme and with this growth his
symbolism grew more complicated. The changes that
came with maturity were changes in degree not in
kind.

The rich experimental nature of O'Neill's work,
which has given new life and fresh impetus to an
American drama that was hopelessly enthralled by a
fixed tradition, may be traced, in its major part, to his
bold and imaginative use of symbolism. His first great
success was *The Emperor Jones,* and it was his use of
symbolism in setting, in action and in plot construction

that stirred his audience to wonder and admiration. O'Neill had realized that modern drama need not necessarily be bound by the realistic set. Like the Elizabethans he rose above the limitation of his stage. He made his stage a servant to his art, refusing to accept the limitation imposed by tradition. Of him it was often said, and still is, as it was said of the Elizabethans, that it is ridiculous to believe that the stage can one minute be a battlefield and next a room in the king's palace. It is true that it cannot for many critics who are quite often bound so firmly by the tradition of what has been that anything new or experimental often disturbs them much more than it does the audience. This has been particularly true of the history of O'Neill criticism.

In *The Great God Brown* O'Neill's symbolism took the form of masks, a technique that was pushed to its utmost limits in *Lazarus Laughed*. In this play the masks are made to bear a heavy load, for each individual mask represents both age and quality. Seven periods of life are characterized by the masks and "Each of these periods is represented by seven different masks of general types of character as follows: The Simple, Ignorant; the Happy, Eager; the Self-Tortured, Introspective; the Proud, Self-Reliant; the Servile, Hypocritical; the Revengeful, Cruel; the Sorrowful, Resigned."

Not only does this symbolism become complex in itself, but as the play develops it is apparent that the combination of these various types and others that follow creates intricate group symbols that offer an interpretation of life-forces at war in the history of our whole Western culture. The play becomes a symbolic interpretation of life in words, in action, in pictorial effect and in pantomime. This marks the extreme of O'Neill's symbolism, and perhaps it indicates the use of symbols beyond their effectiveness for drama. If the audience is to be considered, it seems clear that some explanation beyond that of the play itself would be necessary.

For O'Neill this experiment may have been imperative to his own development. It taught him the value of the mask as well as its limitation. It should be remembered, however, that time and familiarity may still make *Lazarus Laughed* a successful stage play. For the author, it was a step in the direction of a new type of symbolism—that of the aside in *Strange Interlude*. In this play it is again the author's attempt to push back the boundaries of the stage world that gives rise to this type of symbolism. The audience is tacitly required to forget that thoughts are not spoken aloud in the presence of others, in order that it may enter more fully into the psychological analysis of the characters on the stage. His technique thus becomes a means by which he reveals the strange conflict between what man is in reality and what he is in relation to the social pattern of his life.

In this case the technique is perfect as far as the exposition of the idea is concerned, but there may be grave doubts as to its suitability for the stage. Time alone will tell the story of its success or failure. One thing is certain, that if the audience becomes familiar with this type it will establish its own laws and traditions, as has happened to every type that has survived from the past. The stage asks a compromise from the audience. It teaches the audience what it is to accept, and then on the basis of that agreement the play moves on unhampered. It is only the new that is condemned, and as historical perspective teaches us, its newness is its only sin. There can be no doubt about the value of O'Neill's technique in the particular instance of *Strange Interlude*. It was suited to the theme; it emphasized life as a strange interlude between the unknown sinister past and the unexplored and unknown future. It served as a means to the end of a greater understanding of the characters in the play, and at the same time universalized the theme to include the spectators in the tragedy of life.

Following *Strange Interlude* came *Dynamo*. Again he used the "aside" technique to give a symbolic interpretation of man's age-long struggle to find a meaning to life—a meaning to the meaningless. His own account of what he meant the play to be is evidence to the point of this section. He wrote of *Dynamo* that the play is a:

> Symbolical and factual biography of what is happening in a large section of the American (and not only American) soul right now. It is really the first play of a trilogy that will dig at the roots of the sickness of to-day as I feel it—the death of an old God and the failure of science and materialism to give any satisfying new one

for the surviving primitive religious instinct to find a
meaning for life in, and to comfort its fears of death
with. (Quoted from Clark p. 188ff.)

His use of "symbolical and factual" indicates the combination that fits every play. Always there is this symbolism and always the symbolism is used to universal-
ize the theme, to make it important for the race—even
mankind—as well as specifically pointed for the characters in the action of the play. This may be subtly and
almost abstractly represented, as by Dion's mask, or
crudely and too obviously done as in the case of the
money thrown into the sea in *The Rope*.

It is the symbol that matters in an O'Neill play, because he has something more to say than can be said in
plain unshaded words. Directly following the passage
quoted above are these words:

It seems to me that anyone trying to do big work
nowadays must have this big subject behind all the little
subjects of his plays or novels, or he is simply scribbling
around on the surface of things and has no more real
status than a parlor entertainer. (*Ibid*. p. 189.)

The "big subject" of man's relation to the apparently
meaningless world that modern science has revealed
has always been O'Neill's problem. He realizes that
"Long fed on boundless hopes, O race of man, how
angrily thou spurn'st all simpler fare," and his work
has made a powerful gesture in the direction of a solution. There are those who hold that this is O'Neill's

great fault as a dramatist, that he is worrying too much
about the destiny of man and not enough about entertainment in the theater. Then there are critics who will
not even grant him his place as a thinker among the
dramatists. A notable example is St. John Ervine's review of *Mourning Becomes Electra*. No one can say
where the truth lies, but it may be held with some degree of certainty, that if O'Neill is to have a life beyond
that of entertaining his audience of today, it will be
partially due to the fact that he was at least as much
concerned about the universal problem of man and his
universe as he was about the dramatization of a particular situation. He has had something to say that was
worth saying, worth preserving.

The notes to *Mourning Becomes Electra* indicate
how the mind of O'Neill is first of all attracted to the
problem of giving a broad and universal significance to
his theme, a problem he always solves by means of
symbolic representation. Thus in Note #1 is this statement:

> Modern psychological drama using one of the old
> legend plots of Greek tragedy for its basic theme—the
> Electra story?—the Medea? Is it possible to get modern
> psychological approximation of Greek sense of fate into
> such a play, which an intelligent audience of to-day, pos-
> sessed by no belief in gods or supernatural retribution,
> could accept and be moved by?

Note #2, written two years later, places the emphasis
again upon broadening the implications of the original

Electra theme making it include "—most comprehensive intense basic human interrelationships—can easily be widened in scope to include still others." And this is followed in Note #5 by a specific reference to the characters: "Work out this symbol of family resemblances and identification."

When it came to the actual writing of the play his theory and practice of symbolic representation become even more clear. Thus he writes:

> "Mourning Becomes Electra"—Technique—for first draft use comparatively straight realism—this first draft only for purpose of getting plot material into definite form—then lay aside for period and later decide how to go on to final version.—what departures necessary—whether to use masks, soliloquies, asides, etc. (Note #9)

Here it is clear that the straight realistic technique is for O'Neill nothing more than a convenient way of organizing the plot; it is but a means to an end and that end is symbolic representation.

The next step involves the selection of the type of symbolism to be used for this particular play. It is the crucial problem for O'Neill in any play. In this case his own words give objective evidence. He ponders various types that hark back to earlier practices, even going so far as actually to perform the labor of working them into the play and later discarding them as unsuited for the Electra theme.

His first draft, following the straight realistic technique, gives him some satisfaction but on the whole he calls it "lousy—not enough meat." His meaning is brought out in his next comment, "not enough sense of fate hovering over characters, fate of family—living in a house built by Atreus' hatred (Abe Mannon)—a psychological fate—." What it lacks is the symbolic implication, the one element needed to express O'Neill's meaning. He feels this so deeply that a few lines further in the same note he adds:

> Use every means to gain added depth and scope—can always cut what is unnecessary afterwards—will write second draft using half masks and an "Interlude" technique (combination "Lazarus" and "Interlude") and see what can be gotten out of that—think these will aid me to get just the right effect—must get more distance and perspective—more sense of fate—more sense of the unreal behind what we call reality which is the real reality!—the unrealistic truth wearing the mask of lying reality, that is the right feeling for this trilogy, if I can only catch it!

* * * *

> Pattern of exterior and interior scenes, beginning and ending with exterior in each play—with the one ship scene at the center of the second play (this, center of whole work) emphasizing sea background of family and symbolic motive of sea as means of escape and release—

* * * *

> Develop South Sea Island motive—its appeal for them all (in various aspects)—release, peace, security, beauty,

freedom of conscience, sinlessness, etc.—longing for the primitive—and mother symbol—yearning for pre-natal non-competitive freedom from fear—make this Island theme recurrent motive——

Then follows emphasis on the resemblances in appearance, which is intensified by the use of masks. (In the final version abandoned for the "life-like mask impression" of the Mannon features.) This is followed by:

'Shenandoah'—use this more—as a sort of theme song —its simple sad rhythm of hopeless sea longing peculiarly significant—even the stupid words have striking meaning when considered in relation to tragic events in play—

It must not be inferred from this discussion of O'Neill's use of symbolism that he deprecates the drama which aims at and achieves success in straight realism. He lays down no inflexible dogma, but for himself he needs the wider field and the deeper, often dimly felt meanings that some form of symbolism will give. He has written: "Not masks for all plays, naturally. Obviously not for plays conceived in purely realistic terms." (*The American Spectator*. Nov. 1932) In the same article his criticism of modern drama points towards the further and more universal use of masks for rendering:

The profound hidden conflicts of the mind which the probings of psychology continue to disclose to us. He must find some method to present this inner drama in his work, or confess himself incapable of portraying one of the most characteristic preoccupations and uniquely significant, spiritual impulses of his time.

Which is but further evidence of what the drama as an art form means to O'Neill. The drama to him is a powerful medium through which the dark surging of man's inner life sheds for a moment its unreal mask. His plays reveal the unreal reality, the concealed truth; they give form and substance to the dream; they lend to that airy nothing which is in reality everything, "a local habitation and a name."

4

A technique which makes use of symbolism and at the same time remains true to the best traditions of modern realism must eschew the deadly temptations of mysticism. O'Neill likes to believe that there is a strong mystical urge in his nature, but he knows better than to give it a free rein.

There have been times when his strong sense for realistic technique has been tempted beyond the border-line. Examples are rare but may still be found in many of his plays from his earliest to his most recent. *Fog* offers a typical example. A poet, a business man, a woman and a child are adrift in a life-boat. They are survivors from a shipwreck. The ending is climaxed by the arrival of a rescue ship whose officer claims that he was guided through the fog to their boat by the cries of a child. The child has really been dead for twenty-four hours. This type of Maeterlinck technique does not ring true in O'Neill. To the realist it is a violation of truth.

In *Desire Under the Elms* there is a situation that comes within the realm of the possible, but by implication it leads the audience to accept more than a rational mind will countenance. The scene reveals Abbie and Eben in their respective rooms in the upstairs of the house. Only a wall divides them. Then comes this in the stage directions:

> Eben and Abbie stare at each other through the wall. Eben sighs heavily and Abbie echoes it. Both become terribly nervous, uneasy. Finally Abbie gets up and listens, her ear to the wall. He acts as if he saw every move she was making; he becomes resolutely still. She seems driven into a decision—goes out the door in rear determinedly. His eyes follow her.

These instructions imply the transference of thought without words or visible actions. If telepathy had any basis in fact, it could be a very powerful medium in drama, but it hasn't and any temptation to use it must result in a weakened structure. O'Neill knows this and only at rare intervals does he use scenes such as that quoted above, and in this case it might even be argued that coincidence and not telepathy is implied. In either case it would be weak, for coincidence that functions in a series of actions to a second of time is too rare to have any value in the realms of probability.

Strange Interlude and *Dynamo* have scenes which suggest comparison, although in both these plays the "aside" technique gives more probability to the situations presented. In *Mourning Becomes Electra* there is one situation which bears a close resemblance to those already mentioned. When General Mannon discovers that Christine has given him poison, he cries out: "Help! Vinnie!" As if in answer to his call, Vinnie appears in the doorway explaining her presence by saying: "I had a horrible dream—I thought I heard Father calling me—it woke me up—"

This attempt to explain her appearance seems a trifle far-fetched. The implication that is unavoidable is that there was a mystical transference of thought. It must be admitted that from a psychological point of view it is perfectly reasonable to believe that Vinnie should have dreamed of her father's danger and imagined that he called her, but it is the perfect coördination in time that casts doubt on its probability. It is all the more significant in this case, because all the future action of the play hangs upon the discovery that Vinnie makes by her appearance on the scene at this critical moment.[*]

Too much emphasis must not be placed upon this type of symbolism in O'Neill. It may be a weakness, or it may be evidence of his desire to push symbolic representation to its limits. If so, these are examples in which the limits have been exceeded. They serve as an inter-

[*]Cf. Also Father Baird's premonition of John Loving's spiritual distress and his arrival on the scene at exactly the right moment. (*Days Without End*.)

esting study in the impatience and rebellion of the creative mind. It demands more than earth will give, and as it flutters on the very borderline of human adventure in the chaos and mystery of life, it is not strange that at times it should go beyond the limits which are rationally possible. Interesting parallels to O'Neill's practice in this particular might be found in Dreiser's account of his earlier literary expriences, and also in the character of Eugene Witla in *The Genius*. Convenient as the method is in solving difficult problems, it is of doubtful value. Even the satirical note of *Marco Millions* scarcely excuses The Great Khan's use of crystal gazing to discover what happened in Venice after Marco's return.

5

Every title O'Neill has chosen for his plays is strongly symbolic, and in addition to the symbolism there is irony. This combination of symbolism and irony in the titles reveals the serious analytic nature of O'Neill's mind, for his irony is not scornful of man's tragedy, but sympathetic and bitter. His bitterness springs from his sympathy with man's suffering, and the bitterness accompanies his realization that man submits to poverty in the midst of plenty. Poverty and plenty must be understood to apply to things of the mind as well as of the body. In an O'Neill play there is a wealth of potential happiness barred to those that suffer in his imagined world, and the barrier could be torn away if man had the power and the wisdom to know that his slavery is self-imposed.

The early one-act plays show by their titles that O'Neill has always regarded his art as serious and symbolic. *The Web* which comes first in the order of composition is symbolic of the web of life from which man escapes only by escaping from life itself. In this play it is Rose Thomas, a prostitute whose destiny is controlled by the meshes of life's ironic web, just as nearly twenty years later it was to be Lavinia Mannon whose life was to be portrayed as hopelessly entangled in a net of circumstances which her struggles to unravel led only to a deeper and firmer imprisonment. *Thirst* and *Recklessness* are less important in this early group, but *Fog* and *Warnings* are decidedly and clearly symbolic. Fog and Web are typical symbols in O'Neill's plays. To him they have a definite place in the analysis of modern life. Not only is man caught in a web, but his life is confused by a fog in which he sees nothing clearly. In at least one other play, *Anna Christie,* is the fog used as a symbol. Chris Christopherson may be able to guide his old coal barge through Atlantic fogs, but the fog that surrounds his mental life is too dense for his powers as a navigator. He avoids the dangers of the sea, but he wrecks his life and that of others in the dense fog of ignorance.

In the next series of one-act plays the combination of the symbolic and the ironic is definitely revealed. Thus *Bound East for Cardiff* becomes another way of saying that Yank is "going west." *The Moon of the Caribbees* suggests the romantic glamor of a tropical night, but instead the moon looks down on struggle, disappointment and sorrow. *The Long Voyage Home* lays final stress on the long voyage, for home is never reached.

Then comes *Beyond the Horizon* a title which suggests that longed-for haven which man forever pursues, but is by the laws of logic eternally forbidden to reach. There is a combination of pity and irony in this title that is carried out consistently in the subject matter of the drama. The same ironic touch is intensified in the next title *The Emperor Jones*. There is something that approaches the ludicrous in the association of nobility with the name of Jones. As the play develops and the phantom forms of Jones' past appear before him, each one demanding a remnant of his self-acquired noble rank, the ludicrous changes to sympathy, and pity and terror attend the disintegration of the Emperor into the fear-stricken figure of a poor Negro fleeing imaginary evils into the arms of death.

His use of symbolism in his titles is well illustrated by *Gold,* a play in which Captain Bartlett's passion for buried treasure leads him to being an accomplice in murder, and later, in the ruination of himself. The irony is bitter and tragic, for Captain Bartlett wanted gold in order that he might give his wife and children happiness and social security. Instead he destroys their happiness and brings them misery and sorrow. In an earlier one-act version, this play was entitled *Where the Cross is Made,* a title which shows the idea he meant to convey by the title *Gold*. Captain Bartlett crucified himself on the cross of his passion for gold.

There is no need to prolong this particular analysis to include every play. The point is evident and its relation to the other phases of his technique clear. The ironic symbolism of *All God's Chillun Got Wings* should not be overlooked. Nor should one forget *Desire Under the Elms* which recalls vividly one of O'Neill's constant themes, that of the deadly effect of the Puritan ideal. In this play the elms signify and suggest the New England Puritan. Thus the title implies the theme, that of suppressed desire, bitterness and tragedy. The ironic note in this play is only exceeded by the startling title *Lazarus Laughed*.

His own discussion of the title for *Mourning Becomes Electra* has a direct bearing on the subject of this selection. From his own notes on the play is taken the following comment:

> Title—"Mourning Becomes Electra"—that is, in old sense of word—it befits—it becomes Electra to mourn— it is her fate,—also in the usual sense (made ironical here), mourning (black) is becoming to her—it is the only color that becomes her destiny— (Note #7)

"Made ironical here" could be said of almost all the titles. It is not by accident that O'Neill wrote a play dealing with the life of Ponce de Leon and chose for his title *The Fountain*.

6

The final test of his technique is exemplified in the imaginary world which lies beyond the endings of his plays. If one allows his imagination to journey into the world beyond the ending of Dickens' *David Copperfield*, he will soon realize that Dickens violated the reality of the world he had created. He forces his ending to fit a desire for justice which exceeds the limitations of the world he has described in his novel. Pleasant as that may be, it is false art. It needs no voice come from the grave to tell us that Mr. Micawber will be as desperately involved in I.O.U.s in Australia as he was in England. Uriah Heep will soon be out of jail and pursuing the same deception that led to the evil recounted in the novel. The same would be true of all the characters. Dickens deceived his readers into believing that all the problems that caused confusion have been solved, but a moment's thought shows that his method was deceptive.

In O'Neill the reverse is true. With skill and artistic justice he makes his ending consistent with the world he has revealed in his plays. Only once have the critics denied his faithfulness to his subject matter in this respect, and that was with reference to the ending of *Anna Christie*. O'Neill's own answer was that they misunderstood his meaning. Only a romantic judgment would see a happy ending to *Anna Christie*. The storm is over for the time being and there is a period of calm, but that Mat and old Chris will be permanently reconciled to each other, and to Anna, does not seem very certain. The ending is not solved by having Anna die, but it must be recognized that it is not always desirable to purchase life at any price. Anna's honesty may save the day, but "the scar of that encounter, like a sword," will lie forever between her and her troubled lord.

The world beyond the ending of O'Neill's plays is as grim, true and fascinating as is the world his poetic imagination has created. It is a world of strife, victory, defeat, noble courage and brave spirits. There is no possibility of imagining final solutions in his plays. He is too close an observer, and too honest with his materials, to force his endings into a promise that evidence from his work would prove false and untrustworthy. It may be said with safety that O'Neill has not permitted his ideal of the good life to falsify his art.

XI

This Sickness of Today

"One's outer life passes in a solitude haunted by
the masks of others; one's inner life passes in a
solitude hounded by the masks of oneself."
(O'Neill, the *American Spectator*, Vol. I, No. 1,
p. 3.)
"Thinks I at this juncture, well, he's run away as
far as he can get in that direction. Where will
he hide himself next?" *Days Without End*

I

Days Without End comes as a sad surprise to all those
who already *knew* O'Neill's final position as thinker
and dramatist. The chorus of critical comment has in-
toned with monotonous regularity a disparaging attitude toward what they considered the dominant idea
of the play. It has been called "dull, pedestrian, un-
poetic, unconvincing." It has been labeled "a wraith-
like wrangling of thought rather than a flowering of
the soul." In general this tone of disapproval has been
tinged with a touch of bitterness, a bitterness all the
more keen because to most of those who reviewed the
play it seemed that O'Neill failed to live up to their

high expectation. They write in the vein of disappointed lovers, men who believe that their high hopes and just expectations have been destroyed. Thus in all the critical comment there is a note of sadness that permeates the general tone of disparagement.*

In all cases it is quite clear that the critical comment is not made on the basis of *Days Without End* in itself. Nor is it due to such technical imperfections as the play may reveal when it is seen on the stage. The honest critic may find in any single play by any author elements that displease him. He may see technical limitations, but he does not therefore necessarily condemn the structure in its entirety. It follows that there is something outside and beyond *Days Without End* as a play in itself that gives rise to this general voice of disfavor.

The search for an explanation of the critical attitude that prevailed when *Days Without End* appeared on the stage and in print must lead back to O'Neill's earlier works and into the whole critical structure of his interpretation of life in our modern mechanized world. The first point, but not the most important, which bears upon this discussion is the manner in which the play ends. Here it must be noted that the objection is not to the dramatic appropriateness of the con-

* For the sake of accuracy it should be noted that not all comment has been adverse, nor has the play failed as an acting piece on the stage. H. T. Parker's criticism in the *Boston Transcript,* written without Catholic bias, is worthy of high praise as a fine critical evaluation that is not unfavorable to the play. *Days Without End* has been successfully produced at The Abbey Theatre, Dublin, and it will be performed both in Holland and Sweden in 1934.

clusion that gives rise to dissatisfaction, but it is that the final scene appears to imply that profound psychical and ethical conflicts may be solved in a position of humble prostration before the cross of the crucified Jesus. If this were O'Neill's real meaning, and if he intended to imply that the conflicts of the modern world were all to be resolved by turning back to the church, there might be grounds for a profound difference of opinion. Even then it would have to be admitted that for dramatic purposes and as the expression of individual opinion it can not be wholly disregarded, for the fact remains that there are people who still believe, or think that they believe, that all evil is smothered in the dust before the Cross.

It is not the conversion of John, the principal character, in this last scene that gives rise to protest, for that in itself may be relatively unimportant. But John's conversion, if it is to express a fundamental change in the whole critical attitude of O'Neill, is of vital importance. It is this latter idea which has fastened itself upon the minds of all those who have dealt with the play and its meaning. Thus Mr. Krutch in *The Nation* writes: "Hence if the play does not mean that he is at least contemplating surrender to an old faith rather than a new one, it is difficult to see how it can mean anything." (*The Nation*. Vol. 138, No. 3577, p. 111.) And why not? Because Mr. Krutch sees the play not as a work by itself, but in relation to the whole body of O'Neill's dramatic creations. And so have all the others who are dissatisfied. Like Mr. Krutch they try to see this play in relation to those that have preceded it, and it does not seem to "belong." In the same article, quoted above, Mr. Krutch writes: "The fable seems hardly relevant to any discussion of that 'sickness of today' which has always before concerned him."

It is, then, not the ending alone, nor is it the theme in itself, that gives rise to adverse critical comment. It is that in analyzing the play everyone considers it in the light of the past work of O'Neill, and on this basis, finds its values either false or futile or at best ill conceived. I hasten to add that I have no disagreement with the method of approach, nor do I hold that this play should not be treated in relation to the whole body of O'Neill's work. In that then I accept the method of Mr. Krutch and all the others who have commented on the play. The questions then arise, is it true that a thorough examination of *Days Without End* reveals a distinct break with the older plays, and is it true that it is not "relevant to any discussion of that 'sickness of today'?"

2

The answer to these questions must come from a close study of the text in relation to the whole body of O'Neill's work, and in relation to the preceding chapters of this book. The first question then is what relationships that are really significant to the whole body of O'Neill's work and expressive of his attitude to life as revealed in it may be traced in *Days Without End?*

It must be noted that the eternal conflict in personality which has been a dominant factor in O'Neill's work is also the theme of this play. John and Loving are at war with each other. The device of having the two personalities represented by two separate characters is a new device with O'Neill, but the idea is common to almost every play that he has written. Here as always he sees life's battle fought on two fronts. There is the obvious struggle with the outward aspects of our world, but there is also the more sinister battle that is inward in its nature, a conflict that is intangible, subtle, fierce and not infrequently culminates in a disaster far more terrible than any consequence that may follow from the struggle with the outward forces. The greatest disaster that may result from the battle with the forces of nature is lack of food, clothing and shelter. This, it is true, may lead to death. But a rational man must admit that death is not the greatest evil that can befall a man. Death brings peace. As Loving expresses it, "Death is final release, the warm dark peace of annihilation."

More terrible than death is the living despair of a psychologically thwarted life. Few would be such irrational lovers of life as to claim that the incurably insane are better off in their padded cells than they would be in the quiet of the grave. But that is the extreme case. Examine O'Neill's characters to see how he has conceived the problem in *Days Without End* and in the earlier plays. From Captain Bartlett to Lavinia the terrible torture of an inward life that is in conflict with itself has made the dramas of O'Neill powerful trage-

dies of the modern world. John and Loving belong in
this tradition. They are at war, as have been all their
brothers and sisters in this "mad brewage" of a world.

The play opens with this conflict and once more the
old familiar struggle is before us. It is clear that O'Neill
has definitely related it to his past. It is also clear that
John and Loving are revealing a living conflict and that
all the help John gets from Father Baird is not enough
to dampen the spirit of Loving whose contradictions
are quick and pointed to everything that John tried to
do. Thus when Eliot says, "You actually tried to prove
that no such figure as Christ ever existed," Loving replies, "I still feel the same on that subject." But John,
even though this doubt is in his mind feels that
"He must go on! He must find a faith—somewhere!"
To this Loving answers, "Is it your old secret weakness
—the cowardly yearning to go back—?" This is
a familiar touch. The old yearning for an answer to
the unanswerable. The theme of *Lazarus Laughed* is
here, but in this case it is as though the author had at
least faced the issue squarely. He will not accept an
excuse or an evasion. He is open and direct in his self-
criticism, even brutal to himself. He shows that he
understands his own deep yearnings for perfection, and
that he recognizes their futility in relation to any sort
of an absolute.

Thus he plunges into a review of the ideas and ideals
that have dominated his life. This he puts in the mouth
of Father Baird who in his smug certainty of the final
truth may be trusted to put them in the worst possible

light. In this review Father Baird assumes the superior attitude of the one who has answered all questions by solving none, and while he seems to make John ridiculous, he really reveals the true character of John's mind as inquiring, skeptical, inquisitive and, above all, experimental. The evidence as Father Baird presents it is that John has been at various times in his young life an atheist, a socialist, an anarchist, a Nietzschean, a bolshevist, a Marxian, a devotee of "the defeatist mysticism of the East," a follower of Lao Tze and of Buddha, a Pythagorean and an Anti-Christ. In spite of the fact that Father Baird seems to regard these various adventures in the realm of thought and faith as the expressions of a wandering mind and a lost soul, the reader cannot avoid the feeling that the mind of John must be infinitely more fascinating than that of the priest who holds it ridiculous.

Not only is this a review of John's past, it is also a review of O'Neill's own past—a past that gives the lie to the superficiality that Father Baird seems to imply. The mind of O'Neill has created play upon play out of this turmoil of experience which stands as evidence that his intellectual adventures bore a rich and a varied fruitage in the realm of art. It further shows that in *Days Without End* O'Neill is offering a dramatic review of his past struggles. It is in this sense one of the most profoundly self-analytical plays he has ever written, one in which he has not spared himself. In it he has said of himself the things that his critics did not dare to say. In the midst of his life, at the very peak of his success, he asks himself what in the nature of a positive answer has so far been achieved. Nor does he limit it to the realm of the mind, but associated with the analysis of his intellectual attitudes is the whole problem of enduring emotional values in love. When Lucy asks John, "And who are you revenging yourself on, John," he answers "Who knows? Perhaps on love. Perhaps in my soul, I hate love!"

When he comes to reviewing the plot of his proposed novel, John goes even further into the subject of self-criticism and self-analysis:

> JOHN. There always remained something in him that felt itself damned by life, damned with distrust, cursed with the inability ever to reach a lasting belief in any faith, damned by a fear of the lie hiding behind the mask of truth.

O'Neill does not allow this to pass without comment. While it brings a very satisfying "Ah!" from the priest, from Loving it provokes: "So romantic, you see—to think of himself as possessed by a damned soul!"

John continues the analysis of his hopes and fears for himself and for life. He gives an account of his horror of death and the strange fascination it held for him as though there were "something that hated life." These feelings that John describes are not new to those who have followed O'Neill's plays. These intellectual problems and emotional conflicts that John describes have permeated the whole of O'Neill's work; they must be identified as his own problems. In this particular play

they get a more direct expression than they have ever
before had, and they likewise get the most ruthless
treatment. The mind of Loving must not be forgotten,
for it is to Loving, the critic, that we must look for the
final answer. Loving like Milton's Satan is the real answer to the problems posed by the poet's mind. And in
this case Loving's answer is very sharp:

> LOVING. A credulous, religious-minded fool, as I have
> pointed out! And he carried his credulity into the next
> period of his life, where he believed in one social or
> philosophical Ism after another, always on the trail of
> Truth! He was never courageous enough to face what
> he really knew was true, that there is no truth for
> men, that human life is unimportant and meaningless.
> No. He was always grasping at some absurd new faith
> to find an excuse for going on!

This is severe criticism of O'Neill's own past, and it
is also unique as a type of self-analysis of a successful
author. That it contains an element of truth must be
admitted, but it must also be apparent that out of this
tempestuous crusade through many years and into
many strange dwelling places of the human mind has
come a rich and beautiful reward. That O'Neill should
express a profound dissatisfaction is evidence that the
quality of his mind is genuine, something that cannot
be satisfied by either popular praise or large gate re-
ceipts. Just when the world has come to his gate to pay
him a measure of homage unsurpassed by any American dramatist before him, he turns a deaf ear to their

applause. He looks inward and finds his old yearning
for truth and perfection still unanswered. He has been
the prospector in search of a mine of fabulous worth.
Each strike has led to a pocket rich in itself, but not the
deep inexhaustible vein his insatiable passion for eternal
things demands.

There have been times when a bold outcropping of
gold has led him with fever heat to deep excavations,
Dynamo, only to prove a blind lead, a something to be
either abandoned or surpassed. There have been great
and intricate developments, *Lazarus Laughed, Strange
Interlude* and *Mourning Becomes Electra,* which
yielded wealth in the terms of life-meanings far beyond
anything else that American drama has produced. Still
he is unsatisfied, even scornful. The quest is still on.
Days Without End is a review of this interesting and
complicated past. If it is a failure as an acting play,* or
if its concluding scene is unconvincing, the critical implications of the whole argument reveal a mind
alive to the limitations and the values of the past, a
mind high-strung and intense, keyed to new ventures
and further explorations.

3

In studying this play in relation to the "sickness of
today" O'Neill's subtitle must not be forgotten. He calls

* This may truly be considered relative, for it ran seven weeks on the
New York stage, and was successfully produced in Boston, not to mention its
European record.

it *A Modern Miracle Play*. Just as *Mourning Becomes Electra* was meant to be a modern psychological treatment of a Greek theme, so *Days Without End* is a modern psychological interpretation of the medieval Catholic, a Faustian theme of a man with a damned soul, which he has given to the devil as he cursed and denied his God. Thus too great an emphasis upon this play as some new confession of faith on the part of the author tends to obfuscate his meaning.

The modern world has changed its terminology and its outward forms of living, but the Faust theme as expressive of an inner conflict is still true to human experience. O'Neill believes that the modern drama, if it is to have a real significance, must deal with these inner emotional conflicts. In *The Great God Brown* he used masks for the first time to dramatize this theme. He has stated his attitude in the following passage.

> I hold more and more surely to the conviction that the use of masks will be discovered eventually to be the freest solution of the modern dramatist's problem as to how—with the greatest possible dramatic clarity and economy of means—he can express those profound hidden conflicts of the mind which the probings of psychology continue to disclose to us. He must find some method to present this inner drama in his work, or confess himself incapable of portraying one of the most characteristic preoccupations and uniquely significant, spiritual impulses of his time. (*The American Spectator*, Vol. I, No. 1, p. 3.)

His technique for dealing with modern psychological problems has entailed the use of the mask—or some symbolical form of mask. *Days Without End* makes use of a symbolic device in dealing with an ancient theme in a modern setting. It is thus not primarily conceived as a piece of personal history, but rather as an old problem that is universal in its appeal. It is O'Neill's version of the Faust legend. In *The American Spectator* article, quoted above, he states the germ of the idea that finds full development in *Days Without End:*

> Consider Goethe's *Faust,* which, psychologically speaking, should be the closest to us of all the Classics. In producing this play, I would have Mephistopheles wear the Mephistophelean mask of the face of Faust. For is not the whole of Goethe's truth *for our time* just that Mephistopheles and Faust are one and the same—*are* Faust?

In O'Neill's play John and Loving are *one*. The conflict that is dramatized in the play is a struggle between John Loving's faith in God and his faith in himself. In this modern version God is Love, and John has denied himself love. He has given himself over to hatred of love, which has led to a fear of life, a longing for death. In this state, severed from love, which is the only thing that can give his life meaning, he pursues endless theories of man's relation to the universe. Each explanation in turn proves to be a baseless chimera, an empty vessel to a pilgrim thirsting for truth in the desert of unbelief.

Finally his wanderings lead him back to love, represented in the play by John Loving's wife. So far all has been easy for the Tempter, Loving. Just as Faust signed his soul away to Mephistopheles, so John had given his to Loving, to the pursuit of temporal, transitory values. Loving leads John to commit adultery, the sin against love. Having accomplished this the demon tries to implant the belief in John's mind that he desires the death of his wife, for now it is of crucial importance that he destroy his faith in love. If John can be made to believe that he desires the death of his wife, then it will become clear to him that he has lost his last opportunity to find a meaning in life. He will then realize that the desire to murder his wife is really his own death-longing. When that is established he will be at the end of all experiments and lost in the clutches of the demon. From this dilemma he is rescued by a revived faith which slays the demonic power that had held him enslaved. Love becomes once more his true guide. He cries out in rapture, "Life laughs with God's love again! Life laughs with love!"

4

Like the former plays, *Days Without End* is rich in social criticism. The very title comes out of O'Neill's interest in some solution to the social and economic chaos of our modern world. He wants to "Begin to create new goals for ourselves, ends for our days!" Here as in *Anna Christie, The Hairy Ape* and many of

his earlier plays, he is again burning with a passion for
some meaning in our economic world that will have
significance for the good life.

The theme of the novel which forms the basis of the
plot in *Days Without End* is that of a man lost in a
meaningless world, a world which has grown psycho-
pathic in its pursuit of wealth. O'Neill has attempted to
deal with that "sickness of today" in the terms of its
effect upon personality. He is analyzing it from its
psychological implications, which is the true function
of the artist. Some of the modern economic critics have
found grave fault with his analysis because he has
failed to show man finding a clear answer in the midst
of the chaos. They imply that if he would only think as
they do he would see that there is a definite solution to
this modern madness in a new economic order. A quotation here from V. F. Calverton's *The Liberation of
American Literature* will illustrate this attitude and
place the issue clearly. He writes,

> "Overwhelmed by the age that is upon him, and
> driven within himself for a solution of the contradictions
> which the age represents, O'Neill has fumbled and floun-
> dered in every direction in an attempt to find truth and
> free it from its fetters. Mentally bandaged as he is by a
> world which has provided no faith for him to live by or
> accept, his excursions into the psychic frontiers of per-
> sonality have resulted only in a kind of magnificent con-
> fusion. In play after play he has endeavored to escape
> that confusion—but confusion only mounts and multi-
> plies. Brilliant with insights into individual personalities

as his plays always are, nowhere do they catch up with those personalities in terms of those deeper values, which reveal the relationship between personality and civilization."

The essence of Mr. Calverton's objection is that O'Neill has found no sure solution to the problems of our modern world. Mr. Calverton would be satisfied if O'Neill could only have all of his characters triumph over their deep-seated ills by becoming earnest workers in a collectivist political party. Perhaps I can illustrate the difference between Calverton and O'Neill by a brief story of a passage at arms between Dr. Rebec, my former professor of philosophy at the University of Oregon, and a visiting clergyman. The clergyman preached a baccalaureate sermon in which he condemned the philosophers as people who are imprisoned in a dark room, searching for a black cat that isn't there. At a banquet following the address Dr. Rebec rose to make a speech, and in it he replied to the clergyman's condemnation of philosophers. He said: "It is true that the philosopher searches in a dark room for a black cat that isn't there. The difference between the philosopher and the clergyman is that the clergyman finds the cat."

Now it is quite clear that if Mr. Calverton hasn't already caught the cat he knows where it can be found, and he is not very well satisfied with the artist who spends all his time searching, but is unable to make the proper discovery. It might be said that in *Days Without*

End O'Neill has found a cat, but if he has we can be pretty sure that it is not the kind of a cat that Calverton would want him to find.

O'Neill does not find a conclusive answer to this "sickness of today" because he cannot convince himself that there is any final answer. The latest panacea is Communism in one form or another. That Communism may easily offer us a better economic system than the anarchy of capitalism might be admitted, but what does it offer the creative artist? It may offer security at the price of slavery. As John puts it, "Slavery means security—of a kind, the only kind they have the courage for. It means they need not think. They have only to obey orders from owners who are, in turn, their slaves!" O'Neill, it is true, is disturbed, but he is also critical. He sees no sure answer, but he sees the need for analysis of ideals, discussions of values, even if need be a re-definition of old values, in the hope that the experiment may bring something to light that will help to cure the sickness which is driving Western culture into a deadly decline.

Days Without End deals with this problem. It presents it in every scene in one form or another. It is studied from various angles and finally forced to a conclusion that may not be convincing, but serves the need for a dramatic ending. John and Loving who are nearly always in conflict come very close together on this subject of social sickness. The speech of the one follows almost without distinction the argument of the other. Both are clear that society is drifting in a world without ends, without objectives that are worth seeking. John's speech is to the point:

> JOHN. I listen to people talking about this universal breakdown we are in and I marvel at their stupid cowardice. It is so obvious that they deliberately cheat themselves because their fear of change won't let them face the truth. They don't want to understand what has happened to them. All they want is to start the merry-go-round of blind greed all over again. They no longer know what they want this country to be, what they want it to become, where they want it to go. It has lost all meaning for them except as a pig-wallow. And so their lives as citizens have no beginnings, no ends.

To this Loving adds a satirical touch by condemning the romantic idea of freedom, and pointing out that in our modern world of science "we are all the slaves of meaningless chance—electricity or something, which whirls us—on to Hercules!" And with this John expresses perfect agreement, asserting the same positive attitude toward life that has always characterized O'Neill's thought:

> JOHN. Very well! On to Hercules! Let us face that! Once we have accepted it without evasion, we can begin to create new goals for ourselves, ends for our days! A new discipline for life will spring into being, a new will and power to live, a new ideal to measure the value of our lives by!

No matter what opinions may eventually predominate
as to the final dramatic value of this play, it is certain
that O'Neill is keenly alive to the issues social, economic and philosophical that confront the modern
world. Communism, Fascism, Socialism, youth move-
ments, all the chaos of thought cries out for a meaning
that will give direction. No more stirring drama ever
was enacted by civilized man than is now being performed before our eyes in all parts of the world. Now it
is no longer the individual king who may lose his
throne, it is Western civilization. O'Neill has felt this
and given it expression in *Days Without End*. That
his dramatization of our endless days may not be all
that we could wish such a play to be is not the question.
He has grappled with the monster that stalks our spirit
and we roam in the sinister shadows of our own creation. With John, modern man may well cry:

> JOHN. We need a new leader who will teach us that
> ideal, who by his life will exemplify it and make it a
> living truth for us—a man who will prove that man's
> fleeting life in time and space can be noble. We need,
> above all, to learn again to believe in the possibility of
> nobility of spirit in ourselves! A new savior must be
> born who will reveal to us how we can be saved from
> ourselves, so that we can be free of the past and in-
> herit the future and not perish by it.

The modern world needs leadership, that is admitted, and Loving's comment, that we "have passed
beyond gods" points to the truth that if we would be

saved we must save ourselves. O'Neill knows this well, but he also remembers that man's past history gives but slight promise of wisdom in matters that pertain to the social ideal. He is not blind to the naïve character of John's plea for leadership. Loving knows that "the pseudo-Nietzschean savior I just evoked out of my past is an equally futile ghost. Even if he came we'd only send him to an insane asylum for teaching that we should have a nobler aim for our lives than getting all four feet in a trough of swill! How could we consider such an unpatriotic idea as anything but insane?"

Is there a final answer? O'Neill does not offer anything that is satisfactory or that is in harmony with the critical character of his analysis. For dramatic purposes John is forced to a decision that is a negation of all that Loving defends intellectually.

This is not accomplished without ample indication that the decision cannot be final. John describes his novel-hero's conversion, but Loving adds, "This cowardly giving in to his weakness is not the end," for "there is a mocking rational something in him that laughs with scorn—and at the last moment his will and pride revive in him again! He sees clearly by the light of reason the degradation of his pitiful surrender to old ghostly comforts—and he rejects them!" A little later John affirms this statement, saying, "He realizes that he can never believe in his lost faith again." He admits the hopelessness of a final solution, but holds that "It is man's duty to life to go on!"

Now, as far as the drama is concerned it must carry

on to an ending. The conflict between John and Loving must be resolved. So far the honors have been equal; in many cases where the issue touched on vital problems the two personalities were so dangerously near to harmony as to be almost devoid of conflict. Then comes the serious illness of John's wife, which adds force to the needs of his passional nature. The gap between John and Loving is widened, and finally we are led to believe that the battle will be fought to a standstill, forced to a victory that will be complete and final.

In that conclusion many may disagree and they may justly hold that it is a departure from the usual procedure of the author. The ending may not be convincing, for there are those who will doubt that the victory is complete when John turns from the church, leaving the dead body of Loving on the floor. There is something tenacious about Loving. He is also subtle, clever and at times even wily. Not only that, he may be immortal. Thus when John leaves the church at peace with himself, and confident that the old questioning, doubting spirit of Loving is dead, he may really be deceived. Perhaps when he is sitting in his study late the following night he will find that Loving was scotched but not slain. For there he stands at John's elbow once more. Once more his strong, sardonic laughter rings out through the room. The old argument begins once more. Loving again asks questions, suggests doubts, loses battles, but in the end wins the real victory, for his is the inquiring, the skeptical mind, his is the mind of Eugene O'Neill.

XII

O'Neill and Modern Tragedy

LARRY.   I saw men didn't want to be saved from themselves, for that would mean they'd have to give up greed,
and they'll never pay that price for Liberty.
                                            The Iceman Cometh

HICKEY.   You've all done what you needed to do! By
rights you should be contented now, without a single
damned hope or lying dream left to torment you.
                                            The Iceman Cometh

IN THE final analysis O'Neill's plays must be judged in
the terms of tragedy. That is exactly what he wanted,
for he held that whatever greatness a man may have
his ultimate stature is measured in the terms of his
ability to experience tragedy in his own life and in
the life of man.

Any analysis of the concept of tragedy as it finds expression in modern drama, and in O'Neill in particular,
must recognize that Aristotle's famous definition cannot apply, at least not as it has been traditionally
interpreted. The full implication of the traditional
interpretation as applied to drama from Sophocles to

Shakespeare will not serve for O'Neill. But no discussion of tragedy can avoid Aristotle, nor can O'Neill be discussed as a writer of tragedy without reference to Aristotle's definition. That he does belong in the great tradition of tragedy is certain. No matter how far removed he may be from the poetic form of the past, any evaluation of his tragedies invites comparison with the great plays in this genre, because all lesser ones' sink into a minor place where contrast and not comparison is implied. The form of his tragedy is different, in subject matter and theme it is the same.

There are two points in Aristotle on which modern drama departs from the classic definition, or at least from the traditional interpretation of that definition. Pertinent to the study of an O'Neill tragedy are character and *hamartia,* the fall from high station due to some "flaw", human error, or failure in sound judgment. Aristotle's conception of the tragic character holds that he is a man of high station, a king or a leader of his people in some great cause. General Mannon (*Mourning Becomes Electra*) is the only one in O'Neill's world who in any sense at all measures up to the specific requirements of Aristotle, if he is to be taken in a literal sense. *Hamartia* is a different problem, but even here Aristotle could not conceive of the fall from greatness as being tragic unless the leading character was victim of some slight flaw, because to have a perfectly good man fall from prosperity into adversity would be "impious" or "merely shocking"; it would in fact, question the goodness of the Gods. This, in its traditional interpretation by critics found expression in the assumption that at the end of a tragedy there was a *katharsis,* which in turn was interpretated to mean that man was "Brought face to face with universal law" and "The divine plan of the world".

Neither the traditional Aristotelian character, nor the pious belief in a divine order of things has validity in the best of modern tragedy from Ibsen and Strindberg to O'Neill, and of these, it applies least of all to O'Neill. His tragedy, if it has universal appeal, must deal with the fall of man from prosperity into adversity in a manner that is "shocking" and through causes that lie within man himself in relation to the outward forces of his world. He is brought to disaster by forces that are stronger than he is. This attitude toward man has been apparent in O'Neill's plays from the first to the last. The men and women of his world are victims of a cosmic trap, cold and impersonal as steel. Mary, (*Long Day's Journey Into Night*) who has struggled for years with her inescapable despair, says to Edmund, "It's wrong to blame your brother. He can't help being what the past has made him. Any more than your father can. Or you. Or I". And again later when she knows that there is no escape, she thinks of her happiness as a student in the Convent, "You were much happier", she says to herself "When you prayed to the Blessed Virgin. If I could only find the faith I lost, so I could pray again". But impossible. There is no will that can conquer the forces of life that have imprisoned her.

Tyrone asks her to "Forget the past". Her answer is, "How can I? The past is the present, isn't it? It's the future, too. We all try to lie about that, but life won't let us."

All the Tyrones are caught in the same trap. Each character has his flaw, his failure. He is a combination of the inner self, which is the life force, trying to deal with the circumstances of a world he did not make and could not control. The punishment they suffer in spite of all their efforts is out of all proportion to what they deserve, and in the case of Mary, who is the central figure of the tragedy, the suffering is a mockery of a divine plan in the world. The appeal of the play lies not in "order re-established", but in the realization of man's powerlessness to deal with life in any way that would indicate a universal good. He stumbles in the fog, that in this play is the dominant atmosphere, seeking for a pathway that is not there.

Aristotle's man of high estate, who was to him a figure of national importance, is not present in modern tragedy. But the character who falls must still be significant. His importance in an O'Neill play lies then not at all in his station in life, but in his capacity to feel and understand the forces that have brought him from a place of great promise to one where the value of life has lost its charm, all its high promise, where it has no more value that a rag pinned to a clothes line fluttering in the wind. When Lavinia (*Mourning Becomes Electra*) views the wreckage of everything that once made the House of Mannon, she does not ask for exile, the most fearful punishment that Oedipus could imagine, but she does accept its counterpart. She orders the windows of the Mannon mansion boarded up to shut out every ray of light, all the beauty of the world. She then enters the house to live with the dead. Death was something the Mannons understood.

But still the Mannons had something of the outward stature of ancient dramatic heroes. In order to realize most fully the modern tragedy as O'Neill saw it, it is best to turn to *The Iceman Cometh.* In time this play may very well come to be recognized as O'Neill's greatest tragedy. It is easier at the moment to accept the *Long Day's Journey Into Night* as superior to *The Iceman Cometh,* because it deals with a more familiar world. Sentiment, sorrow and pathos are there in every character and every action. It is so poignant that the audience often loses esthetic distance in identification with the characters. The emotional appeal of the mother is irresistible, and the condition of Edmund, sick with tuberculosis, arouses a deep sympathy that verges on pathos. The saving spirit is Jamie whose bitter uncompromising irony pervades the whole play and covers his own sorrowful heart. Both he and his brother in their combined use of poetic quotations help to keep the theme universal, thus escaping from the particular, which always tends, when left to itself, to destroy esthetic distance.

In *The Iceman Cometh,* there is no easy identification with the characters. Gorky's *Lower Depths* is the only play comparable to O'Neill's. It presents a collec-

tion of the outcast and the damned more terrifying
than the inmates of Harry Hope's Saloon, but Gorky's
play tends to give more emphasis to the outward forces
that lie in wait for their victims. Some of the characters
in this play are in trouble with the law, some could
even be saved, rehabilitated through the proper use of
legal justice and a decent income. The characters of
The Lower Depths were meant by Gorky to be victims
of a vicious and unjust social order. Change the order
and all those who had not fallen into crime incompatible with organized society could have been saved.
It is a tragedy of the failure of a social order.

In *The Iceman Cometh* the point of no return had
been reached for all the characters long before the play
opens. Twenty years before the curtain rises Harry
Hope crossed the threshold of reality as he turned his
back on the ward which bridged his contact with the
world. This world of reality he would never see again,
except for one brief moment, and when that moment
was over, he stood shocked and trembling in his saloon
unable to understand why he had ever ventured to go
outside the protection of his prison.

On the stage is one of the most remarkable collections
of human beings ever assembled in a single play. They
represent a wide and rather familiar group, the lost and
the damned. Everyone has failed in his own peculiar
way to make a normal adjustment to the world. Poli-
tician, soldier, remittance man, ward heeler, newspaper
reporter, policeman, bar tender, labor organizer, pimps
and whores. Central, and major catalytic agent, is the

salesman of death in the guise of selling life. Each
in his own way has crossed the borderline of so-called
normal life, and is now living on the edge of starvation
and spiritual death. He dreams of someday recovering
the ideals and standards of a social status long since
lost. Jimmy Tomorrow, the leader of the Tomorrow
Movement symbolizes the ironic strategy for success.
Each person has or develops during the play the rationale of his present position and plans for his own personal rehabilitation. To each it is logical, clear and
certain. Tomorrow the action that leads to the good
life will begin. For some of them this has been the
Tomorrow for years. Others have just joined the Tomorrow Movement. Only one includes *no Tomorrow*
in his philosophy. He is Larry, the ex-I.W.W. He had
invested all that life holds good: love, honor, social
justice, a sense of human value and dignity in *The
Movement,* and when that failed him or he failed it,
perhaps both are present in his complex nature, when
that moment came he had no values left. He was
without knowing it at the time, a member of one of
the great Tomorrow societies of the world, the labor
movement. The only character lacking in this remarkable collection of characters is a disillusioned preacher,
who would have represented the greatest Pipe Dream
of all. The nearest to that is the Ole Doc, Ed Mosher
tells about, whose devotion to medical science was
expressed in the sale of snake oil. He died at the age
of eighty from overwork. But he was a great "Gentle-
man of the old school. I'll bet he's standing on a street

corner in hell right now, making suckers of the
damned, telling them there's nothing like snake oil
for bad burns."

This, then, is the company with which the audience
is to identify itself if the drama is to have that universal
appeal which is the essence of the tragic experience in
the theatre. Also these are the characters which O'Neill
has offered as a substitute for the tragic characters
required by Aristotle's definition. At first glance it
would appear that there is here nothing comparable
to the tragic hero of tradition. Larry is the only character whose social status represents a great ideal and
whose intellect is of a high order. He serves to give the
theme a slightly more dignified quality than the others
and he interprets the futility of the *Tomorrow Movement,* but he also has his pipe dream and it is finally
shattered by his intellectual realization of the complete
futility of life.

The audience is identified with the characters in
Harry Hope's saloon, but its obvious similarity is not
established on the basis of social position, income,
houses, salaries or any of the hundred standards by
which ordinary men live and claim their right to respect and honor. But if one were realistic, he would have
to recognize that what he is as an individual, or as a
member of a social order, he still is far from being on
an equality with Oedipus or Hamlet either. He identifies himself not with Hamlet, Prince of Denmark, but
with the tortured spirit of Hamlet who would kill
himself if "The Everlasting had not fix'd his canon

'gainst self-slaughter!" He is the man who "Could
be bounded in a nutshell and count myself a king of
infinite space, were it not that I have had bad dreams."

The individual reading Oedipus is not so absurd
as to think he has the proportions and the stature of a
king. His identification again in Hamlet lies in the
tortured spirit that finds itself betrayed by arbitrary
and capricious forces over which it has no control. In
sharing this world of the tragic king man meets himself and understands better than he ever understood
before the precarious adventure of life and its intimate
tragic consequences.

This is what O'Neill understood. He reduced the
outer shell of man almost to ultimate negation. Stripped
bare as a forked radish all that remained is the Pipe
Dream, the great *Tomorrow Movement* which is im-
bedded in the hearts of men. It is this abstract ideal of
life that gives universality to the tragic character and
not social status. It is what Matthew Arnold called an
inward condition of spirit, not an outward set of circumstances that measures the meaning of life.

The traditional use of pride as the great flaw which
brings about the fall of the tragic hero has little value
in the interpretation of modern tragedy as developed
by O'Neill, with the one exception of Cornelius Melody, "The embittered Byronic hero" of *A Touch of the
Poet,* and even in this play pride is treated with irony
and not as it is supposed to be developed in historic
tragedy.

The characters in *The Iceman Cometh* do not fall

through pride, but because they wanted from life more than it could in reality give them. They, each in his own way, failed the crucial test. The Pipe Dream which is a universal aspect of the human spirit took possession of their lives; the Siren's voice of the *Tomorrow Movement* became for them irresistible. Without the dream they cannot live and at this point the salesman of death offers them salvation, which at first they fail to recognize as an invitation to the only peace left for them, death.

Larry is the only one who recognizes that the Pipe Dream is the end of the road. "What's before me is the comforting fact that death is a fine long sleep . . . And it can't come too soon for me." He could resist Hickey who had come to save all of them, but Don Parritt, the man who had betrayed his own mother, forced Larry to face the reality of his life. He must, figuratively, sentence Parritt to death, and he must stand by the window to be sure that the sentence is carried out. He had grasped the full meaning of Hickey's preaching. "Life is too much for me." He hopes for death, and "May that day come soon! Be God I'm the only real convert to death Hickey made here."

The others find comfort in the illusion that because Hickey had murdered his wife, he must be crazy. Being crazy, his whole negation of the *Tomorrow Movement* was a fearful lie. Unable to face reality they return to the Pipe Dream by which they must die. The irony of life is irresolvable. "To be or not to be" has been stated in modern terms, as *The Iceman Cometh* ends with Harry Hope calling "Hey there, Larry! Come over and get paralyzed," and the final message from Hugo " 'The days grow hot O Babylon! 'Tis cool beneath thy willow trees!' " And so the "Second feast of Belshazzar" came to an end "With Hickey doing the writing on the wall." It is the universality of this theme freed from the too intimate pathos and personal experience of *A Long Day's Journey Into Night* that may in time rank it as O'Neill's greatest tragedy.

The Iceman Cometh does not stand alone. There is a consistency to all of O'Neill's work from *Bound East for Cardiff* to *A Touch of the Poet*. All are developed out of an inner conflict of values as this eternal problem finds new depths of meaning in the modern world. Yank in *Bound East for Cardiff* belongs in the company of the mask-tortured figures in *The Great God Brown,* of Nina Leeds, the Mannons, the Tyrones, Jim in *A Moon for the Misbegotten* and the heart-stricken Larry. Their tragedies are built out of irresolvable conflicts that are a part of the modern world. It may even be that now with science triumphant, *Dynamo* may have a deeper meaning than it appeared to have a generation ago. The Dynamo is the new cross on a new Golgotha as it really was to O'Neill. These characters are all wanderers seeking shelter in the Garden of Eden, but knowing that the road is washed out and overgrown with weeds, that the Garden has withered into a barren desert.

O'Neill does not deny that there are moments of insight and peace for man. Paddy in *The Hairy Ape* has such a vision when he identifies himself with The Absolute. O'Neill many years and plays later comes back to the same vision in *A Long Day's Journey Into Night*. Here Edmund and Paddy are one and the same. Their visions are O'Neill's dream. Edmund says to his father:

> "You've just told me some high spots in your memories. Want to hear mine? . . . When I was on the lookout in the crow's nest in the dawn watch. A calm sea, that time. Only a lazy ground swell and a slow drowsy roll of the ship. The passengers asleep and none of the crew in sight. No sound of man . . . feeling alone, and above, and apart, watching the dawn creep like a painted dream over the sky and sea which slept together. Then the moment of ecstatic freedom came. The peace, and the end of the quest, the last harbor, the joy of belonging to a fulfillment beyond man's lousy, pitiful, greedy fears and hopes and dreams! And several other times in my life . . . I've had the same experience. Became the sun, the hot sand, the green seaweed anchored to a rock, swaying in the tide. Like a Saint's vision of beatitude . . . For a second there is meaning! Then the hand lets the veil fall and you are alone, lost in the fog again, and you stumble towards nowhere, for no good reason . . . It was a great mistake my being born a man . . . A stranger who never feels at home . . . Who must always be a little in love with death."

These moments of mystic insight are but flashes that leave the spirit in greater darkness than it was before they occurred. The same thing happens in the opposite extreme where a conscious awareness of physical reality seems the perfect answer. But it too fades leaving man desolate and alone. Hickey presented that view at the moment when he had "saved" the men and whores in Hope's saloon. He speaks with bitterness:

> "By rights you should be contented now, without a single damned hope or lying dream left to torment you! But here you are, acting like a lot of stiffs cheating the undertaker . . . Can't you appreciate what you got, for God's sake? Don't you know you're free now to be your-selves, without having to feel remorse or guilt, or lie to yourselves about reforming tomorrow? Can't you see there is no tomorrow now. You're rid of it forever."

There is no ending or point of rest, there is no answer to the bite of conscience nor is there a rationale that offers peace. At the end of *The Iceman Cometh* there is no one left to summarize the story and give it mean-ing, for the meaning of life has been lost in Pipe Dreams. Kafka's Castle is visible on the hill, but there is no road through the tangled thicket that surrounds its base. This is the meaning of tragedy.

In the last four plays *A Touch of the Poet* is closely related to *The Iceman Cometh,* while *A Moon for the Misbegotten* is a sequel to *A Long Day's Journey Into Night.* Cornelius Melody is a man who had generated a *pipe dream* of himself as a true aristocrat. He main-tains his ideal in the terms of lofty speech, elegant dress and freedom from toil. He is the master of his *estate* which in reality is a cheap saloon. He is ashamed of the simple manner and low Irish brogue of his wife, he barely tolerates his daughter, while on the other hand he worships his horse, since it is the symbol of his aristocracy. He always celebrates the anniversary of the great victory at Talavera where he had won honor on the battlefield. The *pipe dream* has become his reality, even as the inmates of Hope's saloon had each his own pipe dream. Major Melody disregards the fact that he is impoverished, that his wife must beg for credit at the local store, while he struts in his uniform unable to understand why the Yankee scum should not be honored to extend him credit until his pipe dream comes true.

In the end the dream fails. He shoots his beautiful thoroughbred, because by killing her he can kill the Major, for now he speaks in Irish brogue and refers to the Major as another person not his true, low born Irish self.

His daughter Sara asks in astonishment, "But why did you kill her?"

> MELODY. Why did the Major, you mean? Be Christ, you're stupider than I thought, if you can't see that. Wasn't she the livin' reminder, so to spake, av all the lyin' boasts and dreams? He meant to kill her first wid one pistol, then himself wid the other. But faix, he saw the shot that killed her finished him, too . . . So he didn't bother shooting himself, because it'd be a mad thing to waste a good bullet on a corpse!"

At the end Major Melody sheds all his glory, his pipe dream dead, he goes through the door into the bar. He is now a member of Harry Hope's saloon, where a new kind of pipe dream can develop.

There is one frame of reference in which Major

Melody's dream relates him to O'Neill. Major Melody
sustains his idea of himself by accepting the Byronic
character as his own. He quotes Byron's poetry on all
those occasions when he wanted to establish his superior
position in the world. One special quotation is repeated
several times and should be quoted here, because it was
a favorite with O'Neill. He quoted it with a touch of
irony, while at the same time it was also clear that he
accepted it on its face value. Major Melody was a long
lost brother of O'Neill's youth. They both shared, each
in his own way:

> " 'I have not loved the World, nor the World me;
> I have not flattered its rank breath, nor bowed
> To its idolatries a patient knee,
> Nor coined my cheek to smiles,—nor cried aloud
> In the worship of an echo: in the crowd
> They could not deem me one of such—I stood
> Among them, but not of them . . .' "

The tragedy, *The Moon for the Misbegotten,* picks
up the story of James Tyrone about nine years after the
ending of *A Long Day's Journey Into Night.* It introduces in direct action a scene that was merely reported
in *A Long Day's Journey Into Night,* and in so doing,
makes O'Neill guilty of an anachronism, which while it
may deserve notice as having a bearing on the way
he worked with this autobiographical material, has no
other significance.

In this play James has no illusions left. His father and
mother are dead. He makes no reference to his brother

Eugene, who has obviously moved out of the sphere of James' own life. All that is left for him is an endless series of gray dawns creeping over dirty windows to reveal some fat tart snoring by his side. For him "There is no present or future—only the past happening over and over again." The memory of his mother's death has anchored him to a guilt that nothing will obliterate. She had died in California. He had spent the long train trip home, his mother in the baggage coach, he in his stateroom with a whore, drunk the whole time, so drunk when he arrived that he could not attend his mother's funeral. He is broken in spirit. There are no pipe dreams for him, only death can bring him relief from the burden of his life.

For an instant he catches contentment and rest in Josie's arms. When he awakes he sees once more the beginning of the agony. As he walks down the road Josie pronounces a benediction. "May you have your wish and die in your sleep Jim, darling . . . May you rest forever in forgiveness and Peace."

This is Eugene O'Neill's final word to the brother he had loved just this side of idolatry. This whole play must be interpreted as an elegy. The dramatist forces himself to see all the faults of the one he immortalizes, and then beneath a thousand failures, recognizes the great worth of the man betrayed and driven to disaster by the Fates, relentless in their determination that he be destroyed. All the outward appearances of callous disregard for others were but forms to conceal the specters that haunted his spirit. This was O'Neill's farewell to his brother, just as *A Long Day's Journey Into Night* had been his In Memoriam to his father and mother. The dedication to *A Long Day's Journey Into Night* applies to *A Moon for the Misbegotten* as well. To Carlotta he wrote that he had been able "To face my dead at last and write this play—write it with deep pity and understanding and forgiveness for all the four haunted Tyrones."

Index

(All characters from the plays are listed under their first names.)

313

Index

Index 319